PETER O'TOOL

# PETER O'TOOLE
## A Biography

Nicholas Wapshott

NEW ENGLISH LIBRARY

# To my mother and father

The Author and Publishers gratefully acknowledge permission to include the following extracts:
From *Confessions of an Actor* by Laurence Olivier, published by Weidenfeld and Nicolson Ltd.
From *An Open Book* by John Huston, published by Macmillan Ltd.
From *That Despicable Race* by Bryan Forbes, published by Hamish Hamilton Ltd.

First published in Great Britain in 1983 by New English Library

First NEL Paperback Edition October 1984

NEL Books are published by
New English Library,
Mill Road, Dunton Green,
Sevenoaks, Kent.
Editorial office: 47 Bedford Square, London WC1B 3DP

Made and printed in Great Britain by
Richard Clay (The Chaucer Press) Ltd, Bungay, Suffolk

**British Library C.I.P.**

Wapshott, Nicholas
   Peter O'Toole.
   1. O'Toole, Peter
   791.43′028′0924    PN2598.0
ISBN 0–450–05754–2

# CONTENTS

# ACKNOWLEDGEMENTS

As one who writes regularly about politics, I am well used to writing about people who would prefer not to be written about. I had, however, not expected that actors and directors would be so cagey about their memories. Peter O'Toole did not want me to write this book, but I thank him for leading such an interesting and amusing life. I apologise for any inconvenience and distress that this biography might cause. It was not intended to offend: merely to record the goings-on of one of Britain's most entertaining actors.

I am indebted to those who know O'Toole and have been close to him for most of his lifetime. They have been of extraordinary help to me and I regret that O'Toole's reticence means that their contribution to this book must go unrecorded. I must respect their confidence, but acknowledge the debt I owe them. I could not have been sure of being right about so much of O'Toole's life without their generous assistance. For those close to O'Toole who politely refused to help me, many thanks also.

I must thank in particular Kenneth Griffith, who trod a delicate line between his friendship and loyalty to O'Toole and his friendship to me. Among the dozens of friends and colleagues of O'Toole who have talked to me and endured my probing into their memories, I especially thank: Bob Willoughby, Dirk Bogarde, Alec Guinness, Harry Andrews, Anthony Hopkins and Timothy West. Many thanks to those librarians, particularly of the British Film Institute and the Royal Shakespeare Company, for enduring my constant enquiries. I also owe a great debt to all those reporters who recorded O'Toole's words throughout his career.

Above all, thanks to my wife, Louise Nicholson, for her constant support and patience and for criticising the work so effectively; to Jacqui Grainger-Taylor for her enthusiasm and her work on preparing the typescript; to Simon Scott for his calm in editing; to Alison Peacock for finding the pictures; and to Giles Gordon for lending his extensive theatrical knowledge.

# The Summons

THE SUMMONS came by telephone, a discreet enquiry such as might have been made by Buckingham Palace. It was Kenneth Griffith, Peter O'Toole's closest friend.

'O'Toole has asked me to ask you whether you would be prepared to see him,' said Griffith.

For all the years they had been friends, they had remained on surname terms. It was a sign of endearment, a means of showing their closeness by slightly distancing themselves from each other. In the world of the stage, where the use of Christian names is commonplace, considered even formal, and where 'Darling', and 'Love!' are showered on vague acquaintances, the schoolboy formality of Griffith and O'Toole amounted to a recurring oath of allegiance to each other.

Griffith continued: 'He's come over from Ireland to talk to you. He wants to tell you himself. He's not happy. He wonders if you will go and see him in Hampstead.'

'Of course I will go and see him,' I answered. Then, after a pause: 'He's not going to hit me, is he, Kenneth? I want to keep my teeth.'

It was a serious question, even though, to ease my nervousness, I had asked it as if it were a joke. Word had been filtering through friends that O'Toole was not happy for me to continue writing about him. Someone reported him as saying he wanted to kill me. Melodramatic? Of course. And even more melodramatic to take such a threat seriously. Or was it? Shortly after hearing of O'Toole's anger, I had met at a party his London theatrical agent, Steve Kenis, who works for the William Morris Agency in London. It was Kenis who had tracked down O'Toole on my behalf and discovered that he had decided against helping me write about his life. But at the party, Kenis went further, confirming the rumour which threatened violence.

Kenis, an American, was sympathetic. 'I wish you luck, but you can't count on O'Toole's help. He doesn't want it written by anybody. He said he'd put the Irish Mafia on you, but I told him not to be stupid. The only advice I would give you is to lodge the manuscript with his lawyers when you have finished. It would be a wise thing to do.'

The Irish Mafia? That means only one thing to me: the IRA, with its unchristian attitude toward human life, its Black and Decker drills and its booby trap bombs. Life as a writer doesn't usually invite such hostility or danger. And who knows what excuse was needed before a set of irrational thugs flexed their muscles a little in my direction? Even if I was safe from the Irish, a more direct threat was possible. O'Toole may not want to punish me for continuing with his biography, but he had a reliable record for taking a swipe at people whose occupations cramped his liberty. A photographer in Rome; a restaurateur in Dublin; why not an author in London? Before I walked into the lion's den, I at least wanted some assurance that the beast had been sedated. Not for the first time I mentioned the threat to Griffith.

'I wouldn't worry about that,' he said. 'Put it right out of your mind. He won't hurt you. He used to have contacts among that lot, but not now, not for many years.'

'But you are sure he is not going to hit me, Kenneth?'

'No, he won't. But when you first meet him, tell him that Kenneth Griffith has assured you that he won't give you a black eye. He's got a good sense of humour, you know. It is going to be a very interesting meeting. I wish I was going to be there.'

The next morning, I pressed the bell on the door set into the high wall surrounding O'Toole's front garden. He lives on the busy main high street of Hampstead, but is secure from prying glances behind a brick wall eight feet tall. The door was opened by a young woman, a former actress who was now O'Toole's private secretary.

'My name is Wapshott. Mr O'Toole has asked to see me.'

She led the way through the small front garden, green and mature, then into the house. It is an enormous Georgian home, bought from the proceeds of *Lawrence of Arabia*. O'Toole paid a laughably modest £20,000 for it twenty years ago. It must have increased in value at least ten times since then. Inside, it is warm and expensively decorated. The furniture is a mixture of antiques and good quality sumptuous modern. I was shown into the study and sat down on a huge sofa. In the place next to me was a script of George Bernard Shaw's *Man and Superman*. That in itself was a piece of news. There had been a quiet announcement that O'Toole was returning to the London stage to make amends for his disastrous previous performance in *Macbeth* at the Old Vic. So it was true. O'Toole had been billed to appear in many different plays and films over the years, none of which had materialised. But here there was hard evidence that O'Toole was at least in a position to read through his lines. London really might see O'Toole on the stage of the Haymarket Theatre in one of the longest parts in the English language.

O'Toole was late. I was told to report at ten-thirty. It was ten to eleven. O'Toole has a reputation for being at his worst in the mornings and this was not a day for breaking rules. At five to eleven I was given a cup of coffee. The tray held three cups and saucers. So O'Toole had not breakfasted somewhere else in the house. He would be waking up with me. A little American girl about five years old came into the room and introduced herself. Her mother, out of sight, was preparing for a shopping expedition. The little girl said she came from New York, which made sense. O'Toole had recently made two films, both of them in New York. She waved goodbye and left with her mother, who remained invisible.

I was miles away, deep in *Spotlight*, the jobs wanted notice board for actors, when O'Toole bounded in. He had come from a bath and his hair, dyed blond and hanging to his collar, was a mess.

He shook my hand. I stood up. He turned to his secretary.

'I wonder, would you run down the road and buy me one of those large clown's combs. I would be most grateful.'

And she left.

He poured himself a cup of coffee and sat down in a large leather chair with high wing sides. He sat floppily, his elbows resting on the arms of the chair, his hands limply dangling from the ends of his upstanding forearms. His legs were crossed at the knee. His fiftieth birthday had been only two weeks before, yet he looked at least ten years older. His skin was pale, slightly yellowing. His staring blue eyes looked as if they were just ending, not just beginning a full day. His dishevelled hair looked much as it had looked when he had played the mad Earl of Gurney in *The Ruling Class*. He was wearing an ivory double-breasted suit, with wide lapels, which he had buttoned with some flamboyance in front of me. He was wearing a shirt with a collar too large for him, so it hung down at the neck in a vee, like those on old men whose wardrobes have not kept pace with their wasting away. He was wearing the green and pink striped tie of The Garrick Club, the gentleman's club which attracts eminent actors and men of letters. He was wearing his mandatory green socks – through superstition and a love of Ireland he will wear no other – and on his feet were a pair of lush plum velvet slippers, on the toes of which were embroidered in gold brocade a crown. He looked a sight. It was difficult to guess whether he was putting on a show for my benefit or whether he always dressed as strangely – as theatrically – as this. I suspected the latter.

He began to make small talk. He wanted to know the origin of my name. He told of his investigations into the derivation of the word 'left'. He asked after Jack Crossley, a journalist with whom he used to work in Yorkshire. Then he got down to business.

'I do not want you to carry on. I do not wish you to carry on. It is causing me great distress and will cause me further distress. I simply do not wish it.' It was an unreal request. The book was nearly complete. He seemed surprised to learn that I had been paid money by a publisher to write it, as if somehow I would write such a thing on spec. I apologised for the distress that I had unwittingly caused him, we shook hands and parted company. And as I walked down Heath Street on my way home, I thought of the opening scene in the film which had made O'Toole an international star: David Lean's *Lawrence of Arabia*.

Down the steps of St Paul's Cathedral, after a memorial service to the memory of T. E. Lawrence, comes a crowd of military dignitaries. General Allenby, played by Sir Donald Wolfit, denies having known Lawrence well at all. Then Jackson Bentley, the American newspaper reporter who wrote about Lawrence and dignified his wild, daring deeds, acknowledges that he knew Lawrence.

'Yes. It was my privilege to know him and make him known to the world,' he says, then adds, 'He was a poet, a scholar and a mighty warrior. He was also the most shameless exhibitionist since Barnum and Bailey.'

He is upbraided by a stuffy and well-meaning bowler-hatted officer, who has overheard the last, damning remark.

'You, sir. Who are you?'

'My name is Jackson Bentley.'

'Oh, well, whoever you are, I overheard your last remark and take the gravest possible exception. He was a very great man.'

'Did you know him?' asks Bentley.

'No, sir, I can't claim to have known him. I once had the honour to shake his hand in Damascus.' And the film flashes back to a scene from Lawrence's early life.

I can't claim to have known O'Toole very well. I met him first in a private cinema off Soho Square, watching one of Kenneth Griffith's radical, campaigning documentary films, the life of the American revolutionary Tom Paine. I was, at that time, considering the prospect of writing this book.

My knowledge of him was that he had been a startlingly precocious young actor who had established an early success in a season at Stratford. He then landed the role of Lawrence in Lean's *Lawrence of Arabia*, one of the most artistically satisfactory and commercially successful films of the 1960s. A moderately high plateau of film projects had followed, with O'Toole wandering without any discernible direction through a succession of disparate films – some, like *Becket* and *The Lion in Winter*, quite creditable; others, such as *What's New Pussycat*, inexcusably self-indulgent.

O'Toole then slipped from the top line of stardom into a succession of moderate to very poor films. Grandiloquent actors like O'Toole had become anachronistic, overtaken by a new generation of young stars who seemingly didn't act at all. O'Toole drifted out of fashion with little prospect of ever attaining again the fame that he once briefly had achieved in the mid-1960s. But at the same time he was turning up in extraordinarily good, if modest, films which had something of a cult status. There was Clive Donner's *Rogue Male*, a glorious British film, made for the BBC, with O'Toole as a young aristocrat who had to go to ground in the West Country having taken a failed pot shot at Hitler. O'Toole's performance was exceptional. Then there had been, only recently, Richard Rush's *Stunt Man*, about a sadistic, half-mad film director who subjects a man on the run to the terrors of film stunt work, just to test his grasp of the thin divide between illusion and reality: an existential nightmare. Again, O'Toole's acting had been extraordinary, compulsively watchable.

Then there had been the *Macbeth* affair, O'Toole's intended triumphant return to the London stage after more than a decade. Amid an enormous theatrical *brouhaha*, the like of which had not been seen at least since the war – some say this century – O'Toole had landed flat on his face. It was a terrible, sad episode for anyone's life, yet O'Toole was unrepentant, defiant of critical opinion and pledged that he would be back.

O'Toole was no mere has-been actor, but a full-scale tragic figure. He had pulled himself out of his parents' poor circumstances by an ingenious application of his keen wit and a fantastic capacity for self-education. From early on, acting for him became not simply a release from pressures within him which needed to communicate and lusted after attention, it became a political campaign. In meritocratic Britain, which had been unable to provide him with the wherewithal for easy self-advancement, he found that the theatre had been taken over by grammar school boys. Acting had become the domain not of self-determined individuals interpreting their lines direct to audiences, but as ciphers for the bright young men who both administered and directed simultaneously. O'Toole was not happy with that and saw the handing over of ultimate interpretative power to directors as a betrayal not only of living actors but the honourable tradition of every great, spirited, independent actor that ever trod the stage. O'Toole might not quite have seen himself as Edmund Kean, the ultimate actors' actor, but he was certainly a disciple and saw himself as a direct descendant.

His film and stage career, which has seemed so unprepared and haphazard, began to make sense. First, to establish his independence from the theatre directors whom he saw as mere puppet-masters, he needed a successful film career and he lost no time in making contact with film makers. He was simultaneously disdainful of money, which, as a socialist, he saw as a shallow reward for work – the true reward being the enjoyment of acting and the comradeship of other actors – and, at the same time, he enjoyed to splash money around, the ultimate expression of disrespect for a commodity which he despised as unfair and irrelevant to rewarding human worth.

But the large fees that film work brought him did give him an enviable independence. He promptly set up his own company, Keep Films, with his partner, Jules Buck, which would provide him with projects of his own choosing, and – less successfully, as it turned out – would give other independent projects an airing. And more than anything, his large film income gave him an independent attitude to the theatre. He maintained a strong and close link with the stage and more than once attempted to found an actors' company which would restore the dominant position of actors in theatres. Even the débâcle of *Macbeth,* which only O'Toole himself considered worthy of him, was about restoring the Old Vic, every British actor's favourite London theatre, to actors instead of the directors-cum-bureaucrats who had dominated it for so many years when it housed the young National Theatre company. The more I dug around O'Toole, the more it turned out that this story of an actor's climb to fame was truly heroic, even if, as was evident, O'Toole's self-important character and fierce individuality would prove persistently distasteful.

Above all, the thing which attracted me to O'Toole and his life was that he is such an intelligent comic. From his Irish parents and his smattering of learning, most of all from his capacious memory and the plays which he appeared in, he became capable of wonderful off-the-cuff remarks. Like all actors, there is an identifiable repertory. He slips into familiar phrases, a barely conscious quoting from texts which he has otherwise forgotten, and many of his remarks are, like those of us all, worn in with age; he remembers them from a series of renditions and is rarely likely to reword them at this stage. But there is running through everything he says evidence of his keenness of wit. He can describe an actor's dilemma like few others.

He is lucid on film directors, other actors, stage directors, politics, religion. He is articulate like so few others, when in full flight, he is almost entirely quotable. And what he says is wickedly, outrageously, gloriously funny. For an actor who has worked to so little effect in comedy roles, his comic repertoire is sensational. Just to describe his antics is to describe a man who, in many ways, is more like a fictional character that those to be found in most novels.

In the last five years O'Toole has found himself alone, divorced, without work, critically ill, near death, ridiculed, abused and down-hearted. Where had he gone wrong? What factors within or without his own character conspired against him, leaving him a star without a base, an actor without a refuge, an actor-manager without a theatre? And part of the reason for his downfall was the air of unreality which he showed that morning in Hampstead. O'Toole really had little idea of how the world was operating. He believed that to ask an author to stop writing about him would be the end of the matter. He did not appeal to my better nature; he asked me politely, like a man pointing a remote control box at a television to turn it off. He gave no reason for his inhibition but, using a small dose of pathos, imagined that his wish would come true – he repeated many times the phrase 'I do not *wish* it', putting great emphasis on the word 'wish' – that what he saw as an irritant would dis-appear.

His life is one of dodging reality. Riddled with ill-health from as soon as he could remember, he was regularly removed from everyday life in the limbo of hospitals. His father, an illegal bookmaker, worked in the nether world of the black economy. He was brought up in the Roman Catholic Church, where he learnt his theatricality and the escape from the miserable world about him. As soon as he was old enough, he took to the bottle. It buried the physical pain that was so often with him, leaving the harshness of real life for a more amusing world of blurred thoughts and dampened feelings. He has always preferred the company of those who like the no-man's-land of public houses. He has always worshipped the ways of actors, with their ability to plunge out of their own existence into the simulated reality of another.

His favourite remark from an actor of the old school is from Wilfred Lawson, who would tell young actors to 'Stop acting!' Like Jean-Paul Sartre's explanation of Edmund Kean, O'Toole has found himself happy to be confused as to where the boards of the stage or the rehearsal room end and where the unsteady reality of life begins. Since illness caused him to go teetotal, O'Toole has lost one method of retiring from reality when he needs to and has to depend upon less convenient methods. The reason that he is still so alive when half his insides is missing, the reason he can relentlessly hurl himself into projects which would be exhausting for any normally fit actor is that he holds on to his notion of unreality and retreats there. His lack of worldliness is his salvation; anyone else who faced what he now has to face would already be dead.

So, why should he be so reluctant for his heroic life to be recorded? An answer suggested to me by more than one actor is what might be called the Niven Syndrome. Since David Niven wrote *The Moon's a*

*Balloon*, the autobiographical best-seller, every actor has thought that he might have a book in him. O'Toole has certainly thought so. He once started an autobiographical book, part of which even reached publishers who enthused and begged him to finish. He never got round to it. And there is a thought in many actors' minds now – and certainly those with a life as amusing and ludicrous as O'Toole's – that to tell any story to anyone is to throw away seed corn which may, in old age or when their talents are abused or ignored, be translated into a book of their own. Newspaper interviewers have found a marked reluctance in actors to tell their stories – at the very least they prefer to tell them to chat-show hosts who at least give them a fee.

A more serious reason for O'Toole not wanting to spend time with a biographer is that he feels that he may not have much longer to live. He certainly came close to death a few years ago and has been reluctant to spend any time thinking about the past, not least because his serious illness coincided with the break-up of his marriage with Sian Phillips, which he found horribly painful. O'Toole's natural hyperactivity was magnified by the prospect of a truncated life and he has gone hammer and tongs at everything he has done since. He is a middle-aged man in a hurry. He is not much interested in his past life, he is too busy living in the present. His brief time in journalism, in any case, confirms to him that there is no such thing as objective, definitive truth and that anyone who attempts to write his life will only glance at what really happened. Why co-operate in something which he thinks will never do him justice? And he has been lucky so far in that he has always had enough money and enough work to avoid the lucrative lures of publishers to bless an official biography or spill his version of events to a ghost.

There is an element of humbug in O'Toole's reluctance to be written about. He has always courted the newspapers and encouraged publicity stunts. Many of his public misdemeanours with drink suited the image which encouraged people to write about him and he was glad of the notoriety – and enhanced fees – which such publicity encouraged. O'Toole is no natural Garbo. He would much prefer to talk than not talk. Even on the morning after the first-night fiasco of *Macbeth*, O'Toole invited all the press to his house to give his side of the story, knowing only too well that they would also be wallowing in his disaster. But he is happy to be the centre of attention, whether for what he has done well or what he has done badly. He relishes the comparisons which theatre people make at the latest O'Toole outrage, that that is how Kean behaved and that all great actors of mythical stature have been involved in failures as well as successes. O'Toole needs an audience if he is to become a legendary actor and audiences troop to his performances like few other figures on the British stage. But he also needs to be written about. The legend, like that of Lawrence, needs to be recorded.

# 1  The Connemara Boy

IF THERE is one single fact which would explain Peter O'Toole's wayward character, it is that he was born an Irishman. By his own admission it accounts for his passion, his love of conversation, his unruly behaviour, his disregard for authority – and above all, his natural capacity for acting. Few without an Irishman's gift for blethering could so easily consume, digest and later relay the poetry of plays. It has been O'Toole's gift, even from the first time he inflated walk-on parts into major roles, to inject his lines with a magical lilt, an ability to charm *en masse* – the weapon of the confidence trickster as well as the actor.

And this gift for casting a spell upon others does not abate when he leaves the stage. That he can win women with his golden tongue is well known. But he also wins men to his cause. Few who have met him refer to their 'acquaintance' Peter O'Toole. To everyone he is a friend, as if by engaging another in conversation he has imparted a secret, shared a conspiracy which is respected and valued. He seduces nearly everyone he meets, whole audiences in the theatre and – the rare quality which has lifted him from mere actor into that elusive and exclusive freemasonry of stardom – he is able to charm through the lens of a motion picture camera and win souls to his cause from the cinema screen.

O'Toole is proud to be an Irishman and his knack of converting others to share his feelings he would claim as an Irish gift. But he was barely an Irish boy. 'I can't really claim to be a soil-reared Irishman, I'm more free than battery running.' He was born on the promontory of Connemara in the county of Galway in the Republic of Ireland on 2 August 1932 and, like a child to its mother, it is to a cottage in Connemara that he has always retreated when under pressure of work or illness or personal disaster. His parents were poor. His father, Patrick Joseph O'Toole, could not find much of a living in Ireland and the arrival of his second child, Peter, was confirmation that the beauty of Connemara would not pay the rent. Within a year of the boy's birth, Patrick O'Toole, aged forty-four, began the traditional move eastwards, via Kerry, Dublin and Gainsborough, to England. There, Patty O'Toole, his Scots-born wife, Constance, his daughter Patricia and baby Peter, nicknamed 'Bubbles', settled in a mean one-down, two-up with outside lavatory terraced house in a cobbled street in the working-class area of Hunslet in Leeds.

It might have been a poor area, but it was one which spawned a number of literary lads. Playing the streets of Hunslet during the 1930s could be found O'Toole, Keith Waterhouse, the *Daily Mirror* columnist, and Willis Hall, the dramatist, who, in 1959, wrote *The Long and the Short and the Tall*, which was to help launch O'Toole's acting career. O'Toole neither met Waterhouse nor Hall during childhood.

Yet, although O'Toole has spent all but one year of his life out of Ireland, he has always been an Irish patriot. Like a spy who must shelter within the established order, O'Toole has enjoyed the split personality of being an Englishman, perhaps the most archetypal Englishman, the English eccentric, to a cinema audience around the world, while in his own mind he remains stolidly, four-square an Irishman, with Irish sympathies, a genuine respect for Irish Republicanism and a suspicion of the English ruling order. There was certainly nothing about the suburb of Hunslet which would have encouraged a more generous view of the English and their ways. The O'Tooles moved to Hunslet on purpose, to join a well-established community of expatriate Irish – what O'Toole has described as 'a Mick community'. There was not much wealth around. Hunslet was about as poor as any area in the north during the 1930s. But the attraction for the Irish and for Patrick O'Toole, the reason why he moved his wife and children so far from home, was that, as mean as the existence was that Hunslet offered, it was away from the outright poverty of the west coast of Ireland. For the O'Tooles, a move up in the world, from the bottom of the pile to the first, uncomfortable rung of the ladder, meant emigrating to England – the land which through myth, tradition and understandable grievance has been the object of hatred for any upright, self-respecting Irishman. O'Toole still harbours this inherited resentment for the colonising English.

O'Toole also sees himself as in good company – part of a group of talented, artistic, articulate men of letters and the arts who had to flee the Emerald Isle to make good. In the diatribes which O'Toole regularly delivers to his friends, one of the recurring themes is this brain-drain from Ireland. 'Tell me one Irish artist that ever produced there – just one! God, Jack Yeats didn't sell a painting in this country. And all the talent. You know what Ireland's biggest export is? Men. Shaw, Synge, O'Casey couldn't stay.' And another time: 'No one's ever flourished in Ireland: her greatest export is men. Look at the theatre, for instance. Run through Farquhar, Sheridan, Goldsmith, Wilde, Shaw, Synge, O'Casey, Brendan Behan and Samuel Beckett – all wild geese who flew the coop.'

And O'Toole is honest and immodest enough to see himself in the same bracket as the Irish greats. He is grateful to Ireland for all the stubborn, crazy, furious qualities which make him an extraordinary man, but he knows that he is well out of it. 'God, you can love Ireland but you can't live in it. It's a frightening thing.' He knows that from his father's experience. Patty O'Toole left Ireland in 1933 for a self-imposed exile in a land he distrusted, yet he never returned to his home country, not in the forty-two years that he lived in England until his death, aged eighty-six, in 1975.

Peter O'Toole has often returned to Ireland, although some of his memories are highly selective. Great moments of his childhood he will transpose to Ireland. He remembers taking long walks around Glendalough, a small loch between two small mountains outside Dublin, though when that could have happened is not clear. He remembers walking jubilantly through Irish countryside in 1945, screaming and shouting with delight that the Americans had dropped a nuclear bomb on Hiroshima, but again, how he came to be in Ireland is unclear. He had, in fact, been evacuated to Lincolnshire during the war.

Ireland has always been an important dimension of O'Toole's life. He has used it as a bolt hole. When in trouble or unwell, which is quite a lot of the time, O'Toole departs for his cottage in Galway. He describes his attitude to Ireland in this way: 'Life is chaos and confusion. When the hammers start to pound and it all becomes too much, I cut off and disappear. I go to Ireland for a rebore and a refit, just like a car.' Although he has never properly lived in Ireland, he still remains a citizen of the Republic of Ireland. When he wants to think things over, sort out his life, prepare for a particularly gruelling project, he retreats there.

For instance, when doing the groundwork on his Old Vic *Macbeth*, he went to his home in Galway and even encouraged other members of the cast to visit him there to rehearse together in the quiet of Connemara rather than the bustle of London. And it is in Ireland that O'Toole has consecrated all of his most important personal decisions. It was in Dublin that Peter O'Toole and Sian Phillips, his actress ex-wife, finally were married. And although his first daughter, Kate (named after Katharine Hepburn), was born in England, it was considered to be an error. For the birth of his second daughter, Pat, he personally visited Dublin and made the arrangements for Sian to be in an Irish maternity ward for her labour.

And O'Toole has constantly returned to Ireland for work whenever he can arrange it. In the early seventies he played in *Ride a Cock Horse* and *Man and Superman* at the Gaiety Theatre in Dublin and in *Waiting for Godot* at the Abbey Theatre, Dublin. Although the film

*Country Dance*, known in America as *Brotherly Love*, was set in Scotland, O'Toole caused half of it to be filmed in countryside similar to Ireland. And O'Toole has been a regular sponsor and proponent of Irish dramatists. He played in Beckett's *Waiting for Godot* at least once a year for many years. In 1966 he hired the Gaiety in Dublin for a production of Sean O'Casey's *Juno and the Paycock* in which he played Captain Boyle. In 1976 he opened in Peter King's *Dead Eyed Dicks* in Dublin.

He is happiest in Ireland, yet dare not live there for a long time lest he is swamped by the Irish inertia. Ireland must remain a promised land, a resting place, a holiday home, for once it becomes a daily habit, O'Toole knows that the verve and ambition which drove him to leave Hunslet behind him has gone. But in Ireland he can relax and, before illness finally drove him from the booze, he would go there to prop up a bar, natter with a few saloon bar poets, politicians and philosophers, knocking back the whiskey. 'Whenever I'm not working I go to Galway and Connemara, provided I can get past Dublin. With Dublin the only thing you can do is turn up the collar of your coat, pull your hat down over your eyes and walk straight through it: otherwise you're there forever.'

Since his illness, Ireland has lost this element of diversion. It is no longer a place to get sozzled in: quite the reverse. The constant drinking in Ireland is now a sadness to O'Toole who can no longer join in. That essential thread to Irish life – the bar and the booze – is now off-limits to O'Toole, and what worse than to have once enjoyed so wholeheartedly a place for its most sociable vice only to find that it is now forbidden him. And with the best will in the world, even O'Toole cannot enjoy exchanging wisdom with a drunk in an Irish bar if he himself is forbidden the essential lubricant to answer back with any effectiveness. The teetotaller will find it hard to while away a few hours, let alone a few days, in a country which so closely embraces alcohol as does Ireland. For that reason, Ireland is losing its magic for O'Toole who can now find inebriating company more easily in the United States.

O'Toole was a good looking child. His own description is: 'I was very pretty and rather tubby, with a mop of golden hair that I've tried to keep straight ever since.' And his earliest memory is of being lost in Leeds, seeing a man painting a telegraph pole green and, when the man left for home leaving his paintbrushes and paint behind, O'Toole remembers finishing the job for him and painting the rest of the pole. Whether this is a real memory or an amalgam of dreams, a false memory made up of family stories of when he got lost, it is difficult to say. But for O'Toole the memory is real. He even remembers being found by a policeman and taken to the station – the first of a lifetime's glimpses inside police stations – and he remembers clearly looking up at the desk, beyond the duty sergeant to the ranks of white tiles which lined the wall.

His mother instilled in him a sense of poetry, reciting verses and stories to him. But the main influence upon O'Toole's character formation, if not his upbringing – O'Toole says that he was brought up as a girl for the first dozen years of his life – was undoubtedly his father. O'Toole likes to quip: 'I'm not from the working class. I'm from the criminal class.' His father was an off-course bookie – illegal before the war – and the law was therefore always seen by the O'Toole family as an inhibition to earning an honest penny by taking bets for the neighbours. As time went by, the off-course work became on-course, and Captain O'Toole, as Patty or Paddy O'Toole liked to be known, was a commonly-seen figure at all the Yorkshire race courses of Wetherby, York, Catterick, Beverley, Doncaster and the numerous hunt point-to-points.

The young Peter idolised his father and was allowed to help at the racecourse. He learned to speak a little Yiddish from his father's Jewish clerk. On course, the Captain was always impeccably dressed in broadcloth, billycock, spats and the rest. He was even awarded the nickname of Spats because he was such a snappy dresser. But while his clothes were always in order, often his judgment was not. It was quite a regular occurrence for Spats O'Toole to make a quick getaway, pulling young Peter by the arm, when he had miscalculated the odds of a favourite winner. To grow up with a father who lived so recklessly, so close to illegality, who depended for his trade upon drumming up business in the Silver Ring, who lived from day to day upon the certainty of chance, inevitably caused Peter O'Toole to approach life in a similarly happy-go-lucky way. It was a reckless-ness which stayed with him until cinema stardom made him wary of attractive offers and smooth-talking producers and until he was personally dented by the blow of his divorce and the *Macbeth* affair.

It is from his father that O'Toole has acquired his most peculiar Irish superstitions. For instance, he always wears green when he can and always, without exception, wears green socks. As he explains: 'In the late eighteenth century, Britain made it a capital offence for the Irish to wear green, their national colour. So they made a point of wearing it, and this was handed down to my father from his father.' He touches wood whenever he tempts fate by a boastful remark. And, like every other actor, he refuses to name Shakespeare's *Macbeth*: his solution at the Old Vic was to call it *Harry Lauder*. And he has more inconvenient superstitions. He never wears a watch, never carries a wallet and never takes house keys with him: 'I just hope some bastard's in.' When they are not, he has, more than once, had to explain to the police why he should be breaking into his own home.

His friendship with his father lasted a lifetime. His parents continued living in the north during their forty-seven years together and O'Toole was heartbroken when, in 1975, his father died, aged eighty-six. He had been an inspiration to his son and had encouraged him in the career that he wanted to follow. It was in Leeds that O'Toole first tried out acting, in amateur theatricals, and he was given every encouragement by his parents. They would also take him to the theatre and the cinema. He saw Robert Donat in *Goodbye Mr Chips* when he was eight and he still remembers every frame. In particular, Patrick O'Toole gave his son a spirit of adventure. He was a thin, wiry, athletic man who was dependent for stability upon his wife Connie, much as O'Toole became dependent upon Sian Phillips.

It was a childhood like few others. There was no money in the family. The only heirloom which O'Toole could look forward to was a fob-watch which was stolen during a false bomb warning to the Old Vic when he was playing *Macbeth*. It came from his mother's father. Otherwise the income of the family was variable, depending upon chance, the success or otherwise of the horses. O'Toole remembers: 'When he'd come home from the track after a good day, the whole room would light up. It was fairyland. When he lost, it was black. In our house, it was either a wake or a wedding.'

Patrick O'Toole was a rascal who liked to drink – too much when he could afford it – and was not averse to picking a scrap with a policeman when drunk. The neighbours used to whisper behind their curtains: 'What would poor Patty do without Connie?' But for all his wayward ways, O'Toole never lived to regret his father and never would he deny what he was really like. As soon as he became famous, O'Toole came clean. His father was an off-course bookie and often fell foul of the law, he would boast to any interviewer who asked. The film company publicists would often try to cover up his father's dubious pursuits. The press handout given to critics for the film *Becket*, described him like this: 'His father travelled wherever his accounting business took him . . .' And when Patty O'Toole visited his son and daughter-in-law in their grand house in Hampstead, more often than not he and his son would become totally drunk, as befitted a man who was born at midnight on St Patrick's Day.

When Patty and Connie came up to London to celebrate the birth of their first grandchild, Kate O'Toole, there was a party at which father and son became drunk. When the rest of the family had gone to bed, O'Toole the younger was laying spreadeagled on the floor 'not asleep but crucified'. His father, out of the room to fetch another bottle, returned and tried to lift his flagging offspring to his feet. It was no good. The old man could not lift the deadweight of the plastered O'Toole. And so Patty O'Toole opened the bottle and joined his son on the floor. And that is where the pair of them were found the following afternoon. O'Toole was fond of his father's wit, even though it came nowhere near the standard of his own. That made it all the more touching when bragging of his father's remark, when more than a little tipsy: 'You can lead a horse to water, but rhubarb must be forced.' It was a mark of O'Toole's strange but undoubtedly happy childhood that he would indulge his father so.

O'Toole can thank his father not only for a love of drinking but a plague of ill-health. O'Toole remembers with affection: 'He was physically quick – whatever else I got from the old sod I got that. A little while before he died he was hit by a car as he came out of the bookie's and knocked into a saloon bar without being much damaged.' But, like his father, O'Toole suffered from ill-health, particularly to his eyes. During his childhood, his schoolwork was totally disrupted. 'You mention it, I had it. Peritonitis, eye trouble, TB, the lot.'

His eyes were so deficient that he was subjected to a series of painful and discomforting operations. Eight were performed on the left eye alone. The damage was lasting. He still has trouble with his sight and, seen in close-up – for example, at the beginning of *The Stunt Man* – they are permanently blood-shot, the white has turned to pink. He still goes cross-eyed very easily and strong light affects him, causing lumps on the eyeballs which must be removed. Added to these disabilities, during childhood O'Toole suffered from a stammer and a lisp, and, among other indignities, he was forced to be right-handed even though he is naturally left-handed. He was beaten each time he used his left hand – his right hand still bears the scars – yet with his left hand he can still write his name backwards, in mirror writing.

The constant illness which O'Toole endured as a child led to a chronic poverty of education. Although he could read by the age of three, he did not attend school on a regular basis until he was eleven years old and then he stayed for only two years. He disliked school intensely. He was rebellious and a bad pupil. The O'Tooles were good Roman Catholics and so the boy was entrusted to nuns and Jesuit priests for his education. Despite the Jesuit boast of keeping a child and winning a life, O'Toole resisted the charms of the Roman Catholic Church and today describes himself as 'a retired Christian'.

But his schooldays were not entirely a disaster. He was good at English composition and can still remember one story he wrote when about twelve years old called 'A Sound of Revelry'. It is not difficult to guess what a child psychologist would make of this. In his own words, the story 'was all about a village idiot I once met, an old twat named Obadiah, who heard a sound of revelry. He got into this pub where everyone was playing darts and enjoying themselves and he joined in the darts match, and they all poured mixed drinks down him – crème de menthe and after-shave lotion. Then they kicked him out; he got thrown through the door. But when I met him in the street outside, he felt perfectly happy; he'd been accepted at last.'

Peter O'Toole left school with no apparent benefits from those who tried to teach him. He was glad of the instruction in rugby football, which would lead to the cure of his stammer several years later. But otherwise it only left him with a feverish and antagonistic relationship with the Roman Catholic Church. In an early attempt at schooling, in a rare spell of attendance between illnesses, he had drawn a picture of a horse. And when asked by the nuns whether there was not something else which might be added to the drawing, he agreed and drew in the horse pissing. It caused a furore and he was beaten by his guardians, 'flapping nuns with white, withered hands. They'd never held a man, those hands.' It was O'Toole's first encounter with sin and, when a child and trying to imagine what sin was like, O'Toole would picture a pile of black horse manure.

Being punished for something which appeared to him so innocent was an early lesson in injustice. But for O'Toole, a Catholic boy, the injustice was backed up by the might of the black and white hawks of a nunnery. From so liberal a home, where drinking and gambling were the staples of life, he found himself puzzled and sneakily intrigued by the vagaries of his religious order. In particular he enjoyed the pomp and ceremony. It was his first introduction to a theatrical experience and he knew that he enjoyed it. It was so exciting to him that he volunteered to be an altar boy. To pretend to be pious was a small price to pay to be involved in such an important ritual. Even a bit part had its responsibilities and most certainly a uniform. O'Toole's memories of being an angelic altar boy were brushed off when, twenty-five years later, he came to play three angels in John Huston's film *The Bible*.

Looking back on his church performances, O'Toole regards it as natural that he should have been involved in the services, prompting those taking the ceremony and stage managing priests who often did not know which service they were enacting. It was plainly his introduction to theatre. 'I loved every second of it. The Mass was my first performance: it's as simple as that.' (This is an example of O'Toole contradicting himself. On another occasion he alleged that his first performance was when he was six, playing a character called Professor Toto in a children's concert. He had to feed sugar to a donkey.) The young O'Toole, a poor boy in Hunslet, saw the Church as a window on much wider things and, in those days, he believed in God. Even when sweets were rationed, during the war, he would approach the altar and leave an offering of a toffee – the most precious gift a small boy could give.

The Church was also capable of showing a more human face than the starchy nuns who perpetually scolded him. One day he surprised a priest, a Jesuit, who was smoking during prayers. He had made a feeble attempt to hide the cigarette behind his breviary. O'Toole, with more honesty than discretion, pointed out this apparent misdemeanour to the priest and asked him if it was not a sin to smoke in church. The priest was smarter than O'Toole and told him that the bishop, no less, had once caught him smoking in the church, but, to avoid a reprimand, the priest pretended to take advice, asking the bishop: 'Is it all right if I pray while I'm smoking?'

It was a friendly priest who realised that, despite the lack of formal education and an independence of spirit which made many adults despair, O'Toole was a bright child who deserved better than the menial life which his lack of qualifications would entitle him. O'Toole had left school at the earliest opportunity, at the age of thirteen. The priest took him in hand. The young O'Toole's sole ambition was to sell Jaguars, but, after a brief period working in a warehouse, wrapping cartons – he can still break string without using scissors – he was found a job on the local evening paper, the *Yorkshire Evening News*, thanks to a Catholic priest, Leo Welch, who pulled a string with the paper's general manager, who was a Catholic.

At the age of fourteen he began his career in journalism, starting at the bottom, first as a teaboy, then as a copyboy, taking typed stories from place to place. In the four years he worked on the *News*, he made good progress. He did wretched 'gopher' jobs – 'gopher this', 'gopher that' – including buying horsemeat for the chief photographer. But he also covered the span of the paper's output. He learned about photography in a dark room he instantly disliked. He learned to write captions. He assisted the art director, laying out the fancier pages. He was even allowed outside the office, to cover cricket and soccer matches and he wrote a story about a legless, ninety-two-year-old Leeds theatrical landlady.

But the thing he liked most of all was going to the cinema to see Laurel and Hardy or Buster Keaton, and plays at the Theatre Royal, to write notices. The *News* was an enlightened institution. Two afternoons a week, O'Toole would be allowed to take classes in English Literature. He became affectionately known in the office as 'The Bard of the Bog'. The newspaper office became his schooling and O'Toole is quick to give them credit. And, perhaps most of all, it filled him with a sense of ambition: 'I met people who were, as it were, in the world – who had horizons I didn't have, horizons I didn't know existed.'

It was during this time that O'Toole experienced his first brush with sex. His first sexual adventure, in fact, had been masturbating with another boy when he was twelve. 'I joined the fraternity of M M under the auspices of the reverend brothers. M M stands for Mutual Masturbation, which was regarded as a healthy alternative to ordinary sex. But I got over it. You could say I pulled myself together.' But by the age of fifteen he was ready to make the great leap to the thrilling but scarifying world of women and the real thing.

The encounter happened, ironically, on the steps of a church. He recruited a game friend and they went in search of women. Outside the doors of a church in Leeds they found two women who, looking back on it, O'Toole believes must have been semi-professional prostitutes. They were experienced, but O'Toole had been given advice to take the initiative, so he took hold of her hand and thrust it towards his flies. The result was humiliation. The woman laughed, saying: 'Put that on the mantelpiece. I'll smoke it in the morning.'

For O'Toole it was no laughing matter. It was not a great success, although he achieved penetration and the incident counts as his technical defloration. Nor was he happy about it. He was still a believer and to so wantonly give in to carnal lust was a sin high on the list of Catholic crimes. He felt enormous guilt and decided to confess. The priest in the confessional only asked two questions – 'Was it a woman, my son?' and 'Was she married?' – before condemning him to two rosaries and all the stations of the cross. O'Toole cannot remember having taken confession since.

Having discarded Roman Catholicism, O'Toole has never been able to give up wondering about religion. For all that he is a 'retired Christian', his lapse of the Catholic faith has made him more concerned about belief than had he been a lapsed Protestant. O'Toole has known what it is like to be consumed by an organised Church and to have experienced the buzz imparted by the rituals of a theatrical service. For all that he has left the Church behind him, still he has a fascination with the supernatural, an enquiring mind which demands that he turn over in his head the fundamental questions of existence and the place of man on the earth, which stem from his parental gift of Roman Catholicism. There may be no more zealous Catholic than a convert; but similarly, as O'Toole proves, there is no agnostic better versed in the jargon and mechanics of spiritual thought and the nature of sin than a lapsed Catholic.

To questions about his belief in God, he will try to remain flippant.

He will palm off a serious reply by falling back on stock debating answers. He believes, he says, in what John Le Carré has written, that the Number 11 bus goes to Hammersmith and that Santa Claus isn't driving it. He believes in what Gandhi said when, inverting the central Catholic tenet of transubstantiation, he remarked that God had no right to appear to mankind except in the shape of bread. It took O'Toole a great deal of time to reject transubstantiation and for a long time he persisted in avoiding the ultimate sin of ignoring the Church's ministry by dropping in for the shortest Mass available, the 12 o'clock Mass, known as the Short 12. As O'Toole has it: 'It's there for actors, writers, painters and other drunks, and it's short because the priest needs a drink like everybody else.'

But, as far as the Catholic Church is concerned, O'Toole has no time for religion. Having got over his 'bad case of handmaiden's knee', he is a thoroughgoing agnostic with a full armoury of justifications. On the great Catholic issues of cremation and contraception, he takes the liberal line. He was happy to marry a divorcee and the unhappiness surrounding his own divorce was not because of a theological objection. But he still has a strong view of what sin is and is happiest when indulging in sinful occupations. And he has replaced the unworldly debates of the Catholic Church for a set of more pertinent debates about politics and injustice.

He once described himself as 'a total, wedded, bedded, bedrock, ocean-going, copper-bottomed, triple-distilled Socialist' and even if he would still call himself that, now feeling it necessary to add a few riders to this previously wholehearted support, and would specify where his differences with other socialists lay, it would be to encourage and take part in an ideological discussion of politics as a type of religion. The instincts and foundations on which he builds his political beliefs and his clear view of the rights and wrongs of political actions arise out of the stern morality instilled into him from birth until he drifted away from practising Catholicism in his adolescence.

At eighteen, O'Toole had come to the conclusion that journalism was not going to be his career for life. (A view shared by his editor.) He considered that writers were only witnesses to the deeds of great men and that very few writers, let alone journalists, became great men in their own right. He also found that tripping out to find the Best of Breed result at the Great Yorkshire Show was a little tame. He had been keeping a notebook in which he confided his most private ambitions. There was no doubting his determination to leave Hunslet, Leeds and the rest of his humdrum existence behind. He wrote to himself: 'I will not be a common man because it is my right to be an uncommon man. . . . I will dig the smooth sands of monotony. . . . I do not crave security. . . . I want to hazard my soul to opportunity.'

And he knew what he wanted to do. He had become obsessional about the theatre, reading every play, going whenever possible to see actors at work. He even rehearsed scenes to himself and he was convinced that he had talent. He was determined to see the best productions. He was lucky in that Leeds, at that time, had three fully operational theatres, including a Yiddish theatre, and part of his duties as a copyboy for the paper was to move freely backstage, carrying a camera case for photographers or taking copy from stage reporters. He remembers: 'I began to love the theatre, wholly and indiscriminately, and I attended it more and more frequently.' He remembers the first play he saw, when he was six, *Rose Marie*. 'I fell hopelessly, irredeemably in love with "Hard Boiled Herman".' And, as soon as he was able, he joined the Leeds Arts Centre as a playing member.

In Leeds he was also venturing into the world of jazz, as an amateur musician. He could play the drums, after a fashion, and the bagpipes, a skill which led to his first film performance in the film of Robert Louis Stevenson's *Kidnapped*. The crowd he used to play jazz with in Leeds were an oddball lot, playing Old Leadbelly numbers. O'Toole's hero at the time was Gene Krupa, whom he considered to be the finest orchestral drummer in the business.

But his ambitions to reach the stage, as an actor or even a drummer, had to wait. In 1950, when he was eighteen, National Service was still demanding two years of every young man's life and O'Toole was called up. His verdict on the two years was to be: 'A total waste for everybody . . . particularly His Majesty.' There was no choice of service. He actively considered declining military service on religious grounds, even though his Catholicism was by this time more a habit of association than a genuine faith. He was told that he would have to invoke his Christianity to avoid joining up and he decided that, in all honesty, he couldn't pull that one, particularly as there was no war going on and he was unlikely to be in a position to put his half-baked pacifism to the test. His options were between going to jail, going down a mine or joining up, and the decision did not take long. He has said since that if there was a genuine war he would have no qualms about declaring himself a conscientious objector, but his age will prevent that hypothesis ever being put to the test. And so, for National Service, he had to express a preference between the three services.

O'Toole was guided away from the Royal Navy by the recruiting panel because he didn't have the proper background. It was a risky decision on the Navy's behalf. Once forbidden to do something,

O'Toole's sense of perversity made that forbidden service his goal. He lied rather than be turned away. He told them that he came from a long line of sailors in Ireland and that he hoped to make the Royal Navy his lifetime's career. The Navy swallowed the blarney and O'Toole was in. He was given a test of twenty questions to measure whether he was of officer potential. He only answered one. The question was, how would he lift a heavy barrel over a thirty-foot wall with two ten-foot lengths of rope. O'Toole's too-smart answer was: 'I'd call the chief petty officer and say to him: "Get that barrel over the wall." '

O'Toole was a recalcitrant recruit. He was made a signalman, decoder and encoder in the submarine service and was ordered to serve in the Baltic and the North Atlantic. From the beginning he resisted the traditions of the Navy. He referred to the deck as the floor, the portholes as windows, the funnels as chimneys. And he found out trouble wherever it lurked. He was arrested several times, for taking an extra ration of rum 'because it was a cold day' and for being insubordinate. He was also arrested for an ingenious method of decoding messages. They tried him out, first, on decoding the weather forecast, which was encoded by a Wren on shore. O'Toole was, as a 'brown-card' rating, allowed ashore and, to avoid the hour and a half it would take him to decode the forecast, he would telephone the Wren and get her to read it out in English. This worked well until someone at her end found out what was happening. She was sacked. O'Toole ended in the brig.

There was more trouble for O'Toole during the Fleet's first post-war visit to Sweden. A big ceremony was planned, with the King of Sweden greeting the British Admiral on the jetty. A fog descended and the exact location of the jetty was difficult to find. O'Toole and others were sent out in a boat with a walkie-talkie to tip off the admiral where the King could be found. O'Toole's reaction was accidentally to drop the radio into the sea. He was imprisoned once more.

Soon afterwards he was to be cured of the stammer and lisp which had cursed him since childhood. He made contact with a Swedish woman who said that she would drive him to the rugby pitch where he was to play in a Navy team against the Swedish police. She lost her way, doing a tour of the soccer grounds instead of the rugby fields, and O'Toole arrived late. As a punishment the team captain placed O'Toole, usually a threequarter back and well out of any rough and tumble, in the pack, at the front of the action. After several punishing scrums, he was removed to the full back position as an even more conspicuous target. O'Toole caught the ball with his mouth open, fell upon it and an enthusiastic Swede promptly kicked him on the chin, slicing off the front of O'Toole's tongue. He was rushed to hospital, where the tongue was stitched back together. That much is true.

O'Toole's tendency to elaborate on a good story might explain the rest. Discharged from hospital, O'Toole took the train back to the harbour and his ship but stood on the wrong platform and started his journey in the opposite direction. He spoke no Swedish, nor could he write the language, and his tender tongue made it difficult for him to utter anything other than a grunt. He recognised on the train one of the nurses from the hospital, however, who helped him back to the harbour, where his ship was just ready for departure. To avoid missing the sailing – and the inevitable punishment for arriving late – the nurse helped him to hire a funfair boat, colourfully decorated with balloons galore, and he made it to the supply ship, who threw him a rope ladder. So says O'Toole.

The upshot was that in the bisection of his tongue, the application of the stitches and the tongue-curing therapy, having to count his teeth with the tip of his tongue and so on, he completely lost both his lisp and his stammer. The only other benefits of service life for him had been to play the drum in the Navy band, to play rugby, which he had liked since his schooldays, and to be given the time to read the complete works of Shakespeare. It was also the last time that O'Toole was able to sleep properly. Particularly on watch, 'talking to the seagulls for hours and hours', he was able to doze off when he should have been looking for submarines. Since those days, insomnia has struck O'Toole and he is lucky if he is able to sleep for an hour each night.

At the end of two years, the Navy and O'Toole parted the ways. There were no regrets on either side. O'Toole was in need of a grand gesture to purge the memory of the Navy before resuming civilian life and, if possible, storming the stage for the life of an actor. He took his old Navy uniform to the Thames and threw it down into the water. He remembers that scene most clearly, particularly that the white-topped Navy cap floated downwards like a parachute and turned over just before splashing into the Thames. He remembers that he hoped that it would stay white upwards and that it was a disappointment. The way was now clear for him to return to Leeds and plan how he could enter the theatre and put into practice the motto he had invented while a reporter on the *Yorkshire Evening News*: 'Hesitate, Look, Leap.'

# 2   Learning the Trade

AND SO, after two years as an ordinary seaman in the Royal Navy, Peter O'Toole was ready to put his bold and ambitious ideas about acting into practice. The Navy had taught him little, not even what he calls 'The Eleventh Commandment: Thou Shalt Not Be Found Out'. National Service had been a gruelling sentence, one long charge with hours of lonely personal contemplation in the brig. Now he had to face a world which was not as impressed with his talents as he was himself. His qualifications amounted to only two years formal schooling. There were no exam certificates, for he had taken no exam. All he knew was that he wanted to be an actor full time. He had been able to read through the whole of Shakespeare in the off-duty hours of a signalman and he had his own views about what the text meant and how it should be translated into action.

Yet there was no prospect of becoming an actor as far as he could see. Theatres would take on no one without experience and an Equity card, and as one led to the other and vice versa, he was caught in a trap. He explained once to Kenneth Tynan that his time in the Navy reminded him of Joseph Heller's *Catch 22* and even in civilian life, the absurdities of organisations were clear. None of the acting schools would take him because he had no formal qualifications. Whether he could act or not and whether he understood the subtleties of Shakespeare's language were of no interest to the likes of the Central School and the Royal Academy of Dramatic Arts. If he was going to find himself a place in either of those places, he was going to have to talk his way in the front door.

And that is exactly what he did. On demob from the Navy, he first returned to Hunslet and a photographic job – there, at least, the *Yorkshire Evening News* had given him a skill. And he dabbled in amateur theatricals again. But he realised that to charm his way into an acting school, he would have to be on its doorstep. Armed with a few pounds of demobilisation money, he set off for a grand tour of Britain with Patrick Oliver, a painter friend. They hitch-hiked to Stratford-upon-Avon, taking in as many theatre cities as they could on the way. 'When we got to Stratford,' remembers O'Toole, 'Michael Redgrave was doing *Lear*, and we had just enough money left to buy two back stall seats. Then we had to sleep wherever we could find space, free space, so we went out into the fields and found what we thought was a haystack. Pat went crunching off to sleep. I tossed around in the hay, building a little house of it and making a bivouac, and in the process of building I discovered it wasn't a haystack, after all, but a dung heap covered with hay to keep it nice and warm and alive.' The next morning, they were so broke that they ate a hearty meal in a café then made a run for it when the waiter wasn't looking. (Years later, when he returned to Stratford to act, he visited the same café and left a massive tip. His ex-Catholic conscience runs deep.)

They hitched a ride in a lorry to London and were dropped off at Euston Station. 'We were coming to London primarily to put the arm on my sister for a few shillings, because we were so broke,' explained O'Toole. And, walking south, O'Toole, half accidentally, half wittingly, made for the Royal Academy of Dramatic Art, known throughout the acting profession as RADA. O'Toole had asked among his friends in the theatre in Leeds where the best place to learn about acting was and the unanimous view had come back that RADA was the top – any other place was second best.

So O'Toole arrived at the main building of RADA at 62 Gower Street and enquired of the secretary how he could apply to become a student there. He was told the truth; that competition for RADA places was fierce and depended upon a series of interviews and auditions. But the first requirement was evidence of a solid, broad education to a high level. O'Toole protested. He argued more in disappointment than anger, for he saw that there was no way round the lack of paper qualifications. He was already twenty and wanted to act immediately. He could not afford the time, nor did he imagine that he would have the patience and persistence, to work during the day, then sit at night school each evening, slogging for the magic certificates of virtue.

Then, by a stroke of luck which only an Irishman might expect, he was asked by a distinguished looking man what all the fuss was about. It was Sir Kenneth Barnes, the unfussy principal of RADA, who did not see a great actor in front of him, but was committed to meritocracy irrespective of the rules. Barnes was persuaded, without any prompting from O'Toole, that the young man's beef could be tested and defused by offering him the benefit of an audition. If he was good, he was in; if he was not, then he should go away.

Sir Kenneth took O'Toole into his office and subjected him to two quick examinations: one written, one oral. And the results were so promising that O'Toole was told to go away and come back in a couple of hours for a further test. O'Toole was delighted and decided that he would return looking a little smarter than before. He must have been a sight, having spent the previous night rough in a Stratford field, asleep on a dung heap, then riding in a lorry. He was unshaven and dressed in an old, thick sweater. He made for the YMCA in the Tottenham Court Road and borrowed a blazer, a tie, a pair of trousers and went into the lavatory to shave. Patrick Oliver went into a cubicle and fell fast asleep.

O'Toole returned to RADA to find that he was the subject of an audition. 'I did my test in front of a load of people – I don't know who they were to this day – and sat biting my nails for an hour and a half until Kenneth finally came out and said: "Congratulations." I'd got a scholarship, which meant that my fees were paid. And I was given a grant of five pounds a week. [Four pounds ten, to be exact.] So there it was. My life had completely changed.'

O'Toole's intelligence had won the day. His audition was a bit rough, but shed enough light on the potential that was in him for Sir Kenneth to be happy to take a chance on the young rogue. It was, after all, a romantic idea to act your way in to RADA. The rest of his time there was not to be as simple. For the first time in his life, he was among people eager to learn and people who could not really care whether he made progress or not.

There was no time for encouragement and personal tuition, as he had been used to in his brief schooldays. At RADA you either knuckled under and got on with the job of learning the trade of acting or you were out the door. O'Toole was flabbergasted. He was in. He could legitimately spend all his time thinking of the theatre instead of sneaking it in between dreary jobs. But he was also daunted. Looking at the people around him, they all seemed more articulate, more confident, above all more educated than he. Now, armed with a scholarship and provided with grants to allow him to live, it was up to him to show what he could do. The first year he did little. 'I was a bit of a child and the whole idea of London rather stunned me. The only thing I remember of that first year is gin and giggles.'

It was a most impressive collection of young actors at RADA in 1952. O'Toole's classmates included Richard Harris, an Irishman whose wayward manners could rival O'Toole's; Ronald Fraser, the solid London actor who remains one of O'Toole's dearest friends; Alan Bates; Bryan Pringle; Roy Kinnear; Tim Seely, and another Yorkshire bookmaker's son, Albert Finney, who was not only to prove a stern friendly rival for attention at RADA but would provide a parallel career of robust stage work married to well-chosen film appearances which would necessarily invite comparison.

It was at the age of twenty also that it became clear to O'Toole that the illness which had dogged him throughout his life would become a fixed part of his life, not merely a temporary childhood condition but a chronic state of ill-health which would be permanently with him. He would be admitted to hospitals regularly – a fact which he kept concealed when he became famous, for fear of frightening off work. The main cause of sickness was his stomach. His intestines were constantly troublesome and he regularly suffered from pain – pain which he would alleviate by drink. His friends testify that his drinking might have been excessive at times, but there was no need for O'Toole to drink a lot because he became intoxicated very quickly, thanks to the delicate state of his intestines.

In the three years he spent at RADA, O'Toole learnt some essential truths about acting which he has taken seriously ever since. He was, for all his boldness and wildness, most sensitive to criticism, and his eagerness to learn, and learn quickly, meant that he took comments from his tutors in acting most earnestly. The first lesson he learnt was that acting is about detail, conviction and concentration and not about wallowing in a large role. O'Toole began under the impression that the only parts worth giving his full attention to were the major roles and that to take a minor role was not only a humbling position but also one of biding one's time until a bigger part turned up. O'Toole's easy facility for memorising scripts gave him an advantage over others when fishing for principal parts. If O'Toole was not given a part fitting to his ego, he would fidget and mess around, giving a sloppy, ill-thought rendition of his few lines.

His first part, of course, was a small one and he made the most of his few words. They were in *The Appleyards* and the line he had to say was: 'It's a nice band.' But after that, O'Toole craved a part more appropriate to his ambition. He was impatient and treated the small roles he was being asked to play with contempt. One day Hugh Miller, a tutor, screamed at him: 'O'Toole, there are no small *parts*, only small *actors*.'

'He gave me the thrashing of my life in front of everybody,' O'Toole remembered. 'He pulled me out of myself, somehow, and I started working with him.' O'Toole took the criticism to heart and realised the small parts could steal a show if the actor playing them had treated them with the same imagination, ingenuity and conviction that he would use for Lear or Hamlet. O'Toole then went out of his way to make the most of small parts, treating them as a useful exercise in miniaturist character building. It was a lesson he held dear and used to great advantage when he joined his first professional company at the Bristol Old Vic.

The second lesson which O'Toole was to learn while at RADA was to use the wisdom of other, older actors as a short cut to avoiding mistakes in his own career. Like all the other student actors in London, evenings were reserved for going to the theatre and watching the old hands performing. One night O'Toole went to see Wilfred Lawson, the great British character actor who had appeared in, among many others, the film of *Fanny by Gaslight* and the 1938 British film of *Pygmalion*, playing Alfred Doolittle.

Lawson was in Strindberg's *The Father* and, by chance or by design, O'Toole found himself in the same tube carriage after the performance. O'Toole was reading a play, trying to memorise his words for a RADA lesson, when Lawson glowered across at him and hissed: 'Not in public, my boy. Not in public.' O'Toole struck up a friendship that was to last until Lawson's death in 1966. O'Toole has often given Lawson the credit for teaching him more about acting than any other person. And for Lawson's three words of advice he has been always grateful: acting is an act of conjuring and the tricks of the trade should not be revealed to the public.

O'Toole pays tribute to him. 'You know the greatest influence in my life? Wilfred Lawson. He's lent me money, taught me to drink, been my guide, mentor and friend. He's an actor to be cherished. And there aren't many. Certainly not in films.' And he delights in another piece of acting advice that Lawson liked to snap: 'Stop acting.'

A third lesson which O'Toole took away from RADA was that theatrical agents can be more trouble and expense than they are worth, particularly if you are talented. O'Toole toyed with several agents during his time at RADA, none of which gave him the value and attention he thought he deserved, and he has been wary of agents ever since. He has, of course, been most fortunate in his rapid rise to fame, rarely needing a third party to drum up business. But in principle he rejected their services before he could pick his own work and only now and then has he been tempted to employ an agent.

One play and one part which O'Toole learnt at RADA was to be of particular interest later on: that of Captain Cat in Dylan Thomas's *Under Milk Wood*, the sailor who starts scrapping on the harbour front and ends as a solitary blind man, imagining the events in his village. Nearly twenty years later, in 1971, O'Toole played the part again, persuading his friend Richard Burton and his then wife Elizabeth Taylor to join him. It was one of several favourite plays which O'Toole returns to again and again throughout his life.

On the way to RADA's public production, O'Toole suffered his first serious car crash – one of a series of motoring disasters throughout his life. This first was undoubtedly one of the worst. He was in the passenger seat when the car hit a lorry on the A1. He and a friend, who was crippled for life by the injuries sustained, were taken to hospital. O'Toole's leg was immensely painful and he was given an X-ray. O'Toole was impatient, for he was due to appear on stage that evening. After five hours lingering around in hospital, O'Toole discharged himself, took the train to London, found a doctor to prescribe pain-killers for the throbbing leg and turned up on time for the performance, giving a highly dramatic display in the traditions of 'the show must go on'. When he returned to hospital, the X-ray results proved that he had broken his leg.

He has never had much luck with driving since. One of his acquaintances said that he was better able to drive a camel than a car – which he was later able to prove most conclusively. He once fell asleep while driving his Riley on the M1 and woke up to find himself careering down the grass of the central reservation. 'There was nothing for it but to put my feet up on the dash and wait for the crash,' he recalls. He walked away from the accident, hitched a lift to the nearest town and told the AA to please go and tow the wreckage away. 'I never did see that heap again.' And he also wrote off an MG. A woman who took a ride with him swore that she would never accept the offer of a lift from him again. In a little less than half an hour, he had ignored a keep left sign on the grounds that it was 'silly'; greeted the suggestions from a well-meaning pedestrian that he ought to turn his lights on with the shout 'And keep the Pope off the moon' and had only just avoided driving down a flight of steps.

Since he has been wealthy enough to hire a chauffeur, he has left driving to others, preferring to travel in the back of his Rolls Royce and leave the dangers of the road to his driver. (His chauffeur only defied him once: during the 1964 General Election in Britain, O'Toole had demanded that everyone in his house should vote Labour. His driver declined and drove down to the polling booth in the Rolls to vote Conservative.) In 1960, O'Toole, who was then living in Hyde Park Mews, was fined £75 and disqualified from driving for a year when he pleaded guilty at Bristol to driving while under the influence of drink. 'I like a drop, you know,' he explained later. 'That's why I don't drive any more. I was banned for a year at Bristol, and even though the time's nearly up, I'm not going to drive again. I'm not very good at it, anyway; I've already written off two cars.'

O'Toole left RADA in 1955, not a star pupil exactly. Few guessed that of his intake, he would prove to be the most exalted star, if not the best-respected actor, among the class of 1952. But his talent was evident and he found no trouble in finding a permanent place in a repertory company. O'Toole says of his entry into RADA: 'I never looked back.' And he didn't. From Gower Street in London he went to King Street in Bristol and three crowded, tough, energetic years with the most thorough provincial company in Britain: the Bristol Old Vic.

'The high spot of my life was walking up the steps of the Bristol

Old Vic for the first time at the age of twenty three,' O'Toole says. 'It always will be.'

His first role was a seven-line part as a cab-driver in *The Matchmaker* and that was the first of seventy-three parts that he would play in the next three years. Although the part was very small, as the old horseman, O'Toole took his lesson hard learnt at RADA and made the most of it. He decided that an old horseman would come on to the stage and heads would turn because the old man smelt of horses: and so O'Toole did smell of horses when he arrived.

It was a trick that he played in a Chekhov production in which he was to play a Georgian peasant with the sole line: 'Dr Astrov, the horses have arrived.' The part was almost insignificant. 'I decided this Georgian peasant was like Stalin and so I played it with a slight limp, like Stalin's, fixed my make-up like Stalin and when I came on the stage, smouldering with resentment for the aristocracy, so very sinister, I could hear a hush come over the audience. Then I glared at Astrov and said 'Dr Astrov, the horses have arrived.' Once again he had turned a nobody into an attention-seeking part.

The Bristol Old Vic company is small but ambitious and O'Toole was into everything and refused no part, however small or insignificant. He explained it like this: 'Catapulted as one is through repertory, there isn't much time for deliberation. One relies on tested technical allies in what is a terrifying battle to establish contact with an audience. The most one can hope for in repertory is to give a pretty fair shadow of what would be the substance of the part, given more time.'

It is fascinating, when looking through the list of parts which O'Toole played at Bristol, to see on which roles and on which plays his passion for the theatre and actors was built and which plays and roles convinced him that stage-acting and stage-plays were the true force for acting anywhere. And in those Bristol parts, it is possible to see already the pattern he was to follow in the roles he chose later. It is not just that he was to choose 'theatrical' roles, plays which had larger than life characters to play, for he was naturally a larger than life character himself. He chose roles which had been created by a literary author. He was never to be interested in film direction; he saw it as an irrelevance to what he was about. Instead he chose parts which arose out of literary scripts, scripts by identifiable authors who, irrespective of the story and the plot, were to offer subjective views of characters, true characterisation which did not just demand an actor of intelligence to play them but needed a resourceful actor to understand them and then represent them to an audience much as a barrister would adopt and digest a brief before delivering a convinced, passionate account of his client's case before judge and jury.

When asked what contribution an actor had to give to a play or a film, O'Toole answers: 'I am the author's advocate, no more than that.'

The Bristol roles also gave O'Toole an education in literature. Unlike his contemporaries in RADA and those new colleagues he found in Bristol, O'Toole was uneducated about literature and plays. He had read through Shakespeare many times. He had, in amateur theatricals in Leeds, read and even memorised a wider range than just Shakespeare, but it was traditional amateur farce, not a rigorous education in literature. And he had gone as often to the theatre as he could, learning from actors the meaning of the plays they were delivering and the meaning of the words they were speaking. But for understanding literature, O'Toole was left to himself.

He brought his own understanding to bear upon each new play as it came before him and he did not miss the educational advantage that others had over him. He noticed the difference between those who had formally read the classics and concentrated upon books and plays as part of an exam syllabus, but he was determined that it should not prove a handicap and, when it came to it, his lack of formal education proved an advantage. He was able to bring to the lines of a play a freshness of approach which was genuine. He had not been bored by the repetition and familiarity with the text that frighten most schoolchildren from literature. He was forced to be ingenious and interpret the lines as he saw them.

Yet, perhaps most of all, O'Toole was there at the Bristol Old Vic simply because he wanted to be an actor and wanted to understand and interpret plays. The others around him had reached their first jobs by design, by a well-trodden route of hard work, rote learning, received wisdom and good chance. He had been determined to become an actor and that was all that he needed to know. He was uncluttered by the tedium of science, the drudge of mathematics, the dreariness of geography and all the other schoolroom assault course obstacles which line the traditional route to employment. Ill-health had allowed O'Toole to miss those dulling activities and it provided him with an unbridled enthusiasm and passion for acting which few others had.

The roles which Bristol gave him were therefore not simply a succession of parts, useful practice for a lifetime on the stage. They were O'Toole's education. At RADA he had been taught the theory and practice of acting, but Bristol was to teach him about plays and players, about dramatists and their intentions.

For O'Toole, Bristol was a university education. RADA may have been his principal education in name and intention, but Bristol was the true Alma Mater, for it was here that O'Toole could stop play-acting and rehearsing for the real thing. Here rehearsals were rehearsals for genuine performances in front of a paying public; lines were learnt not to impress a tutor but so that the audience would hear the play as the author wrote it; lines were delivered not to express how clever you were or find an ingenious twist to the commonplace but were to form an integral part of a whole play's worth of meaning for an audience who should not be able to notice the cleverness of interpretation – for them a line was just what a character said, as if he had invented it on the spur of the moment.

So, what were these assumed characters that formed O'Toole's personal repertory? Which plays have become so instilled in O'Toole's brain that he will quote them unwittingly in his general conversation? What are the plays by which O'Toole would come to judge the scripts sent to him by eager film producers? Which authors did he work with so closely and understand so quickly that he became a lifelong devotee to their cause? For in those seventy-three roles, O'Toole found the character he was able to slip in and out of for the rest of his career. And some of the plays and characters O'Toole has come back to again and again: they have changed from being his founding repertoire to being plays in a lifetime's repertoire.

Between 1955 and 1958, O'Toole dedicated himself to the Bristol Old Vic, which he calls 'the best repertory company in this country and the most beautiful theatre in the world'. He had made his professional debut with a seven-line part as a cabman in *The Matchmaker* and thereafter had a series of roles in which he was made up to look like an old man. It was so convincing that one observer wrote of him: 'This old man of sixty or seventy, this Peter O'Toole, who is never going to make it big, but isn't it a delight when you find someone who clearly shows no bitterness or resentment?'

He went on to larger roles. He played Corvino in *Volpone*; Bullock in *The Recruiting Officer*; Peter Shirley in George Bernard Shaw's *Major Barbara*; Lodovico in *Othello*; Alfred Doolittle in Shaw's *Pygmalion* (years later he was wooed for *My Fair Lady* the film musical version of Shaw's play); Jimmy Porter in John Osborne's *Look Back in Anger*; Lysander in *A Midsummer Night's Dream*; Jupiter in *Amphitryon 38*; he played in Peter Ustinov's *Romanoff and Juliet*.

His first Shakespearean role was as the Duke of Cornwall in *King Lear* in which Eric Porter played the mad king. O'Toole was very impressed by Porter's ability as an actor and unashamedly took notes and hints from him. 'Eric was one of the two great Lears I've seen. The other was Donald Wolfit. He was the best young actor I'd ever seen, a real catalyst for me. Eric was similar to me in all sorts of ways that I was uninhibited about using. He released a lot of my own energies because of his great looseness and power.'

And repertory brought its variety. The cast of *Lear* alternated with *Dick Whittington* and Eric Porter had to switch from king to pantomime dame. And O'Toole was also drawn into panto, an essential winter money-raising ritual. One year, when playing in *Alladin*, O'Toole had to sell ice creams in the interval dressed as Mrs Ali Baba. One evening, dressed in drag in the stalls, he sold an ice cream to Cary Grant.

Other parts were more demanding. It was at Bristol that O'Toole first played in Samuel Beckett's *Waiting for Godot*. For the next fifteen years, O'Toole performed in one version or other of *Godot* at least once each year. He has acted in three proper, full-length versions and has performed Sunday night readings and extracts. In 1959 he worked on a film script of it, with the intention of filming it with his own money, but the project fell through. He has also worked on a television script of it, to no avail.

He saw it first at the Babylone in Paris and since then he has been obsessed with it. 'I saw it for the first time with a boy who was mentally disturbed at the time and I remember him turning round to me halfway through and saying with a great smile on his face, "Someone else knows".' After Paris, he read the play in English, saw a production at the Arts Theatre in London directed by Peter Hall, which he loathed, and was then cast as Vladimir in the Bristol Old Vic production. It was the first part which really personally affected him. Before the first night he was discovered in his dressing room 'screwed up in a kind of agony, as if he was in labour. It was the nearest artistic equivalent to giving birth.'

That first night O'Toole has described as the turning point in his career. 'Nat [Brenner] came to see me before the opening night of *Waiting for Godot*. I had gone in an hour and a half early – a thing I hadn't done before. I used to go in a half hour before, make up quickly and go on. That night Nat told me to lie down and put on eye pads and pretend I was a foetus. That night something began to click and I realised what it was all about – me, waiting for Godot. It was a rebirth, probably. Now I always have to be there an hour and half or two hours early, even when I'm making a film, and I put on eye pads and became a foetus.'

Later, O'Toole explained: 'I can't rationalise why it meant so much to me. I know that when I played it it had its own meaning for me. It meant a great deal to me at that particular period. I think it was a wedding of both my growth as an actor and as a man. For the first time I think ever, I really felt that marvellous – I suppose it is the only word – power. It began to work. I had my head against a wall for

42

years with the most basic things – timing, movement, even double takes. As far as I was concerned, that was the great click.'

So impressed was he with *Godot* that some years later he persuaded Beckett to give him the film rights. But Beckett was pessimistic. When O'Toole spoke to him about the film project, Beckett said he wished he had never given him the rights and that he thought it would never be made into a film. He was quite right.

O'Toole's unhampered mind took *Godot* very simply and literally. 'Happily none of us ever questioned it. We simply took it literally as a piece. It never occurred to us to sit down and chew what it was all about. No symbols where none intended, and all that Beckettiana. He was called Lucky because he'd got nothing to say in the second act. And the same thing happened again when we did it in Ireland. Everybody took it literally, comma for comma, and it seemed to make total sense. It's the well made play of all time.'

In other plays he was a little too accurate for his own safety. In a play called *The Pier*, he played a Teddy Boy (this was the mid-1950s) so convincingly that a certain section of the audience took exception. When O'Toole left the theatre that night, walking along the dark, high-walled King Street, a bunch of Teds jumped him and gave him a dusting down. O'Toole, who was used to a little rough and tumble from his days in Leeds and the Navy, was unperturbed and only slightly bruised, and he took the attack as a perverse compliment. He had plainly made such an impression that people were prepared to put up their fists against a character of his creation.

The Bristol Old Vic was also to take him to London. His London debut was at the Old Vic in the Waterloo Road, as Peter Shirley in Shaw's *Major Barbara*. It was a thrilling moment for him. But the London appearance in his early career for which he is most remembered was in 1957 in a strange musical, *Oh My Papa*, which had been a great success at Bristol. It opened at the Garrick Theatre in Charing Cross Road. O'Toole shared the star billing with Rachel Roberts and he had the title song to sing. It was not a success. On the first night there was booing from the stalls and the long-running success which everyone in Bristol had hoped for folded quietly. That opening night did, however, give O'Toole something to celebrate and celebrate he did, drinking home-made mead, as he told the policemen who arrested him at three the following morning for harassing a building in Holborn. O'Toole spent the night in the Theobalds Road police station cells.

Of all the productions at Bristol, the one that made him best known among the critics and theatre establishment was his highly original interpretation of Hamlet. He was only twenty-five when awarded the part and the play was changed about to suit his talents and capabilities. He rehearsed the Prince of Denmark for a bare three weeks while, each evening, playing a pantomime dame and thinking of *Man and Superman* which was to follow. It was not so much ill-prepared as scantily prepared. 'There was no time for great intellectual work. For me, *Hamlet* is an essay in the passions, in the Elizabethan sense. I was anxious to make the play work and not use it for head back and sonority of utterance, what I call the sonneteer school of acting, which I can't bear.'

He was aware of the importance of the part he was about to play. In *Godot* he might have broken through the barrier of self-confidence and realised what acting could be about. In *Hamlet* he was being given a chance to show how substantial those advances were. It was also a chance to prove to the rest of the company that his brash behaviour, his boastful, critical personality and his drinking did not disguise incapability. He had a chance to prove to them that he was a serious actor, that he was going somewhere and that his ambition was more than pie in the sky. It was this pressure upon him that led to last minute nerves unlike anything since *Godot*.

On the first night, before the curtain was raised, he suffered a last minute crisis of confidence. 'It was the most humbling, humiliating experience of my life. As I went up some steps for my first entrance I suddenly knew, before I even got on stage, that the energy wasn't there, that it was not going to be good. It gave me a split second to prepare myself – the old pro, able to perform decently – but I realised I'd lost. It was awful, Awful.' That first night, on 23 April 1958, was to open the month-long run and the critics disagreed with O'Toole. His performance was far from awful.

Under the heading 'Now an Angry Young Hamlet', *The Times* gave this verdict: 'This Hamlet feels and thinks more subtly than [Rosencrantz and Guildenstern] and twice as quickly; his soliloquies reproduce mental process with a gripping freshness. Before the play scene Mr O'Toole sits with his head between his knees, like a nervous tennis player before his first appearance on the Centre Court and he listens to the Ghost rigid in suspense. This is as near to repose as we get in a restless interpretation, crudely staccato in diction and gesture yet blessed with uncommon energy and staying power.' It was an exceptional notice. Although the 'angry young bearded rebel' of John Moody's production was, apparently, 'handicapped by a pair of boots which make nonsense of any pretensions to nobility, Mr Peter O'Toole holds this perverse conception together with a Hamlet who would seem hopelessly miscast but for the fact that he conveys thought and feeling in a kind of instantaneous neurotic fashion.'

It was just what O'Toole had hoped. The old-fashioned notion of Shakespearian acting, with a stilted delivery of lines, found no sympathy with O'Toole. 'I meet Shakespeare on his own terms. Shakespeare's a theatre man, for Christ's sake, not a deity. His people are real. You can smell their breath. They piss against the wall. That's the way I play Shakespeare.' The critics were convinced and that Bristol Old Vic production has gone down in history as a landmark of post-war British theatre, the moment when the theatre loosened up and abandoned the gulf between a formal theatre audience watching 'respectable' Shakespeare played with decorum. O'Toole's Hamlet was a real figure, easily understood by a new generation of urgent, serious, intense young theatregoers for whom O'Toole would remain a life-long representative of their generation.

It was that exceptional Hamlet which caused O'Toole's name to be bandied about by critics, producers, directors and other actors. And when his contract with Bristol ran out, he was in demand. But O'Toole left the company with many regrets. For him it was like leaving home. For all the rows and the disagreements, for all the jealousy and the accidents – he twice set his dressing room on fire accidentally – he had met a lot of good friends and been properly launched on a profession which appeared at that stage to be promising. He was proud to have been a member of what was a golden period of the Bristol Old Vic company. Since then it has rarely regained that standard of production, that verve and quality of original acting.

Perhaps' O'Toole's closest and most dedicated friend is Kenneth Griffith, the Welsh actor and film maker. He is so close to O'Toole that O'Toole's ex-wife, Sian Phillips has said to him: 'Only one person knows Peter better than I do – and that is you.' And that extraordinary friendship was formed during O'Toole's days in Bristol. Rediffusion were filming a television version of James Forsyth's *The Pier*, the play in which O'Toole, inspired by the television version, put on and so convincingly portrayed a Teddy Boy in Bristol. For that reason he was invited to join the cast for nine days of rehearsal and shooting at an Irish club in Islington which has since been knocked down. Three days passed and there was no sign of O'Toole. Peter Vadeck, the play's director, had no idea where he was.

On the fourth day, the doors of the hall were pushed open and there in the doorway was a tall, young tramp. 'Sorry I'm late, darlings,' he said and he came down the steps, staring Griffiths straight in the eyes. He sat in the corner and watched as Griffith went through his lines. O'Toole sat silently, gazing at Griffith in admiration. When the scene had been finished, O'Toole stood up, strode towards Griffith, staring all the while, and kissed him, saying: 'I think you're bloody marvellous.' Griffith was horrified and intrigued. After rehearsing with O'Toole, Griffith surveyed the tall, gangling young man, sat backwards on a chair. He remembers: 'I knew it was the most formidable opposition I'd seen.'

They went to Manchester to record the play and Griffith, ten years older than O'Toole and already an established actor of note, recognised the young man's energy. He asked the assistant floor manager to ask O'Toole to share his dressing room. O'Toole was quick off the mark: 'Which fucking half of the dressing table are you having?' he asked. They soon became close friends and Griffith visited him in Bristol several times. Among O'Toole's crowd was Patrick Dromgoole, who was to become programme controller of Harlech Television, and Tom Stoppard, the playwright, then working as a journalist on the *Western Daily Press*. They would drink a lot and get up to tricks.

And when O'Toole left Bristol for good, he got in touch with Griffith and asked him if he could come to live with him in his flat, a shoe-box in Dorset Mews, Belgravia, the only unsmart part of Belgravia, behind the National Coal Board. And the three of them – Griffith, his girl friend, later to become his second wife, Doria Noar, and O'Toole – lived happily there together. O'Toole often brings that small flat into his stories. 'My bed was held up by postage stamps,' he will say. They were Griffith's postal history collection.

O'Toole did not live a London bachelor life for long. He went on a tour in 1958 with Sian Phillips in a play called *The Holiday*. It was intended, eventually, to reach the London stage but they had another reason for taking the parts of brother and sister. 'We both took parts in this play because we wanted to have a look at each other,' she explained. 'I'd always imagined him to be a short, fat man and when we met I discovered he was tall and thin. It was quite a shock.'

Sian Phillips had been married and divorced. Her father was a policeman and later a caretaker of the Dyffryn Educational Centre at St Nicholas in Wales. She was educated at Pontardawe Grammar School and graduated from University College, Cardiff, before joining the BBC as a Welsh Region radio announcer. In 1955 she won a scholarship to RADA and, in August of the same year, she married Donald Roy, a lecturer in French at Glasgow University, but the marriage was not a success. 'I never lived with him so I like to think it never happened.'

She left RADA in 1957 with the Bancroft Gold Medal, the Academy's highest award, as well as the William Poel Prize for delivery in stage rhetoric and the Arliss prose-speaking competition. She went to Oslo to play the lead in Henrik Ibsen's *Hedda Gabler* and the notices hailed her as 'a fully fledged, utterly delightful Ibsen actress'. The *Sunday Times* described her as another Sarah Bernhardt. It was inevitable that O'Toole and Sian Phillips should want to meet each other, but they did not guess at what would result.

Sian Phillips describes the tour of *The Holiday* like this: 'We were playing brother and sister in a show which did the disappearing act. You know, they tell you you're doing a pre-London run and when you get to Birmingham they say we'll just do a few more weeks in Nottingham and then you go on to Leeds and so on right up to Scotland where the whole thing fades out. But we got married at the end of the run, so it wasn't total disaster.'

They married in secret in a registrar's office in Dublin. Perhaps the one thing that O'Toole has not forgiven Griffith for is that he refused to desert a film job to be best man. Sian's divorce and his inclination made it an obvious thing to do, although it was difficult to keep quiet. All of their friends guessed that, at the very least, they were intimate with each other. Kenneth Griffith knew exactly what had gone on because they were living with him and Doria Noar in the tiny flat in Dorset Mews. Griffith had even been consulted by both partners before they decided to marry. But they kept the whole thing quiet for a year. It was when they had finished a BBC television play together, Saunders Lewis's *Siwan*, recorded in Cardiff, that Sian told Griffith that they were planning to marry and they finally decided to let the secret out. When they had both visited the Llangollen Eisteddfod, where Sian was admitted to the Gorsedd, the press questions and rumours became so annoying that they fled to London in a taxi which cost them £25.

For O'Toole, that last tour of Britain was the last routine theatrical experience of his life. Never again would he be able to taste that raw experience and genuine appraisal of an audience. From then on – by coincidence, from the moment he married Sian Phillips – his life would take off. Success would follow success. He would no longer be judged as merely an actor but as a star. That meant that failure or mediocrity were themselves news. It meant that his private life, which was never likely to be quiet and well ordered, would become the raw material for gossip columnists. His marriage, his indiscretions, his brushes with the law would all be prominent news.

He was very ambitious, of that there was no doubt. He had a high opinion of himself and, since the Bristol *Hamlet*, he was invested with expectations from the press and from theatre people. He was prepared to change his looks to advance his career. He was toying with having his prominent nose, which had been further increased by bashings about in rugby and in scraps, lose its humpbacked shape by having a plastic surgeon nip it into a pert snub. So he was prepared for success. But he could not guess how soon and how fast the process would be.

Before the secret of his wedding was out he was famous, hailed once more as a superlative actor. And from that would come more acting honours and the lucrative offers of film parts. Within a year of that clandestine marriage, most of London would have heard of him. Within two, most of Britain would have heard of him. Within five years, he would be a worldwide star. And all would be achieved while maintaining the high principles of a young, serious actor. He did not guess it would happen that simply, although he believed he had a chance. And when he went on that one-way ticket tour with *The Holiday*, he had no idea that it would be the last he saw of the normal actor's life, flogging from one city to another, taking what jobs came along without the luxury of being choosy. He came back with a wife and walked with her onto an escalator to wealth, fame and not a little unhappiness.

# 3 From Sloane Square to Stratford

IT WAS important for O'Toole to consolidate the gains he had made so far. His Bristol Hamlet had certainly caused a sensation, but memories were annoyingly short when it came to success. He was not sure whether his performance really was as good as the critics had said, or whether they were using hyperbole for their own ends. After all, theatre critics like to be ones to discover great new talents and every now and then an unwarranted superlative was in order. No biographer trawls through the files holding up to ridicule a critic who went nap on a nobody – they only notice those who back an actor who makes it. O'Toole knew that praise came cheap for those who wrote for newspapers and his proud cuttings of the notices for his angry young Hamlet would soon yellow. He needed another substantial part, one that would attract a good press and in a theatre more prominent than the little Georgian theatre in Bristol.

Then, out of the blue, he was sent a script of Willis Hall's *The Long and the Short and the Tall*, a play about soldiers lost in the Japanese campaign with a wireless on the blink. It was a lively but contrived theatrical piece, with a representative sample of British young manhood: a nervy Yorkshireman, a serious-minded Scot, familiar with the Geneva Convention, a naive Welshman, who saw little further than the gossip in the letters from home; and the part that O'Toole was being asked to consider – that of Private Bamforth, a loud, cocky and blatantly cowardly Cockney, the most conspicuous role in the play, which would go on in the most prominent showpiece theatre for young talent, the home of angry young actors, the Royal Court in Sloane Square, London.

O'Toole read the part quickly and sent back his reply. 'I wrote back saying it's marvellous, whoever plays it will become a star and please let it be me. Next thing I know, Albert Finney's playing it, and the next thing I know after that is that Albie's got appendicitis and they're asking for me again. At first I turned them down, because Albie and I had joined the Royal Academy together and we were both tottering about trying to get our feet in the door – in fact we still have a certain sort of dark, professional rivalry – but in the end I took the part and I'm very pleased I did.'

49

O'Toole makes it sound more straightforward than it was. *The Long and the Short* began life as *The Disciplines of War* on the Edinburgh Fringe, where it was a great success. George Devine, at the Royal Court, saw it as a natural play for his theatre and quick preparations were made for a production. Albert Finney was offered and accepted the central part of Bamforth, then fell ill. O'Toole, among others, was sent a script. Since the Bristol Old Vic, he had been barely in work. Suddenly he was in demand to play the part of the artist Henri Gaudier-Brzeska in a BBC Television production. The producer, John Jacobs, had met O'Toole at the home of Kenneth Griffith in Dorset Mews and Griffith had enthused about his young friend, declaring him one of the best actors in Britain. When Jacobs laughed, O'Toole left the room in a sulk. But Griffith was not joking and, when Jacobs was stuck in Paris, unable to find a suitable actor for his Brzeska film, he rang Griffith and asked him whether he was being serious about O'Toole. Griffith said he was and O'Toole was offered the part.

O'Toole wavered. He wanted the Bamforth part more than anything, but was tempted by the television offer. It would be his first leading role on television. On Griffith's advice, he accepted the television role, then, again on Griffith's advice, he stormed round to the Royal Court, to George Devine's office and told him to take the script back in a way which made Devine's secretary remember the exact, impolite, wording many years later. The ploy worked. Denial is a short step from wanting and O'Toole was promptly offered the part and accepted. Both Bamforth and Brzeska were his.

*The Long and the Short and the Tall* was directed by Lindsay Anderson, who later was to direct the film *If* and *O Lucky Man*, and included a cast led by Robert Shaw, the only well-known actor among a clutch of young hopefuls; Edward Judd; Alfred Lynch, David Andrews, Bryan Pringle, Ronald Fraser and O'Toole. O'Toole had no qualms about upstaging the others. He had been too long off the stage. The critics were bowled over by his performance as an uncouth, blaspheming but ultimately noble Cockney.

Harold Hobson, theatre critic of the *Sunday Times* and then the most powerful voice among stage critics, wrote: 'The big part is Private Bamforth. It is taken by Peter O'Toole, whom one critic (before ever he appeared in London) greeted as an actor who would reach the heights of his profession, and who was called by another (me) the best young player in Britain. Is Mr O'Toole too exuberant at the start? Perhaps; but then, I don't like bawdy jokes. But he is the point of active life in the play; and to the piece's unexpected and beautiful lyric passage in the second act he supplied a subdued musical accompaniment or comment, traditional, ribald and ironic, which is not easily to be forgotten.' The general critical consensus was that both the play and O'Toole were a great success. And when the Variety Club came to make an award for the best actor of 1959, it was given to O'Toole for Private Bamforth.

The important thing for O'Toole was that he was in a prominent showcase. Here, close to those who took important career decisions, was a chance for them to see for themselves what all the fuss surrounding O'Toole was about. They did not need to rely on flattering press cuttings; they could see for themselves. And significant in conjuring up work for O'Toole, according to him, was not an impresario or a producer or an agent, but another actor: Katharine Hepburn. 'She came round one night after the show and said she liked it very much, but I was too overwhelmed to speak, so we just said bye-bye. Then suddenly my phone never stopped ringing – producers and directors all wanting me, which surprised me because I was bad news at the time; they'd written me off as a Cockney savage. But she'd gone around and done a Barnum and Bailey for me. I met people – and I keep on meeting people – who'd say: "Kate Hepburn told me all about you." What a sweet thing, I thought. I hope I can do the same for someone someday.'

And others went to the Royal Court to see O'Toole's performance, among them Sam Spiegel, the American producer for Columbia Pictures, who was looking for suitable actors to play in the film which he and David Lean were planning as the next in a successful partnership which had just completed *The Bridge Over the River Kwai* – it was to be an epic story of the life of T. E. Lawrence.

Another important visitor was Peter Hall, who, at twenty-nine years of age, had just been made the director of the Shakespeare Memorial Theatre at Stratford-upon-Avon. He was determined to follow up the spirit of youth which his appointment signified, by finding some bright young actors to sparkle in his first Stratford season. After *The Long and the Short and the Tall*, O'Toole was on Hall's wanted list. And O'Toole's availability in London led to a number of small film parts which, he hoped, would lead to a proper film career.

Since RADA, O'Toole had been doing small parts in films and television – many of them uncredited. 'I did lots of stunts when I was at RADA under all sorts of names,' he remembered. 'Walter Plings, Charlie Staircase, Arnold Hearthrug. The first proper thing I did was called *Once a Horse Player*, which was for television. Then a thing I wrote myself called *End of a Good Man*. A little Sean O'Faolain story. Then I played a journalist on an airplane with Patricia Neal.'

His television debut, however, was earlier still, in an episode of *The Scarlet Pimpernel*, with Marius Goring as the British aristocrat whisking French gentry from execution at the hands of the French

Revolutionaries. 'I played his aide-de-camp,' said O'Toole, 'Chaubertin, the man who chases him. I was at RADA. I had to say – what's that bird: "A sea mune, citizen." And he said: "Shoot it." And I said: "It's night, citizen." Then I had to chase somebody on a horse. I mean I was on the horse. Filled it with sugar lumps. It was rattling with them. I had to chase after this coach. Lost an iron, swallowed a fly, lost a wig and said: "You are to make the acquaintance of Madame Guillotine." End of part.'

And he remained in costume when he came to play his first substantial film part, in Robert Stevenson's production of Robert Louis Stevenson's *Kidnapped*, for Walt Disney, with Peter Finch. It was Finch himself who suggested O'Toole for the part, one in which Finch, as Alan Breck, duels the son of Rob Roy MacGregor with bagpipes. When Finch had first read the script, he said: 'There's only one actor I know who could play the part and the fucking bagpipes', and that was O'Toole. He had learnt to play the pipes as a boy in Lord Kolmorry's Own Hibernians, an Irish piping and dancing group based in Leeds, and it was one of many extra-curricular skills that would stand him in good stead for the cinema.

And shortly after *Kidnapped*, where he was wedged in the credits between Andrew Cruickshank and Alex MacKenzie, he was given a larger part in *The Day They Robbed the Bank of England*, adapted from a novel by John Brophy about a group of soldiers, led by O'Toole as a lieutenant in the Scots Guards, who engineers an audacious robbery. Produced by his partner, Jules Buck, and directed by John Guillermin, it was the last film to be made before O'Toole signed for Peter Hall's Stratford season. As O'Toole remembers: 'Buck wanted me to play the tearway Irishman, but I asked if I could play the Guards officer, which was a lesser role, and he said yes.' The film was released a month after O'Toole's Stratford opening, as Shylock in *The Merchant of Venice*. By that time, he was being hailed, once again, as a major discovery of the theatre – and the cinema critics were not to be outdone.

Felix Barker, of the *Evening News*, London, was a cinema critic and a theatre critic and was pleased therefore to be able to use the knowledge of one in his assessment of the other. He was certain he had discovered a major acting talent, and one that moved easily from medium to medium. He wrote: 'It happened again this week – that magical moment in the critic's routine when a magnetic spark seems to come out of the screen and he knows that he is seeing the birth of a great star. It comes too seldom these days. And often the spark of light dies out through neglect or bad use by the producers. But I have an idea that Peter O'Toole is going to blaze a fiery trail over our screens that will make some other reigning satellites look stale.' And

Dilys Powell, the *grande dame* of film criticism, wrote in the *Sunday Times*: 'Peter O'Toole looks like being a gift to the British cinema as well as the theatre.'

For O'Toole, however, *The Day They Robbed the Bank of England* was a humbling experience. He was horrified at his own immodest reaction to seeing himself on the screen. 'I only ever saw myself once in rushes when I did *The Day They Robbed the Bank of England*. I was horrified and for days afterwards I was posing and strutting about. It made me feel self-conscious, which is death for an actor. The I-love-me department; when to twitch what; you know.' He had fallen in love with his own image. 'I was shattered. For the next two weeks I felt like death. I couldn't work, I couldn't talk. I just posed and farted about like an idiot. It made me self-conscious and awkward. Self-aware is one thing; self-conscious is another.' He was so shaken that he determined never to watch rushes of his films again, nor, if he could possibly help it, see his films right through. It is a vow he has kept, not seeing *Lawrence of Arabia* until years after it was released – he gave his ticket to the preview to Kenneth Griffith, then asked him afterwards: 'How is it?' – leaving the image alone until he looks upon it as a piece of history, totally removed from himself.

The final film he made before embarking on his Stratford season – and a film which kept him driving madly for ten weeks between Stratford rehearsals and the set in Pinewood – was *The Savage Innocents*. Also known as *Ombre Blanche* and *Les Dents du Diable*, starring Anthony Quinn and Aldo Ray, it was based on Hans Ruesch's *Top of the World*, set in the Canadian snowy wastes and was to be written and directed by Nicholas Ray, a man whom O'Toole admired, though not for long for his film-making abilities. 'Nick Ray. Good Lord, he was an interesting man. I was more interested in his radio show than anything else. He was employed by the Library of Congress and he was resurrecting old musicians like Leadbelly, Burl Ives, Pete Seeger. He was into all that, as indeed I was.'

But, as far as O'Toole was concerned, the film was a disaster. After two weeks, he regretted that he had become involved. 'It was the funniest thing I've ever been in. There was a small part, in this story about an Eskimo, for an Irish-Canadian mounted policeman who goes to arrest this Eskimo. The Eskimo saves his life and insists he sleeps with his wife. He gets to adore the Eskimo and his wife, but the Eskimo must turn himself in. The Eskimo insists on being arrested and the only way he can get rid of the Eskimo is by kicking him in the face. That's how it started off, but they changed it every day and I suddenly turned out to be a French-Canadian. There was a marvellous moment where they rewrote so much they got stuck. They'd got huskies and polar bears and all sorts of things and they didn't know how to get this sledge made, so I suggested the Eskimo should eat me – that would have given him nourishment – then make a sledge out of my bones and skin. They said: "We want a happy ending", and I said: "Couldn't he whistle?" '

It was a crash course in film-world insanity which O'Toole did well to learn so early in his career. The snow in the picture was really huge piles of salt and there were performing seals who refused to perform who had to be fed pounds of fresh fish. Two polar bears were imported from Dublin and, because they didn't look white enough against the salt, they were covered in peroxide, which drove them mad. O'Toole was becoming quite distracted himself, working hard on the set in Pinewood, then driving too fast to Stratford for his *Merchant of Venice* rehearsals. One day, driving his car, the steering failed and he crashed. He was not hurt, but the rehearsal was abandoned.

*The Savage Innocents* was to cause him more aggravation when he learnt that Ray had decided that his voice, delivered in a strong Irish brogue, was inappropriate and that another voice needed to be dubbed on top. O'Toole was livid. He was vain and arrogant and saw this act of film lunacy as an assault on his integrity. 'I've made them take my name off the picture,' he said, pompously. 'I don't want anything to do with it. As far as I'm concerned, the whole thing is a shambles. The part was cut and cut and is now only about twenty minutes at the end of the picture. Then I was told that the Irish accent I used had to be changed to a Canadian one. So now they've got another actor to put in a Canadian accent. The whole thing's a mess. I've told them I'll sue if my name appears on the film.'

Whatever the rights or wrongs of the case, O'Toole was unwise to make such a public fuss about such a slight film, particularly as he was being closely watched by producers with an eye to casting him in more important projects. His loud-mouthed attacks on his employers and his off-duty drinking habits and uncouth behaviour were becoming well-known – too well-known for his own good – for anyone wanting to hire him for a picture and thus invest a considerable amount of money in his talents, wanted to be assured that he would behave and keep his reservations about projects to himself.

There had already been one bitter disappointment for O'Toole. A film of *The Long and the Short* was planned and, through his success in the part on stage, he was plainly in the running to play the part of Bamforth. Leslie Norman was to direct and the film was to be little more than a screen version of the stage play, with a minimum of opening up. O'Toole was encouraged in the part, but finally a decision was taken against him and Laurence Harvey, then a much more prominent screen personality, was cast instead. O'Toole was thoroughly miffed. 'Upset? I could have shot myself. I could have shot the film company. I was told I could have the part if I signed a contract with them for 155 years. I wouldn't go under contract.'

Life wasn't all disappointments. Six weeks before he was due to open in *The Merchant*, Sian gave birth to a baby girl, who was to be called Kate, a little after the Shrew and a lot after Katharine Hepburn. O'Toole was delighted, but he and Sian were not prepared to allow the arrival of a family to interrupt their careers. A black cook-cum-nannie, called Lonnie Trimble – nicknamed by O'Toole, 'Le Mumbo' – was hired to look after the child while O'Toole was on the stage and Sian was doing television work. And the baby was hauled around Stratford in a carry-cot, taken to parties and generally made a fuss of by the company. Peter Hall agreed to the child being allowed to make a theatrical debut on the Stratford stage the following September in the christening scene in *The Winter's Tale*.

The arrival of a daughter added to the considerable nervous pressure on O'Toole. He was spearheading an extraordinary experiment in theatre under the direction of Peter Hall at Stratford. Hall's intention was to bring together a hugely talented company with which to transform the way the public appreciated Shakespeare. To ensure that the audiences were large and immediately receptive to what was going on on stage, Hall had deliberately chosen people who already had reputations, where possible from the world of films as well as theatre. Hall wanted to widen the appeal that Stratford had. Hitherto it had been a rather worthy institution keeping alive the playing of Shakespeare in Shakespeare's birthplace. It was above all things respectable and to maintain that respectability, it had remained conservative and traditional. Shakespeare was presented with few surprises by actors whose credentials were impeccable.

Hall wanted to change all that and had, at an extraordinarily young age, been granted a mandate from the Governors of the Shakespeare Memorial Theatre to make what changes were necessary to make Stratford not only the showpiece for Shakespeare in Britain, but one of the foremost places for drama in the world. Hall thought he knew what was necessary. He would first inject an element of drama and of glamour into the Stratford company. It should be a place where actors wanted to work – not a remote provincial venue for those whose careers needed an injection of reliable, old-fashioned theatre as a break from the idiocies of commercial managements in the West End.

From the moment that Hall arrived, with his glamorous wife, Leslie Caron, a film actress, he wanted to be the centre of theatrical excitement in Britain in a place where theatregoers of the world must make a pilgrimage: Stratford as a place for enthusiasts not merely tourists. And, to throw off the stuffy, comfortable image, Hall needed young people like himself, above all to bring some excitement to Shakespeare and introduce the plays of Shakespeare to a younger, more lively audience.

The first play in Hall's repertoire was to be *Two Gentlemen of Verona*, a rather odd choice for an opening, but a well-chosen one. It was little staged and would therefore ensure that no one could either accuse the new régime of safety or – just as important – of frippery. This was an unusual revival. It was also unflashy, a quality which disappointed many of the critics who drove all the way from London to see what was going on. But the relative modesty of *Two Gentlemen* also suited Hall's ambitions, for he did not want to be accused of pyrotechnics for their own sake. This was to be a solid, even worthy, production which showed that solid productions needn't be as dull as they had been at Stratford. And, for the existing audience at Stratford, this opening production would seem undisturbing, a reassuring start to what had been billed as a revolution in theatrical thinking.

The real excitement was to start with the second production, *The Merchant of Venice*, directed by Michael Langham, director of the Stratford (Ontario) Shakespeare Festival and boasting a magnificent cast: O'Toole was to play Shylock; Dorothy Tutin was to play Portia; Denholm Elliott was Bassanio. And the rest of the cast included Patrick Allen, Ian Holm, Dinsdale Landen and Jack McGowran. Central to the production was O'Toole as Shylock, at twenty-six, the youngest leading man at Stratford ever. And he was to play it in an original way, as an individual Jew who tries to persuade the audience that his commercial logic is correct and appropriate. He was not going to play the Jew as an old-established avaricious moneylender but as a go-ahead sixteenth century entrepreneur, out to maximise his legitimate profits.

It was an interpretation that had taken a great deal of time to formulate. O'Toole was aware how important this single performance was to be to his career and he took no chances. He prepared for five weeks, then rehearsed for nine. He and Sian spent a week discussing the part with Dr Moelwyn Merchant, a lecturer in English at Cardiff, then he went into the Welsh mountains to learn the part. His conception of Shylock was of 'a man of enormous substance, who loves making intellectual points, as in the distinction between business and usury, the parable of Laban's sheep.' And he did thorough research on the part, so that it would feel authentic to himself and through him to the audience.

'I have no actual experience of what a Jew feels like with his patriarchal responsibilities,' he remembered, 'so I found out one or two of his rites for cursing and the Prayer for the Dead, and the Rending of the Garment. I was assisted by a Jewish Tubal and we composed our own little ceremony.' And he admitted – an extraordinary thing for an actor who was about to play Shylock at Stratford – that he had never seen a production of *The Merchant*. 'I'm in the very happy position of never having seen Shylock before. I gather he has often been played as a grubby pawnbroker from the ghetto. Yet the Jewish father has the power to say the Prayer for the Dead which I mutter to myself after Jessica's flight. There are rivers of irony in the part and at the end he is deprived of his three main supports: family, religion and business.'

After the first night, on 12 April 1960, O'Toole returned slowly to the Georgian house near Anne Hathaway's cottage where he, Sian and their daughter Kate, named after Katharine Hepburn, who had brought him such good luck, were staying. There was a party that night. Sian had watched O'Toole from inside the theatre and reclaimed Kate from an upstairs room in the pub across the way from the theatre quickly after the curtain came down. O'Toole's mother was also in the audience, although she could not get a seat and had to stand for the whole performance. She had given her son a star of David to hang around his neck for good luck. O'Toole was nervous of returning home to the party. He was filled with the same doubts that had attacked him as he was about to take the Bristol Old Vic stage in *Hamlet*. For two hours he wandered around the field where he and Patrick Oliver had bedded down so few years before. When he recovered, he joined the party, but he wasn't content until he had read the London notices the next morning.

He need not have worried. W. A. Darlington, of the *Daily Telegraph*, wrote: 'Peter O'Toole's Shylock is an outstanding performance in what may be called Irving's manner.' *The Times*'s anonymous critic thought that 'in the sealing of the "merry band" scene, Mr O'Toole reaches genuine distinction.' Harold Hobson, more restrained, noted that 'the chief feature of Mr O'Toole's Shylock is his cool, sharp brain, his immense readiness in debate'. Mervyn Jones, in *Tribune*, wrote: 'Peter O'Toole gives a performance of Shylock that will stand as a great chapter in theatre history.' And the *New Statesman* went overboard: 'I don't know what it is that suddenly produces, in all the polished adequacy of English acting, a great performance. Whatever the quality may be, O'Toole has it. Like Olivier, O'Toole has an animal magnetism no matter what he is doing or who else is present.'

But of all the notices, none was more gratifying to O'Toole than the verdict of Desmond Pratt, the critic of his home town newspaper, the *Yorkshire Post*, from Leeds: 'Here is an actor who breathes and lives theatre, who can command and dictate, who is imbued with the dynamic spark of greatness, with an instinct that directs him at the right moment to the right conclusion. He has brought back with him, off-stage as well as on, the grand manner of the earlier actor-managers, the Keans, the Irvings and the Bayntons.'

While the run of *The Merchant* continued, O'Toole was rehearsing for the second of his three plays, *The Taming of the Shrew*, in which he would play Petruchio opposite Peggy Ashcroft. Again, it was a strong cast, which included Elizabeth Sellars as Bianca, Patrick Wymark as Grumio, Jack MacGowran as Christopher Sly and Ian Holm as Gremio. And again the production would break new ground, for the director was John Barton, with his first Stratford production, brought in by Hall after his innovative and exciting work with the Marlowe Society at Cambridge University. A break was made away from the traditional Italianate design with a Flemish set by Alix Stone. Again, there was a high tension after the first night on 21 June 1960 at the party thrown by Peter Hall on the lawn of his Stratford house, Aroncliffe. And again, the nervous cast barbecuing sausages in the garden, listening to jazz on a tape recorder, need not have worried.

Milton Shulman, in the *Evening Standard*, led the praise for O'Toole. 'In Peter O'Toole,' he wrote, 'we have the most aggressive, virile, dominating Petruchio in years. Any woman who stood in his way would be blown apart by a puff or a sneeze. It is a marvellously comic performance which will put heart into even the most brow-beaten husband in the audience.' In the *Financial Times*, the critic T. C. Worsley went further: 'This young actor is now high on the way up, and he fully justifies the hopes that are held out for him. He has swagger, attack, vivacity. He can seize a scene and spin it round his little finger with a minimum of visible effort. His only possible weakness lies in his voice. He yelps when he means to roar.' Felix Barker continued the compliments he had showered on him in his review of *The Day They Robbed the Bank of England*: 'We have here a major actor in the making, an actor with so much personal magnet-ism that he seems to be centre stage even when he is half hidden in the wings. As with Olivier, even his silences excite, for there is no telling how his next line will be delivered, with what whiplash roar or whisper he will assail the ear.' Only Bernard Levin, in the *Daily Express*, avoided hyperbole: 'Mr Peter O'Toole, when he stops barking, gives the impression that in another production he would make a fine, rough Petruchio.'

The good notices from Stratford were making O'Toole an eagerly sought-after commodity for film makers. Among those who were after him were Elizabeth Taylor and her husband, Eddie Fisher, who had been wooing him since *The Merchant* opened to play opposite her as Count Vronsky in a film version of Tolstoy's *Anna Karenina*. Elizabeth Taylor hadn't even seen him, having failed to reach Stratford when a bout of 'flu had kept her bedbound in the Dorchester Hotel in London. Still, she sent Fisher to see him in *The Taming of the Shrew* and he had gone backstage to tell him how 'wonderful' he had been.

Liz Taylor had organised a special screening of *The Day They Robbed the Bank of England* and had even tried to woo him to be her Mark Antony in *Cleopatra*, but he became otherwise engaged with Stratford and she simply became otherwise engaged. The way O'Toole remembered the proposition: 'While I was there Eddie Fisher came up to see me in *The Taming of the Shrew*. "We'd be interested in you playing opposite Liz in *Anna Karenina*," he said. So I drove down to the Dorchester and took forty quid off Liz in blackjack and said I'd be delighted. After I'd seen the script.' It never materialised.

Buoyed up by the extravagant praise, O'Toole began a series of bragging interviews with the press. His arrogance was incredible. He told Evelyn Garrett from the *Daily Telegraph*, who had come down to Stratford to ogle over his new baby: 'I'm marvellous. I must be.' And he recorded a radio interview, later broadcast on the Home Service, which drew this description from Robert Robinson, himself not know for his modesty: 'Mr Peter O'Toole, the actor, spoke about himself and the events of his young life with an enunciation so artificial – a wild fluctuation of all the accents to which, by any stretch of the imagination, he might by birth, environment, upbringing, lay claim – that it was hard to imagine him ever losing his self-consciousness in a part on the stage (though we have ample testimony that he does this exceedingly well). But he spoke in his own person, now seeming to wish to be coaxed, now extravagantly confiding, now mixing knowingness with naïveté until – as his questioner like a doting parent breathlessly brought up the rear – it seemed as if he had abandoned the possibility of real identity in favour of offering himself to the public as a favourite child.'

Nor could O'Toole resist playing up to the tearaway image which he had created for himself. He told the *Evening Standard*, in a typical angry young man pose: 'I get drunk and disorderly and all that, but I don't really think it's true that there is any danger of me destroying myself. I like to make things hum. I like occasionally to shout at the sun and spit at the moon. I have a marvellous life and I'm going to make the most of it seeing I only have another ninety years left. I don't know what I get out of it. What does anyone get out of being drunk? It's an anaesthetic. It diminishes the pain. There are thousands of things one needs to be anaesthetised against. I have a lot of my own personal problems. But it isn't success or failure as an actor that bothers me – if I wasn't sure I could deliver the bloody goods, I would get off the bloody stage. Any actor who doesn't feel he is potentially a king should get off the stage and hide up a bamboo tree. No, it's success or failure as a person that's important.'

But this boasting about the dissolute life was to rebound on him. At the beginning of July, two weeks before the third O'Toole production was due to open, O'Toole was told by doctors that he must give up drinking for his own safety. They also urged him to have an operation, which O'Toole refused, at least until the Stratford season was over. O'Toole tried to keep his illness a secret, underplaying to Sian and telling only Peter Hall the full seriousness of the trouble. Still, he did make an attempt to give up drinking and even had his photograph taken in the Black Swan in Stratford – the actors' local which they call the Dirty Duck – pulling a pint of beer for others while setting up a glass of milk for himself. Not many weeks before, he had broken the house record by downing a yard of ale in forty seconds. O'Toole was almost repentant when the news broke. 'Drinking is one of my hobbies,' he said. 'I just thought I was suffering from hangovers. They have been getting worse lately, so I saw a specialist. He gave me the good news yesterday. I feel pretty awful.'

His confidence was dented further when *Troilus and Cressida* opened on 26 July, in which he played a smaller part than his previous two – that of Thersites. Instead of a barrage of praise, the notices describes him as 'ranting', 'miscast', 'disappointing' and his attitude too much like 'sado-masochistic glee'. Gareth Lloyd Evans in the *Guardian* suggested that 'his accent should learn to forget Shylock for a while'. And the *New Statesman* added: 'Peter O'Toole, dressed as though he had wandered in from a play by Beckett, is toned down to the point of inaudibility. He is allowed to express more with his pathetic knock-kneed stance than with his voice.' O'Toole was conscious that something was wrong and later admitted as much. 'My failure,' he said, 'I couldn't make the words flesh. The idea was to be both part of the action and a commentator. I couldn't do it. Even in soliloquy, nothing is revealed, and there is no development. But I am the better for having played it.'

However, it was not a serious setback. Peter Hall was pressing ahead with the second stage of his ambitious plans for his company. He was negotiating with the owners of the Aldwych Theatre for a lease which would give the Stratford company a permanent auditorium in London. And Hall was not going to wait around. He was determined to be performing in London at the beginning of the new year at the latest – preferably in mid-December – and Peter O'Toole was central to his plans.

At the beginning of October, Laurence Olivier and Anthony Quinn opened on Broadway in Jean Anouilh's *Becket*, directed by Peter Glenville. Hall was keen to take the play for his company, with O'Toole as Henry II and Eric Porter, the Lear whom O'Toole had so much admired at Bristol, as Becket. At the end of October, O'Toole and Hall flew to New York for the weekend, between performances, to see the Olivier/Quinn partnership at work. They both returned convinced and Hall promised himself the direction. A date was fixed for the Aldwych opening: 25 April 1961.

Meanwhile, O'Toole was in secret negotiations with David Lean and Sam Spiegel for the leading role in *Lawrence of Arabia*. O'Toole was determined to get the part and was using the Aldwych opening as a safety net. It was a cynical, if understandable, approach to the new Peter Hall company, which had provided him with so many opportunities. Even more cynically, O'Toole calmly signed a three-year contract with the Shakespeare Memorial Theatre, part of a sixteen-actor deal which would guarantee earnings and allow time off to work in films.

O'Toole was open about the account he owed to Stratford. After one performance of *The Taming of the Shrew*, O'Toole had said: 'People keep telling me I'm out of my mind missing all these film parts by coming up here for seven months, but I'm not. It's done me a hell of a lot of good, and the company pulls together so happily, it's fantastic.' And the truth of the matter was that he wanted to do both: play on the stage as part of a company and also become a rich, famous international film star, recognised wherever he went. Whatever happened, he wanted to do *Becket* and this way he would, either with Eric Porter, if the *Lawrence* deal fell down, or with someone else after the five-month shooting schedule of *Lawrence* had finished. He genuinely hoped that he could do both. And he believed the proposed *Lawrence* filming schedule.

For once, O'Toole had not done enough research on a part. It was an elementary error to believe that David Lean, the perfectionist, could turn in an epic film in five months. It was naive. Worse, it was stupid. When he had left Stratford, he down-graded what they were doing there, but it all sounded too much like sour grapes. 'I flew over to see old Quinn playing opposite Olivier in *Becket* on Broadway, you know. He was awful. Olivier wasn't much better, come to think of it. In the first scene, Quinn looked as if he were about to swim the Channel rather than give a performance. But it was a great play. I wanted very much to do it in London, but I couldn't because of this *Lawrence* film. Films interest me even more than the theatre, you see. Though I'm glad I did that last season at Stratford – even if it is only fifty quid a week and work your guts out. Stratford's an odd place. People go there the way they go to Lourdes. Like pilgrims.'

Years later, he was even more dismissive. 'Actors who go there have the responsibility of doing justice to the works of Shakespeare in an atmosphere of hard-fisted commercialism. It's a tourist industry as bogus as the one at Bethlehem – even more so. The townspeople detest the actors. They tolerate them only because they bring in a turnover of at least two hundred pilgrims a day. There's nothing else to do there except work, and you can't work all the time. I used to drink at the Dirty Duck, by the river, which became our haven and home. Ben Shepherd, who runs it, became the patron saint of us all, bless him. He has an old-fashioned yard measure of ale above his counter and I admit I've downed several yards without stopping for breath. But you only do that kind of lunacy because there's nothing else to do.'

# 4 Lawrence of Arabia

SAM SPIEGEL had read T. E. Lawrence's account of his Arabian adventures in World War I, *The Seven Pillars of Wisdom*, several years before its general publication and had noted then its potential as a film screenplay. It was more exciting than a work of fiction, with the hero a British army officer who organised and mobilised the Arab nations against the Turks and the Germans during World War I. And when his epic *Bridge on the River Kwai* swept the board at the Oscars, Spiegel again considered whether the Lawrence story would be a suitable sequel for the productive partnership he had forged with David Lean, the director of *Kwai*, who had recently signed a further contract to work with him. The rights to the Lawrence story had always remained elusive and resided at the moment with J. Arthur Rank. But an attempt by Rank to film *The Seven Pillars of Wisdom* had foundered the previous year, in 1960, when budget and script problems had proved too great to overcome. At last there seemed a chance of buying the rights.

The cancellation of the Rank project had been a great disappointment to the actor who had been chosen by them to play Lawrence, Dirk Bogarde. The Rank film was to be a modest affair – by no means the showy epic that Spiegel had in mind – directed by Anthony Asquith from a screenplay by Terence Rattigan. Bogarde was ecstatic about the chance to play Lawrence. 'I had never, in my life, wanted a part, or script, so much,' he remembered. Locations had been researched and King Feisal had offered his army as extras. Bogarde did extensive research, reading every available book on Lawrence's work and life. He wrote to Lawrence's friends and, as he put it, 'quite lost my own identity in what the Americans call a period of total immersion.'

But Dirk Bogarde was never to wear the blond wig being made in Rank's make-up department in preparation. A few weeks before shooting was to begin, the project was abandoned, although no one seemed to know why, 'No one ever mentioned *Lawrence* again.' Bogarde remembered. 'I never knew, and still do not know what stopped the plans so suddenly a few weeks before shooting. Neither, if I remember, did Puffin [Anthony Asquith] or anyone else connected with the production.' Rank still held the rights and allowed

Rattigan to rework his screenplay as *Ross*, which opened on Shaftesbury Avenue with Alec Guinness as Lawrence. Bogarde was heartbroken; 'It was my bitterest disappointment.'

But Bogarde's loss turned out to be O'Toole's ultimate gain. The rights to *The Seven Pillars* went back on the market, having reverted to Lawrence's brother, Professor A. W. Lawrence, the literary executor of T. E. Lawrence's estate. Spiegel had to present a hurried script treatment by Lean and Michael Wilson to him, for he was hesitant about film people perverting what was, in any case, a delicate matter within the Lawrence family.

The original script, at any rate, came up to scratch and Spiegel bought the rights for a seemingly modest £20,000. While he was about it, Sam Spiegel decided to head off any opposition by buying up any other book which might be turned into a Lawrence film. What he could do without, particularly with Lean's notoriously drawn-out methods, was a quickie rival to cream off the public's appetite.

He scooped the pool. He bought four books by Robert Graves which contained material about Lawrence: *T. E. Lawrence to his Biographer*; *Lawrence and the Arabs*; *Lawrence and the Arabian Adventure* and *Goodbye to All That*. Spiegel also bought the rights to Lowell Thomas's *With Lawrence in Arabia*. What he could not buy was the stage spin-off from the Rank Lawrence project, Terence Rattigan's *Ross*. The film rights of the play had been bought for £100,000 by Herbert Wilcox, the British producer, who was hoping to sign Laurence Harvey for the Lawrence role. All through 1960, Spiegel was intimidated by the prospect of a rival Lawrence film. In October, it was announced that filming of the British *Lawrence* would begin in March 1961 – two months before filming on Spiegel's film began. But it was to be a false alarm. The project did not materialise.

This left Spiegel and Lean free to make a film of *Lawrence* with the epic proportions they had established with *The Bridge on the River Kwai*. As David Lean explained: 'Sam Spiegel and I felt that *Kwai* had revealed a certain pattern; it worked out a general theme by closely examining the situation of one man [the eccentric Colonel Nicholson] placed by his fate in an interesting and foreign locality. We were convinced that the pattern itself was artistically important and that we could now explore it more fully. Our first idea was to make a film of the life and death of Mahatma Gandhi. We approached this project cautiously, feeling there was perhaps something presumptuous in attempting to film, almost in his lifetime, the activities of a man believed by his own people and by others to have been a saint. It was actually with relief as well as disappointment that we abandoned the project. To dramatise we must simplify. To simplify we must leave something out. To decide what aspects of Gandhi's life and personality can be decently left out and which ones were retained was a responsibility we were not willing to accept.' The collapse of the Rank film of Lawrence's life provided a more practical alternative.

As Lean remembers it: 'The film rights to *The Seven Pillars* became available. Spiegel acquired them and there in India we decided that *Lawrence of Arabia* would be our next venture.' T. E. Lawrence's broad-canvassed autobiography looked a suitable story for the Panavision treatment. It had enough of the right ingredients to make an epic film: a strong spirit of adventure, with the hero an odd Englishman hurling himself into the alien world of Arabs. It had an air of mystery, for Lawrence was not only a secretive character, but his whole personality – his subdued homosexuality and lust for being punished – was a puzzle, and his means of escape from the torment of normality of the respectable English life was to submerge himself and his masochism in the tough, uncompromising, incomprehensible, masculine world of the Bedouin. It was colourful, for the world of the desert, as the audience was to find, was not a drab, empty stretch of sand – it contained a luminous landscape, littered with the colourful wandering tribes of Arabian aristocracy, their camel trains, tents, domestic animals and, last and least, masked women tagging on behind. It had a bold narrative, for the story of a gentle English man volunteering to slip out of his depth among such apparently uncivilised people was in itself a fascinating tale. But added to it was the climate of World War I, a global conflict, the first of its kind, which allowed no party, no nation, not even the nomadic tribes of Arabia to escape its implications and avoid making a decision about which side of the dispute they should support.

And there was an extra dimension, which was intended to woo an audience whose ready appetite for war pictures had become numbed by the bombardment of World War II films that had filled the cinema screens in the fifteen years since the German surrender in 1945. The Lawrence story was set in World War I, a war which offered the prospect of battles between Arabs on horseback or on camels, and infantry, ill-equipped with rifles.

For the British audience there was also a thread of class conflict to enjoy, as the film would show the stuffy, staid old guard being horrified by the open, undeferential attitudes of the shameless Lawrence. And this was a quality which would appeal too to an American audience, who had, for similar reasons as those held by Lawrence, rejected the possibility of the British Empire, led by the fat cats of the British ruling class, being allowed to run half the world after World War II. This was a historical film which would suit the post-Suez political climate of the early 1960s.

For Sam Spiegel, a Hollywood mogul of the old school who had recognised the financial limitations of the studio system and concentrated instead on the better value, all-location films which could add an element of spectacle and originality not to be found on the American domestic screens, nor on the increasingly competitive television screens, the story of Lawrence looked particularly inviting. He had no problem in finding the right director. David Lean was already contracted to him and Lean's style was perfect for this project. It would cost a lot of money – Lean was well known to be a perfectionist who would wait days to get the correct shot – but the result would be extraordinary; a film which was so special, so spectacular and so sensational that the publicity which surrounded it would compensate for the cost of its making, and a film which would demand an audience to go and see what all the fuss was about. Spiegel was himself a master of publicity, but the chief weapon in his armoury was Lean, a man whose name was synonymous in the public mind with a new form of cinemagoing – cinema not as a once or twice a week experience but cinema as a very special treat, as thrilling to the audience as a glittering night at the opera. Lean had reinjected excitement and glamour to what had become a humdrum means of entertainment.

If Lean was the perfect director, then he demanded a perfect script. The hottest British playwright in 1960 was undoubtedly Robert Bolt. With *A Man for All Seasons*, his play about the bravery and integrity of Henry VIII's Chancellor, Sir Thomas More, Bolt had marked a significant shift away from the angry realistic theatre which the 1950s had adored. He had reintroduced high morality and argument into the theatre and, in taking a historical subject, had rejected the mundane preoccupations of the 1950s. But his history was not the dramatised history lesson which the British Ealing Studios had fostered. His use of history was as a vehicle for a wider discussion of issues, so Sir Thomas More was not painted as a wooden figure from the history books, brought to life for entertainment, but as a character who represented and spoke on behalf of those who would put their principles before their own best interests. In looking for a screen writer who could make Lawrence seem interesting and important to a modern audience, Bolt was an obvious choice. If Lawrence could be portrayed accurately and sympathetically, Bolt was the dramatist who seemed most likely to succeed.

The main problem for Spiegel – and a problem which Lean, as the director, shared – was: which actor could best portray this most peculiar Englishman? Lawrence was an introverted character, brusque with those he had little time for; rather vague, but his apparently diffident manner disguising a lively brain and an awkward sense of priorities. He was young and, in real life, physically attractive. He was highly energetic, living the gruelling life of the Bedouin, which entailed camel riding and regular exhaustion due to heat. He had an immediately visible charm which cut through language barriers and encouraged trust and authority: the power of charisma. The actor chosen to play Lawrence would have to have these qualities.

Spiegel, as producer, preferred to have an established star play the part. The dedicated cinemagoer would probably find a good film on their own, but the casual cinemagoer, who ventured away from the television only for a special treat, was undoubtedly influenced by the presence of a star's name in the credits on the poster. There was an obvious candidate to play the role of Lawrence. He had all the peculiar characteristics which T. E. Lawrence had in life; he was also one of the most popular – and sought after – stars in international film making: Marlon Brando.

He was Spiegel's first choice. He was undoubtedly a box-office draw. Spiegel put him on the top of the list and started wooing him. At one stage Spiegel even announced that Brando would play the part and admitted that Alec Guinness, who played the part of Lawrence so perfectly in Rattigan's play, *Ross*, had been considered but rejected. 'We would have asked Alec Guinness to play the part, if he were fifteen years younger,' said Spiegel. 'He's a marvellous actor, but you can't do too much with nature. And to expect the public to accept him as a twenty-nine-year-old would be asking too much.' But the signing of Brando was premature. Filming was continuing on Sir Carol Reed's remake of *Mutiny on the Bounty* and running over schedule.

In any case, Lean was not convinced that Brando was the right actor. Brando showed obvious drawbacks to Lean's style of film making. First, he had an established screen persona which Lean would have to neutralise. Lean preferred actors such as Alec Guinness, solid character actors who could accommodate the role they were asked to adopt. Brando was not incapable of this capacity to adapt, although a succession of lazier directors than Lean had not helped those who wanted to use Brando's by now latent acting abilities. Brando had worked himself into an acting corner, following the tradition of film acting – a tradition which stage actors universally dislike – of offering an established character to the audience around which the script, seen in film acting terms as merely a vehicle for the actor, must hang.

Lean saw at once that Lawrence of Arabia starring Brando would most likely turn out to be Brando of Arabia, based loosely upon the life of T. E. Lawrence. Lean was determined the film should not be this. Lean's films were director's films in which the actors worked to a tight director's brief. The script was more important than the actor, yet even the script had to fulfil the director's purpose. Lean saw difficulties with Brando, who would have resisted the Lean technique. There was not room for two stars in a Lean film, even though it might be made to such epic proportions, and Lean had already been hired and was in possession. Spiegel tried for Brando and failed. Lean shed no tears at the news.

There was a British actor, Albert Finney, who would have served both Spiegel and Lean's best interests. He was already a film star – albeit in very British films of the 1950s such as *The Entertainer* and *Saturday Night and Sunday Morning* – but he was also a good stage actor, currently appearing in Keith Waterhouse's successful comedy *Billy Liar* at the Cambridge Theatre and one who would obey Lean's directions.

Another actor under consideration was Peter O'Toole. Lean had met him once, at the party which followed the première of *The Day They Robbed the Bank of England*. It was not a great film, nor was O'Toole's part, a lieutenant in the Scots Guards, either substantial or significant. But Lean had noticed him and spotted a hint of that elusive quality, the screen presence, an easiness with the camera, an ability to charm through the lens. Since then, O'Toole's reputation as the coming young actor, fuelled by his success at Stratford and the comparisons with Olivier, made him at least worth checking out. Spiegel went to Stratford to see him and became interested, but by no means charmed. O'Toole's reputation as a wild boy was disturbing. Some scandals, such as the current public and well-photographed love affair on the set of *Cleopatra* between Richard Burton and Elizabeth Taylor, could be a commercial benefit. The prospect of O'Toole's drunkenness, however, was hardly as glamorous or attractive. Spiegel took advice and found that O'Toole was not just fond of the bottle – he was also liable to violent revelry and unscheduled publicity of the worst kind.

Spiegel was looking for an actor in which to invest a very large fortune. On his back would lie the entire profitability of the film. This was a film like few others, dependent almost entirely upon the competence of its principal actor for effect. All the Leans, all the miles of film, all the money available would not be able to save a film with a wayward lead actor. And, to take on a potential liability such as O'Toole was commercial nonsense. The original shooting schedule was four months in the desert, four months back in Britain. But Spiegel knew the likelihood of the schedule once Lean had started shooting. It could drag on for over a year – perhaps even two – and the strain of keeping an undisciplined actor well behaved for such a long time might prove too much for Lean and Spiegel between them to manage.

And there were the investors to think about. A film on such a scale demanded a considerable sum of capital and each source would want to know where the weak parts of the investment were. Who were the men who would spend their money? Could they be trusted to spend it wisely? Was there a key figure who could cause the whole project to founder? How reliable was the principal actor to do as he was told? And looking at the career of O'Toole on paper, Spiegel could find nothing to encourage him to think that he would take the commercial responsibility of his position very seriously.

It was true that he had appeared in three films. Otherwise he had a short if impressive career on the stage. He had worked entirely in the noncommercial theatre. He had been trained at the Bristol Old Vic, hardly a money-spinning organisation, and his only venture onto the West End stage was in *Oh My Papa*, a spectacular flop. Since then he had been working in the subsidised Stratford Memorial Theatre, boosting the box office and his ego simultaneously. Still there was no evidence that he was commercially responsible. Indeed, the evidence of O'Toole's private life was to the contrary. He had married in secret a newly-divorced woman although he was financially in-secure. His home life was precarious. Both his wife and he worked and they left their newly-born daughter, brought into the world to share her parents' slender financial circumstances, to be looked after by a black, American male nanny called Lonnie – a homosexual and former US sailor. They rented their house near Stratford and there was no prospect of them joining the great club of owner-occupiers. O'Toole showed a blatant disrespect for money, flying with his wife to Dublin merely to eat lunch. Would O'Toole take seriously the millions which would have to be spent on him?

Spiegel had his doubts. Before going any further, Spiegel wanted to know whether O'Toole was capable of the acting required. The audience would be expected to watch Lawrence for two hours, perhaps more. And they would want to be able to understand how such a peculiar character thought. Was O'Toole capable of carrying such an important part? O'Toole was in Stratford acting Shylock, the most notorious scheming Jew of literature, when he was called to London to test for the part of history's most notorious pro-Arabist.

The screen test was a full-day affair. There were to be no mistakes. If O'Toole was the right man for the job, Spiegel and Lean wanted to know about it for certain. O'Toole was to be dressed as Lawrence and filmed. He was to be asked to extemporise. He was to walk, sit, grimace. In particular, he was to be tested for close-ups. There was little doubt that he was able to act on stage, but what Lean and Spiegel wanted to know above all was whether he would appear to be acting on film. If the acting was transparent there was no use going on. Unlike stage acting, film acting is a more subtle process. There is no need for grand gestures to impress the not-so-rich at the back of the royal circle. O'Toole must be able to play to the camera lens while appearing natural.

For Spiegel and Lean, this was an important test. They wanted to find their principal actor so that they could start shooting. But if O'Toole was not the right man, no matter. Better to wait and get the casting right than to find out halfway through the shooting schedule. For O'Toole it was far more important. His rise had been meteoric. In ten years he had moved from amateur theatricals in Leeds to the most lauded actor at the Shakespeare Memorial Theatre, the most highly respected serious theatre company in the world. He was playing lead roles in Shakespeare in Shakespeare's birthplace and people from around the world were coming to see him do it. He had reached the first division of his profession without really trying. Older actors whom he admired were complimenting him. He was being well received by the cynical critics.

As far as he knew, he had arrived. But even acting in principal parts at Stratford-upon-Avon would hardly make him rich. Nor would it make him particularly famous. He was well-known, but only to a narrow band of Britain, and in the rest of the world his name meant nothing. He was thirsty for money and thirsty for fame. Although he professed to have no interest in material things – he boasted of his socialism and his disdain for money – he still was eager for the benefits that only money could buy. Most of all, he wanted a big family house. Once that was secure he could relax. He described his feelings about getting on: 'In the early days, in the greedy, skint, ambitious days, I would have done anything, practically anything to get on. Money and success . . . I grabbed at it. I was such a greedy little grabber. I never really cared how I looked. It was the other people – they cared. So I had to care, because if I looked untidy, it was an obstacle to making money.'

He had been in films and not much liked the film acting process. But when summoned to test for *Lawrence of Arabia* – the whole of the acting profession knew the scale of the project and were eager to be selected – he realised that this was more than anything he had yet been asked to do. He knew from the producer and the director that this was a big plum which would be offered only once. He was determined to win the part.

O'Toole had taken the decision to have his nose changed. His existing one was a very large affair, a noble nose, but would not do to win the parts, such as *Lawrence*, that demanded a traditional soft-faced screen idol's looks. O'Toole took the decision with his eyes open. He needed to become what he always called 'the pretty boy': 'It was a choice between having a bent nose or a straight one,' he said. 'I thought I would look more beautiful with a straight one.' Later he told April Ashley that it was in his *Lawrence* contract that his nose should be fixed. He knew his nose could be arranged by a good plastic surgeon.

What was more threatening to his winning the part was the formidable opposition. He knew that Albert Finney was one of the hopefuls. They had been at RADA together and he knew how well Finney could act. What is more, Finney had already been doing film work. Lean and Spiegel must be familiar with Finney's undoubted talent. O'Toole started doing his homework. He had not read Lawrence's *The Seven Pillars of Wisdom*, but he got hold of a copy. He studied carefully the photographs of Lawrence as a young man. There at least he had an advantage over Finney. There was already a superficial likeness between himself and Lawrence. If he could make the resemblance closer, there was more of a chance. He was acting in Shylock and, to keep in character as much as possible, he had foregone pasting a crepe beard on every night and had grown a goatee. Lawrence had no facial hair, so the beard was shaved off. And Lawrence was fair haired, while O'Toole's hair was medium brown. He decided to lighten his hair and so dyed it blond. For a day he had to be Lawrence, not Shylock. He would return to Stratford wearing a wig and with a glued on beard for *The Merchant of Venice*.

The test day was certainly the most crucial of his life. It was to divide him between competent, respected stage actor and that most elusive status – the film star. O'Toole was conscious of the pressure upon him. His reaction was not to panic, but to relax. He was quite at home with the paraphernalia of film making and he quickly settled down. He indulged his often inappropriate sense of humour to put himself at ease and relieve the tension. At one stage he was asked to extemporise the part of a doctor in an operating theatre. O'Toole probed around, feigning concentration and concerned anguish. After a little stern face pulling, the worry slipped away from his face and he turned his head slowly to the camera, quietly beaming: 'It's all right, Mrs Spiegel, your son will never play the violin again.'

He was dressed in the full Bedouin drag and still photographs were taken in preparation for the press announcement should the test prove successful. He consciously tried to ape the pose which he remembered from the photographs of Lawrence. David Lean had the same photographs in mind as he posed O'Toole for his own satisfaction. Lean suspected that the camera was going to record exactly what he hoped to see. Through the lens, O'Toole looked exactly right for the part. While O'Toole was driving back that night to Stratford, to return to Shylock, his test footage was being developed. And the next morning, Lean and Spiegel sat down in their small viewing theatre and watched what the camera had seen. Lean had no doubt that O'Toole was the best Lawrence that they could find. And, just as important to Lean, O'Toole was a young actor who was eager to learn. He could tell by the test the previous day that O'Toole would do as he was told and that he would understand how Lean wanted the film to turn out.

Sam Spiegel, too, was impressed by the results of the tests and laughed at the violin-playing joke, but he still had reservations. He was still not sure whether 'the Wild Man of Stratford', as he had been nicknamed, would take the project seriously enough if, as was likely with Lean in charge, the production bogged down. O'Toole seemed capable of tearing up his contract and returning home. Spiegel finally came round to Lean's view. 'At first,' Spiegel explained, 'I wanted Brando for the part. He is a big name and, after all, this is an expensive production. But I was wrong. When I made *On the Waterfront* with Marlon he was magnificent. Now he has become a tortured person and in turn a tortured actor. He no longer trusts himself or his psychiatrist and it is beginning to show in his work. He would have been impossible for Lawrence.'

Albert Finney, the compromise candidate, had been offered the part. He was more reliable, thereby meeting Spiegel's demands, and was an intelligent actor who would understand what Lean was trying to do. At one stage Spiegel was so confident of signing Finney that he declared: '*Lawrence* will make a star of an actor; for that reason David Lean and I have finally determined to forego the established stars in our consideration for the role and to choose an unknown, though necessarily brilliant, performer. It is quite conceivable that Finney fits that description. Our tests indicate that Finney has that rare quality that is required by and accompanies stardom.'

The negotiations broke down, however, over the length of Finney's contract. Finney dearly wanted the part, but also wanted to remain stage-acting. He was offered a reported £250,000 for a five-year contract, but turned the deal down. Finney told Spiegel: 'My freedom as an artist is more important to me.' It was not the role of Lawrence, which he dearly wanted, but the commitment to working with Spiegel for so long that had made him turn the generous offer down. 'Friends said when I was offered the Spiegel contract: 'It's all right, Albie, nobody can force you to do something you don't want,' ' remembered Finney. ' "They can lead a horse to water, but even Spiegel can't make it drink." ' But Finney was nervous of embroiling himself in cramping contracts and decided to stay with the theatre for a while. He went to the Royal Court to play the lead in *Luther*, John Osborne's play about the Reformation leader.

Anthony Perkins, the star of Alfred Hitchcock's suspense thriller *Psycho*, was also in the running at one stage and was most capable of Lawrence's blank, mysterious stare, but he was turned down. And so the part was offered to O'Toole. The deal was struck through Keep Films, the film company which O'Toole had founded with Jules Buck, and was a contract for several pictures. O'Toole was offered far less than the amount offered to Finney, because he was second best. And still Spiegel had his doubts.

O'Toole has a fanciful view of the order in which Spiegel approached the actors. 'You know, I still can't get over the element of luck in this film business,' he explained. 'Do you realise how nearly I didn't play Lawrence? I was twenty-six when they first talked to me about it and afterwards they approached Marlon Brando, Tony Perkins and Albert Finney. See, Sam Spiegel was prejudiced against me at first and you can't really blame him. He thought I was a tearaway; he thought I lived up a tree. When I first went to see him at the Connaught Hotel I took off my coat and a bottle of whisky fell out of my pocket. I tell you, the cold was like the Arctic. After that Sam was understandably a bit dubious; after all, this was going to be a pretty expensive picture. He didn't want to have to go looking for me every day with a net. It wasn't until a long time later that I heard I'd got the part. Sam rang me and said: "I want you to play Lawrence." "Oh yes," I said. "Is it a speaking part?" "Don't make such jokes," Sam growled.'

Once having chosen O'Toole, Spiegel stayed loyal, backing him with the full might at his disposal. 'Peter is absolutely right,' he said. 'And when the film is shown, he will be an enormous star.' Spiegel made that promise with his fingers crossed. Lean was very pleased. Although O'Toole was really a novice to film making, this suited his purpose. Spiegel decided to play up the fact that O'Toole was young and untried and quieten his backers by emphasising the number of well-established actors chosen to surround him.

The original supporting cast which Spiegel went hunting for was certainly an impressive list. Cary Grant was lined up to play General Allenby; Kirk Douglas would play the American reporter; Horst Bucholz would play Sheik Ali and Jack Hawkins would appear as Colonel Newcombe. At one stage, Spiegel went after Sir Laurence

Olivier to play the part of Allenby. The final cast was as impressive as any that had been suggested and, a fact which pleased Lean, more British and therefore more authentic than the original Spiegel line-up. Alec Guinness was to play Prince Feisal; Anthony Quinn, with a false nose, was to be Auda Abu Tayi; Jack Hawkins, to become a close friend of O'Toole, was cast as Allenby; Jose Ferrer was to portray the Turkish Bey; Claude Rains was the scheming diplomat Dryden; Arthur Kennedy the American reporter; Anthony Quayle the ultra-straight Colonel Brighton; Donald Wolfit the practical General Murray; and Omar Sharif was 'introduced' as Sherif Ali Ibn el Kharish. The cast list which Spiegel considered a safety net for O'Toole's performance became an intimidating array of acting competition for O'Toole. He was determined to outshine all of them.

O'Toole found himself in a quandary. He had accepted to play Lawrence for Spiegel, but was still attached to the Stratford Memorial Theatre. On Sunday 20 November 1960, Columbia, the film company for whom Spiegel was making the film, issued a press statement headed: 'O'Toole will play *Lawrence of Arabia*', and continuing: 'Peter O'Toole, brilliant young star of Stratford-on-Avon's Shakespeare Memorial Theatre, will play the title role in Sam Spiegel's motion picture production of *Lawrence of Arabia*, culminating an international search for a newcomer of highest promise, who will be surrounded by an all-star cast.' Spiegel approved the final wording of the release. The only catch was that Stratford had not been bought out for O'Toole's services.

The season ended the following week and O'Toole was expected to start work on *Lawrence* immediately. The theatre was not slow to spot their chance. They had arranged with O'Toole that he would begin rehearsals for Jean Anouilh's *Becket* on 20 March and that the first night would be on 25 April at the Aldwych Theatre. Spiegel's spokesman was saying: 'It's all settled. Stratford are releasing O'Toole so he can play Lawrence and rejoin them after filming,' while Peter Hall, Stratford's artistic director, contradicted: 'In view of rumours now circulating, I wish to state that I have not released Peter O'Toole from his contract to rehearse the part of King Henry in *Becket* next March.' Talks went on behind the scenes. Stratford said that the play could not be delayed and that it was too late to cast anyone else. O'Toole kept out of it, on Spiegel's advice, although he was genuinely distressed at leaving Stratford in the lurch. Meanwhile he prepared for his part as Henry in *Becket* and posed for publicity pictures dressed as Lawrence.

Stratford resorted to the law. The Governors took out a writ against O'Toole, restraining him from performing for anyone else without consent while under contract. On 3 December the case was adjourned and by 7 December the affair was over. The judge in chambers in the High Court found that O'Toole was not under contract to the Theatre and Spiegel was saved a lot of cash. All the same, O'Toole was unhappy at upsetting the principal theatre company in the world and he has never been invited back to Stratford since.

The way that O'Toole explains the court decision is that the Stratford case depended upon their allegation that the *Becket* project and O'Toole were inseparable and that Jean Anouilh had demanded that either O'Toole play the part or all bets were off. For O'Toole to play Lawrence, therefore, meant that the Stratford company would have to abort the *Becket* project altogether. According to O'Toole, he was determined to find out whether this statement was true and he teamed up with a French-speaker and set off for Paris to find Anouilh and ask him. There was some trouble tracking down Anouilh, but finally O'Toole confronted him and asked whether what Stratford were saying was true. The answer came back from Anouilh: 'Forgive me, Mr O'Toole, but I've never heard of you.' This is a rare story that O'Toole has told against himself.

His passion for the theatre was well known and he had to answer the charge that he was deserting the stage for a more lucrative career in films. He denied the accusation. 'Films and stage – it's all acting. Fortunately I can choose what I want to do. I've turned down thousands of film parts. Dozens, anyway.' In fact he had turned down a part in the remake of *Mutiny on the Bounty* in which, ironically, Marlon Brando was to play Fletcher Christian, the *Bounty* mutineer. 'I was going to do *Mutiny on the Bounty*, which would have tied me up. Just think of it. I wouldn't have played Lawrence. I'd have certainly punched Brando on the nose. I'd have probably ended up on the cutting-room floor and had my throat cut into the bargain.'

But he was serious about staying loyal to the stage. 'We all want to do Royal Court and Arts Theatre plays. But you get twelve quid a week at the Arts and I was getting forty quid a week – it went up to forty-five – playing leading roles at Stratford. But I suppose you can't grumble. Indeed, you mustn't. But the plain truth is that actors subsidise the theatre.'

He made two promises about the theatre at that time. The first was that, however grand *Lawrence* made him and whatever offers were made to him as a result, he would only work six months of the year for the cinema. The rest he would devote to the stage. And the other, even more idealistic and ultimately unrealistic goal was to set up a repertory company of actors under his general direction. While one half of the O'Toole/Jules Buck partnership was roaming around the desert in Bedouin gear, the other half of Keep Films would begin a film called *Operation Snatch*, a comedy about Gibraltar during World War II.

This was to be the start of what O'Toole hoped would become a co-operative actors' company dedicated to good theatre, irrespective of producers' demands. 'I will be an actor-manager,' said O'Toole. 'I want to do the same as Igmar Bergman does in Sweden – make films and stage plays using the same company. We would also do television plays. But I'm not having a training ground for young-sters. My company will be made up of good, sound pros. It will be a theatre belonging to actors and writers. And I will have the final say about policy. This is not an attempt to form a sub-Stratford or a quasi-National Theatre but to do one thing at a time and do it well. We will make a lot of money.' It was a hopeless dream and the project soon had to be abandoned, although he has hoped to revive it several times since.

The main hindrance to the repertory company scheme was that the founder and main inspiration was to be out of circulation for over two years making *Lawrence*. While Lean and Spiegel were out in Jordan selecting the final sites for shooting, O'Toole was in Britain preparing. The original filming schedule suggested to him was between six and eight months – half in Jordan, the country in which Lawrence's *The Seven Pillars of Wisdom* was set, and half in the studio in Britain. Everyone connected with *Lawrence* – except, it seems, O'Toole – knew what that brief programme really meant. David Lean was a perfectionist and was unlikely, almost on principle, to bring in the footage on time. O'Toole would be tied to Lean's company for more than two years through seven different countries before the filming finished. And then there would be the lingering around, synchronising the sound and finally adjusting the completed film before O'Toole was free to start another job.

O'Toole's first port of call in mid-December 1960 was the office of Sam Spiegel, where he met Spiegel's unlikely right-hand man, Anthony Nutting. Nutting, aged forty, had four years before been the Minister of State for Foreign Affairs who had resigned over the British invasion of Suez. He was an Arab expert, was writing a book about T. E. Lawrence and preparing another on the Arabs in general. He had just divorced his first wife, Gillian, and was about to marry his second, Anne. He was an Old Etonian and a graduate of Trinity College, Cambridge, who had been honourably wounded in 1940 while serving in the Leicestershire Yeomanry and had then served in HM Foreign Service, until the end of the war when he was elected the Conservative Member for the Melton Division of Leices-tershire.

He was to become an inspiration to O'Toole, for in his cool, quiet manner, he was to teach O'Toole how to act and think like T. E. Lawrence and how to camouflage a well-bred English manner behind the trappings of a Bedouin Arab. It was Anthony Nutting who perfected O'Toole's ability to imitate a gentleman so effectively – a knack which would stand him in good stead for a whole lifetime of film parts. Spiegel knew what he was doing when he hired Nutting, for he would be able to show O'Toole how to talk, walk, eat, even think like a young Edwardian English gentleman.

Anthony Nutting had first met Spiegel at the opening of *Kwai* in New York and was surprised later to find Spiegel offering him a job as his director of public and political relations. It was a smart move on Spiegel's part. By paying Nutting a little more than the £3,500 a year he was getting as Minister of State at the Foreign Office, he was able to tap an extraordinary amount of goodwill for Spiegel in the Arab world – an essential requirement when a Jewish producer wishes to make a film among Arabs.

Nutting knew many of the Arab leaders personally. He was a personal friend of King Hussein and had known him since the King left Harrow to rule over Jordan. 'I remember taking him to lunch at the Commons just after his school had won the Eton and Harrow cricket match,' said Nutting. 'He was delirious with delight – and that sort of link probably helps.' He had smoothed the way when Spiegel and Lean wanted to look at locations in Jordan. 'They asked for one Jeep and were offered ten,' remembered Nutting. 'They asked for a couple of soldiers and were promised a platoon. In fact, they were embarrassed with co-operation to the point where bearded Bedouin would insist on showing them the bridges they helped Lawrence to blow up in their childhood.'

O'Toole first met Nutting in the offices of Horizon Films in Mayfair. O'Toole was dressed in his only suit, slumped in an armchair and he was wearing dark glasses to protect his eyes from the sun after another operation to correct his squint. Nutting gave him a kindly look and said: 'Shortly there will be no trousers. We go to live with the Bedouin.' O'Toole felt like laughing but restrained himself when Nutting's face remained quite serious, for he was not joking. Lean wanted his bright young actor to smell like an Arab before he ever set eyes on him through the camera lens. O'Toole had thought that within three months he would be back in London, acting on a set. It was when Nutting's face declined to break into a grin that O'Toole knew what he was in for. For three months he was to spend his time researching the life of T. E. Lawrence and learning how to live in the desert as if he had been born in it. For three months not an inch of film would pass through Lean's camera.

Nor was there a script to learn. Robert Bolt was working on *The Seven Pillars of Wisdom*, but had not got very far. Sitting in his house in Richmond Green, the venetian blinds drawn to protect him from the distracting view, Bolt was under pressure from Spiegel and Lean to deliver quickly, but it was a slow business. Bolt was trying to understand the particular greatness that T. E. Lawrence displayed and it was no hack's job to rattle it off. At the same time he was bristling at the way that the Lawrence project was consuming him. He was kept working round the clock and complained to visitors that Spiegel and Lean had taken him over, in his own words, 'body and soul'.

O'Toole was shipped out to Jordan where, in between reading the complete works of T. E. Lawrence and every available biography, he was being coached by Anthony Nutting in the ways of the desert. Beverley Cross, who was working on script continuity for Lean, was impressed by the progress that O'Toole had made before the rest of the cast and crew arrived. 'I thought my own research on Lawrence was pretty thorough,' she said, 'but Peter must have read every single word written by and about Lawrence – twice.

'When he got out there he immediately acclimatised himself to that very strange environment and started absorbing the geography and history. He was there for three months before a camera looked at him. Any other actor would have gone to pieces. But Peter sniffed a battle and responded to it. Out in Jordan we met an Arab chieftain who had known Lawrence. He looked at Peter and said: "Very good, but too tall." Without a word, Peter drew his Arab knife from his belt and started sawing away at himself just below the knees.' When Hussein visited the set, he was treated to similar O'Toole humour. He was talking of improving the Jordan economy and O'Toole offered his suggestion: 'Bottle the Jordan River and sell it to the Christians.' It was met with polite laughter. The whole tent broke up. He was accepted.

At that time, the West Bank of the Jordan River was still part of the Kingdom of Jordan, and O'Toole visited Bethlehem, but was unimpressed. 'Very peculiar. Christ commercialised,' he remembers. 'We came out of the crypt and in front of us was the Manger Cinema. It was showing *Circus of Horrors* and the first thing I saw was a large photo of my great friend Ken Griffith wearing my sweater. That was the reason Bethlehem, I'm afraid, did not amount to a religious experience.'

One of O'Toole's first tasks was to learn to ride a camel with the assistance of Bedouin Sergeant Hamed of the Jordanian Army Camel Corps. 'Of course I was a bit scared,' remembered O'Toole. 'I can't say I had a particular liking for any animal, let alone a camel.

And when I realised the height of it, I confess there were doubts in my mind about taking on this role of Lawrence.'

His first lesson demanded that he stay on top of the camel for ninety minutes. When he slipped down the side of the beast at the end of the time, blood was oozing from the seat of his jeans. He was in agony. For the next three days he lay face down in his hotel in Amman. Antiseptic poultices were applied every two hours. He had never caused himself so much pain on purpose. When he returned for his second lesson, he told his Camel Corps tutors: 'You shall be good Bedouin, stones of the desert, but this is a very delicate Irish arse.'

His solution, his 'contribution to Arab culture' as he called it, was to get the Bedouin to use Dunlopillo rubber pads under their camel saddles. 'All they usually use is a bit of wood and a blanket,' he explained. 'Well, after a bit of that caper, my backside was raw. So I went into Amman and bought a lovely hunk of mucous membrane pink Dunlopillo and stuffed it under the saddle. Now the whole of the desert patrol use them.' He put the sponge rubber under the blanket on the saddle and around the wooden pommel at the rear of the saddle, which had bashed and bruised the base of his spine. He clambered on for a second lesson, lasted twenty minutes and spent the next day in bed.

The third ride was the one which decided whether he would continue or not. He gently lifted himself up into the saddle and was making quiet progress when a backfiring car gave the camel a scare and it bolted. O'Toole clung on, more scared of falling than the damage the saddle was doing to his bottom. He lost his hat, his stick and his boots, but stayed on tight. After that, he was able to take anything that filming demanded. His teacher, Sergeant Hamed, told him: 'I never thought you'd make it. But after this I know I can turn you into a camel rider. And when you can ride, I will give you your own camel.' O'Toole had boldly declared before his first lesson: 'If I'm going to play Lawrence, I've got to ride like him,' and within three lessons he was well on the way.

Camel riding was to be a constant danger to him – and a constant source of amusement for those around him on the set. More than once he risked his neck – and Spiegel's investment – because Lean wanted to maintain the film's authenticity. 'My worst experience,' remembered O'Toole, 'was when four hundred city Arabs recruited as horsemen were doing a scene where they officially welcomed fifty Bedouin, including myself. There was bad blood between them in real life and as we rehearsed that scene, I said to David Lean: "The Rafferty rules down there," meaning there were no rules at all, Queensberry or otherwise. I was frankly terrified. We went downhill at a slow trot on our camels and what should have been a welcome became something really nasty. The four hundred Arabs charged at the two wings of our line. They got a twelve-year-old boy off his horse, broke his leg; they knocked me off, too. I went over backwards, only waking up ten minutes later. My camel stood guard over me as they are trained to do and so saved my life, shielding me from serious injury.'

And there were numerous more dismountings. 'Another time I was galloping along and there was a sudden dip. You cannot see that in the desert because of the glare. Suddenly there was nothing there for me and my camel. Again I woke minutes later – safe.' By the end of the shooting of *Lawrence*, O'Toole had ridden five thousand miles on camelback – about a thousand hours of swaying in the saddle.

Shooting began in Jordan in May 1961. For the most part, O'Toole was kept hard at it in the scorching desert heat and he soon won the respect of the rest of the outfit. John Box, the artistic director on *Lawrence*, became an admirer. 'When O'Toole works, he works like nobody else. The man is a complete professional. The role was an enormous strain to put on a young actor, and the picture had to be made under some appalling conditions – heat, sandstorms, soul-killing isolation. He had to learn to ride a camel – that sounds comical, and Peter is comical about it – but it's damned difficult enough to ride one without giving a performance on one, and finally he was riding like a Bedouin and acting. He had to interpret one of the most complex characters ever under some of the worst acting conditions ever, and what he achieved is incredible.'

The desert was tough and O'Toole did not enjoy it very much. Lean was so pernickety that he would wait two weeks to get a shot right. All the time, O'Toole had to be on call, ready for concentration. And the work was thoroughly dangerous. He preferred to do all his own stunts and ended up with a long list of injuries. He lost two stone in weight. A camel bit him and he lost the use of two fingers for a time. The heat of the sand gave him third-degree burns. He sprained both ankles. An anklebone was cracked. Ligaments in both his hip and his thigh were torn. He dislocated his spine. He broke his thumb. He sprained his neck and was concussed twice. His groin was torn and his skull was cracked.

Lean had chosen the most remote place to begin shooting. Jebel Tubeiq is two hundred and fifty miles east of Aqaba in a desolate region near the Saudi-Arabian border. The nearest water is a hundred and fifty miles away. The temperatures reached were so hot that the thermometers taken to record the heat had to be cooled to prevent them from destroying themselves. Conditions for the cast and crew were wretched. Only Lean acted as though it was normal weather. O'Toole was given no privacy. The nearest he could get to being alone was sitting in his camp chair with his eyes shut. O'Toole was often close to despair, although he kept up a stream of bright, chirpy letters to Sian Phillips.

No one had acknowledged quite how unreasonable the conditions at Jebel Tubeiq were until Alec Guinness and Anthony Quinn arrived at the location. They were offered the same accommodation as O'Toole was using – sparse Nissen huts without air conditioning – and immediately created hell, threatening to walk off the set and return to London unless things were improved. They were subsequently given luxury caravans. And the conditions for O'Toole were improved a little: instead of his unprotected canvas chair, he was offered a little hut, which he readily accepted and used until it blew away in the first sandstorm.

Lean kept up the pressure on O'Toole and O'Toole took it all. He was determined to live down the reputation he had brought with him from Britain for being a spoilt starlet. 'I'm a pro,' he declared, 'and what some have failed to realise is that I'm hard and disciplined when it comes to work.' And Lean took full advantage. He was known as a bully and liked nothing better than building up an edge with an actor, a tension on which he could build an extraordinary performance. He pushed O'Toole to the limits of endurance.

One example was a scene where O'Toole, accompanied by the two young boys, is walking to the Suez Canal across the Sinai Desert in a sandstorm; the scene prefaced by the lines: 'What? Are you taking the children?' and O'Toole replies; 'Moses did.' A wind machine was set up to blow sand in O'Toole's face and Lean wanted to show Lawrence's masochistic ability to keep his eyes wide open. They repeated it twenty times, at Lean's insistence, until O'Toole completed a take without blinking, with the sand blasting into his open eyes. Even Lean was impressed: 'I was trying to teach him discipline,' he said, 'and told him that in three months he would keep his eyes open through anything. Peter did it in three weeks, just to prove to me that he could.'

But at another time, O'Toole was close to total despair. Lean's inability to praise his actors or his technicians had led him to the conclusion that he was incapable of portraying Lawrence. It was a major crisis of confidence and O'Toole felt incapable of turning to Lean for the encouragement he needed. He retired to his boiling Nissen hut in a deep gloom, nursing an injured leg. He was considering abandoning the film and many on the site thought that he was close to a breakdown. Still Lean did not help. In the end, John Stannard, the unit chief, spent three hours at night talking with O'Toole, slowly raising his spirits. He removed the air conditioning unit from a kitchen and installed it in O'Toole's hut to relieve him at least of the physical discomfort of the heat.

Gradually O'Toole recovered, although he wrote to Sian Phillips, begging her to come out and be with him. It would not be the first time that he would depend upon her in a crisis. In many subsequent films, when his depression made him feel deeply lonely, he would send for her. She arrived at the location, having turned down a theatrical part in London, and gave him the support he needed. O'Toole recovered. 'Here, you have to be a little mad to stay sane,' he said. And many of the crew who had gone home early, unable to stand the conditions, agreed with him.

O'Toole gleaned some sympathy and understanding from an unlikely source: the Bedouin Arabs. He had misunderstood them at first. 'I was scared stiff,' he remembered. 'Daggers and guns hung all over them and they would sit for such long periods saying nothing that I was sure they were plotting some untimely end for me. Then all at once I felt all right. It was like being in a warm bath. I realised that the Bedouin say nothing unless there is something important to say. I found that for the first time in my life I did not have to keep the conversation going or push it in any way. Oh, the joy of being able to keep my mouth shut.'

But the Bedouin women were another thing. They were of no use to O'Toole as they were forbidden to talk to men outside their own families. And they had not seemed to take in that a film was being shot. The vast majority of the Bedouin used as extras had never seen a cinema screen and, for them, the notion of acting out make-believe was hard to grasp. They behaved as they had been brought up to behave. 'The Bedouin women took it so literally,' said O'Toole, 'that they did what they have always done when their men are away fighting: they looted everything in sight. It took us weeks to get all the loot back.'

In June Robert Bolt returned to London from Jordan, describing the filming as the biggest job since the building of the Pyramids. Life on the set was 'a continuous clash of egomaniacal monsters wasting more energy than dinosaurs and pouring rivers of money into the sand'. He was irritated that he had spent so much time writing a script for it to be changed so arbitrarily on the set. In Jordan he worked ten hours a day on script-writing. By comparison with the film world, the jungle of the theatre seemed to him like the monastic life. He returned to Britain to continue writing the unfinished script and transferred his headquarters from his home in Richmond to the peace of Somerset, where he had once been a schoolmaster.

After six months in the desert, O'Toole was allowed home to Britain for a few weeks rest. He checked straight into hospital to recuperate. 'When I got out of hospital I went mad. After six months in the desert, I should think so. I ended up in jail in Bristol. Bristol of all places; I thought I was all right there. It was my second bit in jail and the film people were upset. You're not supposed to get up to that kind of caper on a film like this.' O'Toole had been stopped by the police and, back at the station, what the policemen had suspected all along had been proven by a blood test: he had been driving under the influence of drink. He was fined £75 and disqualified from driving for a year.

On 18 December 1961, the location work resumed in Almeria in Spain. Lean had, at first, hoped to use the original sites of Cairo, Damascus and Jerusalem for the filming, but the modernisation of those cities in the fifty years since Lawrence was there meant that alternative sites had to be found. All the city scenes were filmed in Spain, mostly in Seville, and although some filming had taken place in Aqaba, a replica of the port city was made in Spain for the spectacular camel charge – with 400 cast and crew, 700 camels and riders and 900 horses – which took the city from the Turks. And miles of railway track and a real steam engine were brought to the Almerian sands.

When the cast and crew arrived in Spain, they were told that they were in the last four months of shooting. It was, at least, more civilised than Jordan, even if the local bureaucracy which prevented the Moroccan camel drivers from entering the country proved a little trying. In the desert at Jebel Tubeiq, water had been hauled in tankers for hundreds of miles and food was flown in from Britain. Everyone hated it. It was too hot to work, too dry to think straight. The only one who was working well in Jordan, who even was reluctant to leave when the six months were up, was David Lean. He had somehow come to be attached to the desert and he was the last to leave. 'When the time came to go,' said Sam Spiegel, 'he was almost tearful. He seemed to have inherited some of Lawrence's own mysticism and love of the desert.'

Spain was altogether more comfortable, though it was hardly more exciting. O'Toole called it 'Pontefract with scorpions', but it was better than the desert. Anything was better than that. O'Toole had learned to cope with the constant discomforts and time-wasting that filming entailed by indulging in quiet resentment. And Lean did not break his stern régime, even if they were in softer surroundings.

His perfectionism persisted, exemplified by the shooting of one scene which has, inevitably, been lost from the twice-cut version of *Lawrence* which is now available. It was an early scene, cut in the twenty minutes which Columbia Pictures demanded to be cut from the final Lean-approved print, with Lawrence poring over maps in Cairo, tinting them to signify where various forces were now deployed. To emphasise the heat of Cairo – and boredom for Lawrence of staff work – before he was despatched, the scene was repeatedly shot while members of the crew tried to shoo a small number of disobedient house flies on to the map and, if possible, on to the brush O'Toole was wielding. Somebody suggested smearing the map with sugar, but Lean vetoed the idea as it would look like smeared sugar and would not ring true. The scene was patiently taken and retaken repeatedly until finally four flies walked boldly across the map of the desert. The crew whooped and applauded. O'Toole, mindful of W. C. Field's warning not to work with children or animals, was being eclipsed by the acting of flies.

O'Toole bought a green cloth cap in Seville one day and used it to keep himself shaded from the sun. After the desert, he was determined never to subject himself to any sun unless he had to. 'I can't stand light,' he explained. 'I hate weather. My idea of heaven is moving from one smoke-filled room to another. I never go out in the fresh air at home. Now here I am filming outside every day. Just horrible.'

Spain was better than Jordan, but the terrain was meant to look like the desert and the arid south of Spain proved almost as rough as the real thing. In fact one of the first things to happen on the new location was a series of flash floods, the worst floods Seville had experienced for a hundred years. After arid Jordan, the sight of camels dripping with rain brought hysterical laughter. And as filming passed its first anniversary, David Lean threw a proper, sit-down celebratory dinner, with food as British as the wandering caterer Phil Hobbs could provide. There were, thankfully, no speeches, but at the end of the evening there was a fireworks display. When it was announced that, after Spain, the Lean caravan would set off for Morocco, the crew were too numb to complain. When a visitor to the set said: 'Cheer up! It can't last for ever', he was met with a po-faced: 'Why not?'

While filming in Almeria, O'Toole was made the subject of a short film biography for 'Monitor', the pioneering BBC Television arts programme. The director was Kenneth Griffith. He had never made a film before, but this was to become the first of a series of highly individual film portraits that he would make. Filming O'Toole at the top of a high sand hill, Griffith remembers being surprised by David Lean, who had run from where the main shooting was going on below. Lean had come all the way to ask Griffith: 'Have you got that wonderful cloud formation in the frame?' He looked through the camera lens to satisfy his worry before walking back down the hill.

Both O'Toole and Griffith were impressed by Lean's generous, impeccable professionalism.

Spain was more accessible and it was therefore easier for Sian to visit O'Toole with baby Kate. And the company was good. Sir Alec Guinness was there playing the part of King Feisal and he got on with O'Toole very well. Guinness, who had been keen to play the part of Lawrence himself, was flattering about O'Toole's acting ability and O'Toole was flattered by the attentions of one of Britain's most celebrated cinema actors. Another whom O'Toole became very fond of was April Ashley.

After a painful and horrifying operation in Casablanca, George Jamieson had re-emerged into the fashionable life of London as April Ashley and had made a fair living as a model. She had first met O'Toole at a party in the house of Duncan Melvin, a musical and ballet impresario, in St Leonard's Terrace, Chelsea. The next time they met was in Villa Verde, the rented home of Bobo Sigrist, an heiress to an aeroplane fortune, outside Marbella – a house which belonged to General Franco's daughter, Carmen, Marquesa de Villaverde. Ashley didn't recognise him at first because of his change of nose. He introduced her to Omar Sharif – O'Toole mentioning nothing of her sex change to Sharif – and they ended up taking O'Toole's studio car home to Villa Antoinette, where Ashley and, soon, O'Toole and Sharif, were staying.

'We went bananas,' remembered Ashley. 'Peter especially. Whenever he had time off he'd dive head first into a bottle.' The three became fast friends, and when O'Toole and Sharif returned to Seville after their rest and recuperation break, Ashley followed. O'Toole became a regular visitor to the Ashley home at Villa Antoinette, as Ashley remembered: 'Peter and I often slept together on these occasions, on the divan in the sitting-room in front of the log fire, chastely. He didn't like my bedrooms. He had his quirks.' And Ashley entertained Sian Phillips and Katie O'Toole for her second birthday. 'She knew of my association with Peter, but wasn't perturbed by it,' said Ashley in her memoirs. 'Nor had she reason to be.'

After Spain the caravan moved on to Morocco and more gruelling desert scenes to film in a wretched, out-of-the-way town called Ouarzazate. 'I shall never forget it,' remembered David Lean. 'A terrible place. During July and August when we were there, they were sending the légionnaires there for punishment. The heat was tremendous.' But there was no prospect of O'Toole backing out. He had become obsessed with the attention being paid to him. He was at the centre of an investment worth four million and he was enjoying the respect of the crew and of the others – many of them, such as Anthony Quinn and Sir Donald Wolfit, substantial stars and great actors. O'Toole realised that something special was going on, that this was no mere film but a landmark in film making. And he was playing the title role. It was him that all this expense, all this misery and discomfort was to benefit. And he realised that he was turning in an exceptional performance which was being drawn out of him by David Lean. He was learning so much from Lean and would be always grateful.

'The most important influence in my life has been David Lean,' he said. 'I graduated in Lean, took my BA in Lean, working with him virtually day and night in *Lawrence* for two years. I learned about the camera and the lens and the lights, and now I know more than some directors do.' Lean had given him 'discipline, patience and tolerance. And I learned them the hard way.' Of these, the most important, perhaps, of the qualities needed for film acting was patience. 'I don't mind the waiting about. *Lawrence* took over two years to make and I got used to hanging around literally two weeks for a shot. I found ways of occupying meself and now I actually enjoy it. Mind you, *Lawrence* wasn't a film. It was an experience. Two years and seven countries. The film even got in the way of the experience.' Lean was also generous to O'Toole, allowing him to contribute significant episodes to the film. For instance, the scene where Lawrence danced in his new white robes and is surprised by Anthony Quinn was made famous by O'Toole's decision to dance and twirl – a contribution which most critics have credited to Lean.

The progress of *Lawrence* met an unexpected and most unlikely hitch with the arrest and imprisonment of Robert Bolt. Bolt was actively involved in the Committee of 100's efforts to have Britain abandon its nuclear weapons. The Campaign for Nuclear Disarmament was filled with artistic celebrities of every kind, from Bertrand Russell through Christopher Logue, the poet, to Bolt himself. The powers ranged against them included most of the established forces, including the normally impartial judiciary.

The CND had decided upon an impromptu Sunday demonstration in Trafalgar Square in September 1961 and had not observed the normal courtesy of asking the police permission to arrange a march through the centre of London. The demo was deemed illegal, yet the Committee persisted, alleging that the attempts to have the march and rally delayed were political and duly ignored the warning that, if the preparations for the march went ahead, those who continued with the publicity work would be considered to have incited members of the public to commit a breach of the peace. The thirty-two organisers stood firm and refused to be budged by what they considered to be an unnecessary and undemocratic conspiracy by the authorities to undermine their efforts. The thirty-two were summoned to appear before the Bow Street Magistrates Court on 12 September and explain their defiant behaviour. They were given the option of recanting and leaving the courtroom free or standing by all that they had said and suffering the consequences.

Bolt was one of the thirty-two and between times was busily writing the screenplay of *Lawrence* – a task which had, like the film, started out modestly and, mainly through Lean's insistence, had become a major work of literature. Bolt could really ill afford the delay and time-wasting that this brush with the authorities entailed. But he was an honourable man, held his views on the tragedy of nuclear weapons most sincerely and, in any case, this was a point of principle. The magistrate should have known better than to challenge the author of *A Man for All Seasons*, which celebrated the noble and creditable defiance of Sir Thomas More against the whole might of his monarch. Bolt did not equate their cases in weight, but in terms of substance they were identical and he was damned if he was going to be silenced by such a transparently undemocratic device. Putting the progress of *Lawrence* to the back of his mind, he declined the treacherous offer of the magistrate to be bound over and was therefore sentenced to a month's imprisonment in the comparative penal comfort of Drake Hall, Staffordshire.

Bolt had misjudged the terms of his imprisonment, however. He had assumed that in prison he would, at least, be allowed to write. The peace of Drake Hall allowed a level of concentration which even Somerset did not offer. But he was mistaken. The authorities forbade him to work while in prison. He and his fellow dissenters complained. Surely any prisoner was allowed to write in his cell? The prison authorities said, in this instance, no. They put forward a suggestion. What if, instead of taking Sam Spiegel's money for himself, Bolt was to donate the money to charity. Then everyone would be pleased. Lean would have his script. Spiegel would have paid the fee. Bolt would have received nothing. The prison governor still would not agree. If Bolt were to continue writing the screenplay for *Lawrence of Arabia* while detained during Her Majesty's Pleasure, it would be confiscated and destroyed. The Committee of 100 members in the prison issued a press statement, outling the restriction of liberty being imposed upon one of their number. To prevent him from writing *Lawrence*, they said, was 'denying him a privilege accorded every other prisoner'.

Sam Spiegel was not amused. He sent a telegram to Drake Hall, demanding that Bolt agree to the magistrate's terms – to sign recognizances to be of good behaviour – so that work on the screenplay could continue and the work on the set be continued. Bolt refused. Spiegel started sending a succession of telegrams. Bolt was holding up the whole production. He was putting at risk the whole of the investment. It was unfair on the rest of the film team. O'Toole would soon run out of words to say in front of the camera. Still Bolt refused.

Spiegel decided to put in an appearance. He was driven to Staffordshire and allowed to speak to Bolt. Spiegel was blunt. The failure of Bolt to deliver the next section of the screenplay was holding up production. Filming had come to a full stop. Technicians' livelihoods were being put at risk. The project could not afford Bolt to be absent for a month. The film of *Lawrence of Arabia* was being jeopardised and could be abandoned altogether if Bolt did not agree to the magistrate's request. The other thirty-one understood clearly the pressure being put upon Bolt and begged him to change his mind which, with great reluctance, he did. He signed the recognizances and resumed his work on *Lawrence*. The filming restarted. Spiegel had not been bluffing.

Towards the end of the shooting, Sam Spiegel began to worry about O'Toole, that he would not last the pace. The film had been very strenuous, very punishing, and not everyone had the stamina for brutal conditions that David Lean had. 'As the film gets nearer the end they worry about me more and more,' O'Toole confided on the set. 'After all, if anything happened to me it would be disastrous. I'm in every scene. They wouldn't let me fly, for instance. In fact, Sam Spiegel treats me as if I were Rin-Tin-Tin instead of a working actor.'

Spiegel's worries were entirely justified. He was a prudent businessman and wasn't about to see his money and his efforts fall away before his eyes while his leading man became unable to continue. The history of cinema is riddled with epics where a large-scale picture has had to be abandoned because of an accident involving an actor. Spiegel would have remembered all too well the history of Alexander Korda's film of Robert Graves's *I Claudius*, starring Charles Laughton as the Roman emperor, and among others in the cast, James Mason and Merle Oberon. It was Miss Oberon who ditched the picture, leaving it in the state that it remains today, popularly called 'The Epic That Never Was', several hundred unconnected and unusable feet of celluloid with hints at the magnificence of the sets and some extraordinary acting from Laughton. On her way to the London Film Studios, Merle Oberon, driving herself, went out of control in her car and crashed, leaving herself with a fractured neck and Alexander Korda with a broken film.

And the same nearly happened to Sam Spiegel in the making of *Lawrence of Arabia*. One afternoon, O'Toole was sitting on a camel waiting to shoot a spectacular scene in which the Bedouin take the port of Aqaba. An effects gun was nearby, loaded with small pellets to kick up the sand and so give the impression of the scatter from the machine-gun bullets of the defending garrison. The effects gun fell over, spraying O'Toole with pellets in his right eye. He was temporarily blinded and his camel bolted in front of the five hundred Bedouin tribesmen, charging on their horses through the enemy encampment towards the port.

O'Toole, his hand up to his eye, could not control the beast and he was thrown into the path of the stampeding horses. The camel, which O'Toole had cursed each day that he had dismounted, saddlesore, from its back, did as it had been trained and stood over the fallen actor, shielding him from the charging horses which ran to either side. O'Toole lay unconscious for five minutes until technicians and the location doctor could reach him. O'Toole recovered with irritating panache. He was flown to hospital to receive treatment but was back on the set – and the camel – the next day.

Ironically, O'Toole came even closer to death filming the final scene of *Lawrence*, which turned out to be the final scene to be shot. T. E. Lawrence died in a motorcycle crash, speeding along a country lane. The traditional way for the cinema to photograph motorcyclists is for the motorcycle to be mounted on a trailer behind the truck carrying the camera and technicians. The actor is free to act, while the motorbike, which appears to be travelling at speed, is in fact stationary on the moving trailer. It is not usually a dangerous technique – indeed, the whole purpose of the procedure is to minimise the danger of the camera car coming close to a moving motorcycle.

In this instance the towing-bar between the camera truck and trailer had been tested and double tested and a length of rope provided a flimsy back-stop. Truck and trailer reached 50 mph and the filming had started when the towing-bar snapped, the trailer swerved and O'Toole was saved from careering into the ditch only by the rope which held firm. O'Toole clambered off the back of the motorbike and into the truck and the whole party returned slowly to the shooting headquarters. 'Afterwards we all climbed in the back of the camera car with Lean,' O'Toole remembers. 'No one said a word. We all sat there in silence, smoking, looking at the floor . . . But I think it was only Lawrence, up there, teasing.'

By the middle of October 1962, O'Toole had returned to Britain for good. His work on the film had ended. Sam Spiegel had brought the work to an end – Lean was capable of continuing on the project indefinitely, such was his passion for perfection – by arranging that the film be given a Royal Film Performance attended by the Queen and fixing the date for 10 December. Lean had a deadline he could not jump or dodge. The most glamorous première had been arranged. O'Toole's sense of relief was absolute. On returning to Britain he admitted himself to hospital once more, taking with him a dozen scripts. 'Sam Spiegel's worried about what I'll do when the film is all over,' he said. 'I'm sure he thinks I'm going to make a quickie called *Abbott and Costello Meet Lawrence of Arabia*. Actually I'm going to do a play.

'Anyway, now it's done. And I must say it was a master stroke on Sam's part fixing the première date and inviting the Queen before we were even through. He knew we were going on too long – David and I had begun to forget we were making a film: after two years it had become a way of life – so Sam nailed us with a date and that was that. Now poor David has moved his bed into the cutting room and is working round the clock to get the film finished. I asked him what he thought and he said: "I think it's the best thing I've ever done." I tell you, boy, when you see those camels charging the screen at thirty-five miles an hour you'll go through the roof. It's just magnificent. Whatever comes of Lawrence, though I must say I feel I've earned it.'

Now came two months of waiting. For all his cockiness and Connemara confidence, O'Toole felt thoroughly nervous. Deprived of the reassuring applause of a live audience since his last night in Stratford two years before, he was no longer sure how good he was – or how good he had been during the filming. Lean was not a man for compliments. He would scold and growl if things were not right – and it was easy enough not to match up to his rigorous standards of perfection – but he was sparing with the praise. Those, such as Alec Guinness, who had worked with Lean before and had steaming rows with him on the set – during the filming of *The Bridge on the River Kwai* Guinness and Lean had not spoken for months on end after a misunderstanding – reassured O'Toole that the lack of abuse from Lean was praise in itself. But O'Toole needed a little encouragement and that was not forthcoming.

He was also in a quandary about what to do next. It was all very well taking two years to complete one picture and he had been handsomely rewarded, but it was a difficult thing to follow. To be offered such a part as Lawrence offered no difficulty. He grabbed at it, as would have any young actor. There was no rational option except to enter for the main chance. But after Lawrence? There was no obvious route. Like a first novelist, O'Toole found that it was the sequel which was so difficult.

He had committed himself to return to the stage, as he decided he would, but beyond that? The stage was now an irrelevance to his career as a film actor. Despite his good intentions, despite his hope that it would be different, film- and stage-acting were quite different skills. And whereas the self-esteem, respect among serious actors and instant gratification of an appreciative public could only be achieved through the stage, still he was set willy-nilly upon a promising and lucrative film career if only he played the next card right.

He ploughed through scripts from his hospital bed. He took advice from his old friends and from Sian. He canvassed advice from old hands of the cinema. He owed Sam Spiegel more films and was contracted to deliver, but even that guarantee of more work had its pitfalls. What if Spiegel wanted him to appear in something quite inappropriate, quite ludicrous? What if, in the event of a hostile reception for *Lawrence* in eight weeks time, Spiegel declined to take up the contractual obligation? His career would be blighted with an epic disaster and a producer who spurned his talents. Should he, then, abandon film work for the theatre and forget the magic of film making and all the knowledge he had gleaned from David Lean?

To defuse the tension and demote the importance of the next decision, O'Toole decided to act in a play. But he also considered a film which had been suggested to him, a screen version of the Rodgers and Hammerstein *My Fair Lady*. David Lean had passed on a piece of advice which he had been given by Noel Coward: 'Never come out of the same hole twice.' O'Toole took the advice to heart and *My Fair Lady* seemed to fit the bill. It was different from Lawrence in every respect. It was a jolly, colourful, comic musical taken from George Bernard Shaw's *Pygmalion* – a far thing from the introverted gloom and arid hardship of T. E. Lawrence's anguished life.

Although he later denied being interested, the more O'Toole thought about it, the more he judged that it would be right for him. He needed a second success to consolidate his career in the cinema and, if the success of the musical on stage was anything to go by, *My Fair Lady* would also mop up in the cinemas. And there was another reason. 'I want to do *My Fair Lady*,' he said. 'The only problem is the film can't be shown until 1965. Something to do with stage rights. But it's a marvellous part and it would be good for me to act with Audrey Hepburn. [Who was already cast.] I need a bird, see. I keep making these films and never get a bird. *The Savage Innocents*, *The Day They Robbed the Bank of England*, *Kidnapped* and now *Lawrence*. Not a bird in sight.'

This problem of being identified entirely with all-male projects became more acute after the release of *Lawrence*. As the American magazine *Esquire* explained: 'People who have only seen O'Toole in *Lawrence* would hardly recognise him in person . . . His light brown hair, which is curly, was straightened and bleached blond for

*Lawrence* making him seem soft and very pretty; and since he camped it up in sand dunes while wearing those Arab desert robes, half of the world's homosexual population came to the delightful conclusion that he was one of them. He is not.'

During the two months of waiting, Sian found a peculiar document which appealed to O'Toole's sense of superstition. At a sale she bought a letter from Lawrence. It began: 'Dear Peter . . .' and it mentioned *The Seven Pillars of Wisdom*, which Lawrence dismisses. 'It's a rotten book, you know.' And it was signed T.E.S. for T.E. Shaw, the pseudonym that Lawrence adopted when in the RAF. O'Toole considered it more than just a coincidence. He toyed with the idea that somehow T. E. Lawrence was trying to tell him something from the other side. But did it mean the film was going to be a success or not?

O'Toole found the suspense unbearable. As the days dragged by, he was filled increasingly with doubts about what the finished film would look like. He was not allowed to see the completed print. Lean, of course, had seen it, but the security was so great that Spiegel and his bodyguard were the only others who were allowed to see it. O'Toole couldn't even remember some of the scenes which had been shot at the beginning, it was so long ago. And he had no idea which parts of those two years Lean had chosen to distil into the two hours of the epic.

And yet these were the last few days that O'Toole was to spend as an acting commoner. After the night of 9 December 1962, life would never quite be the same again. He would have been elevated to the aristocracy of the most successful and sought-after film stars and never would he be allowed to return quietly to the stage and resume the humdrum actor's life. Yet he persisted that, whatever reception *Lawrence* was granted, it would not alter him. 'People keep asking me what I'm going to do when the balloon goes up in December. Well, I'm not going to do anything. I shan't change.' It was an unrealistic combination of a typical false modesty and wishful thinking.

# 5 Films versus Plays

THE NIGHT of 9 December 1962 was the turning point for O'Toole. It was the night that the final version of *Lawrence* was shown to the public – albeit to an especially invited public of royalty and film people – and the night that he met and shook hands with the Queen. He had been instructed by Sam Spiegel to wear white tie and tails and any decorations that were available to him. O'Toole was in a nervous, flippant mood. He was too young for World War II and his National Service had been undistinguished, to say the least. He had no medals and so decided to wear the Star of David which his mother had given him when rehearsing for Shylock in *The Merchant of Venice* at Stratford. He toyed with wearing a badge he had picked up from the St John's Ambulance Brigade, and he took with him a green comb – for luck – which he had pinched from the show business writer Donald Zec after a two-day drinking session. He was feigning nonchalance, but he knew full well how important this royal première was for the success of the film and his future. Asked what it meant to him, he gave the unguarded reply: 'A hell of a lot, mate.'

He told his friend Tom Stoppard that he was not sure what the success or failure of *Lawrence* would do for him. 'It's worse than a first night, waiting for *Lawrence*. I mean, it's all out of my control – just sit there and look at it. A lot of people have talked about being ruined by success, but let's face it, more people have been butchered by failure.' His nervousness on the night prevented him from seeing it all the way through. By curious chance, he finally saw the whole of *Lawrence* for the first time nearly twenty years later, on a hotel television in Amman in Jordan. 'That was quite an experience, I promise you, seeing that film in Arabia and then going out and seeing the Bedouin milling around in the streets.'

Shaking hands with the members of the Royal Family and their party in the cinema foyer after the screening also marked an important stage in the press reaction to the film. The film critics had, as usual, been given a preview of *Lawrence* but protocol demands that no review should be published until the Royal Family has seen a film chosen for a Royal Film Performance. As the Queen extended her gloved hand to O'Toole and David Lean, Sam Spiegel and Sir Alec Guinness, while all the rest of the cast and technicians were being introduced by the cinema manager to Her Majesty and the rest of her party, and all through the celebratory supper party after the film, everyone concerned know what O'Toole knew: that the critical verdict could now be printed.

The press reception was universally ecstatic. Lean was hailed as a genius; O'Toole as the brightest young actor to have emerged for years, a hypnotic screen presence. Even the usually staid *The Times* was enthusiastic. Its critic wrote: 'The film is shot in Super Panavision 70 and whatever that may be it certainly produces spectacular effects. There is the sense of depth, of perspective, and when, for instance, a cloud of dust rises against a background of burning sand and burning sky it is impossible to make a guess at the distance it is away. The big screen has frequently proved to be only too big; here it hardly seems big enough, and the implied compliment to Mr Lean and his camera crew is considerable.

'All this means that Mr Peter O'Toole is obliged to make Lawrence a man of endurance and of action, a born and natural leader of men – and of Arabs in their own country and with their own savage and exacting standards rather than of his own race. Mr O'Toole, although his height is a trifle disconcerting, achieves this supremely difficult task, and at the same time he manages to mingle an arrogant awareness of Lawrence's own contradictory qualities with humanity, and even humility.

'Among those qualities, as the film has it, is blood-lust; the script, however, shies away from any deep exploration of the factors involved in his capture and flogging. At any rate, this Lawrence has the gift, as David Garnett stated the real Lawrence had, of giving to the most commonplace of remarks and sentences the incisive edge of personal style.'

So the two years sweating in the desert had been worth it. O'Toole and Sian were happy and triumphant. Still he persisted that success would not change him and that all he really wanted to do was to return to the stage and get back to acting to small audiences. But it was not going to be as easy as that, as he was aware. He went out of his way to show that success had not changed him, although he was as conscious as all those around him that he had already changed and all his protesting was only evidence of the fact that he could no longer be treated as ordinary – one of the crowd. 'Someone asked me the other day, do I give dinner parties,' he joked. 'Me? Dinner parties! Here, nosh is served for friends. And there's always food, a bed and a jar of something for me mates.' But 'here' was already a long way from the cupboard, as he used to call it, that he shared with Kenneth Griffith.

During the filming of *Lawrence*, O'Toole and Sian left Kenneth

Griffith and Doria and their home in Dorset Mews. Home was now a £20,000 Georgian mansion, built in 1740, in Heath Street, Hampstead, the smartest inner suburb of London. O'Toole was able to return the hospitality given him and Sian when Griffith, Doria and their newly-born daughter Eva stayed with them in Hampstead, *en route* to a new home in Islington.

O'Toole's home has five floors and nine principal rooms, which he filled with works of art. He began collecting art seriously and was able to buy his father's favourite painting, Jack B. Yeats's *The Emigrant*. It was one of a number of Yeats's that O'Toole bought in competition with John Huston. His daughter Kate became fond of using an Epstein bust as a knicker rack. Upstairs in the bedroom was a small Bonnard of the back of a naked woman. And in this large, grand, high-ceilinged house, he reserved himself a study, a den. On its door he fixed a brass plate, which read: The Marcus Luccicos Room. It is a Shakespearean joke. Luccicos is a character in 'Othello' who never quite makes the stage, although in one scene his presence is urgently demanded.

The room's walls are hidden by framed theatrical and cinema posters, prints of famous actors and theatrical trophies, such as the gloves worn by Sir Henry Irving in Tennyson's play *Becket*. Taking pride of place is a portrait of one of O'Toole's favourite cinema star, the deadpan comedian and freelance philosopher, W. C. Fields. On his first trip to New York, to see Anthony Quinn and Laurence Olivier in Jean Anouilh's *Becket*, O'Toole had made a detour to see Philadelphia, the city most abused by Fields, simply to find out whether it was, as Fields had claimed, only marginally more inviting than the prospect of death. Outside O'Toole's front door and before the busy main road, to protect O'Toole from passing star-pesterers, there is a forbidding door set in a high wall through which visitors must first identify themselves by talking into an intercom.

There was a sense of mischievous irony in O'Toole's voice when he told people: 'The only thing that's changed in my life is I've got a new house with a seven-foot-wide bed. I've still got the same mates. Tony Armstrong-Jones [Lord Snowdon, the Queen's brother-in-law] came round the other day for a Guinness and a chat. My middle-aged daughter [Katie, then aged two] looked at him sternly and said: "What's your name?" "Tony," he said. "All right, Tony," she said, "come and play." And there they were on the floor, playing together. I've got some great mates.'

He protested that he was in debt, that he had put every penny into the house and he was actually in the red. 'I haven't got a penny. The difference is that I'm now luxuriously broke.' It was hardly true. He was already contracted to make more films with Sam Spiegel and he was in enormous demand. He would boast how much he was being offered by film companies for the next available film once his Spiegel contract had run out. 'Success is marvellous. I love it,' he said. 'You know, I sometimes wonder what my temptation level is. There was this part the other day – a fat, juicy Hollywood part. I knew I was going to turn it down. Anyway, instead of just saying no, I decided to see how far I could go. So I asked for the earth. You know what they said? Let's negotiate. It's fantastic.' The fact was that he was not certain what he wanted to do. He had a contract with Spiegel and he would have to negotiate carefully to ensure his career was put above Spiegel's short-term interests.

Spiegel had other fish to fry. O'Toole owed him a great deal, but he was not ready to take up his option so quickly. He was a businessman first, a film maker second, and before he could move onto the next, he must first see *Lawrence* through to the end. It was going to make money – that was by now certain – but it was a project which needed careful nurturing and Spiegel did not trust that sort of fine decision-making to anyone other than himself. As soon as the film was released, that was the last time that Lean and O'Toole and the rest of the actors and technicians had to worry about it. They might be drawn in – usually at an extra negotiated fee – to attend premières in cities where showbusiness still demanded the push of a glamorous first night. (O'Toole was already booked to go to New York and Los Angeles to attend the opening of *Lawrence* in the United States.) A film as big as *Lawrence* simply had to have a lavish, flashy launch, complete with a specially invited celebrity audience and as many recognisable faces from the film as possible. And, for the actors and technicians, there would be the arduous but glorious task of attending awards ceremony events if the film were nominated – although of these, only the Oscar ceremony in Los Angeles was essential. But beyond that there was nothing to be done. The job was finished and their work was fixed forever in the final cut. O'Toole was ready to start work again. But Spiegel must take care of his expensive baby and sell it around the world.

He could therefore not immediately cash the contractual obligation which O'Toole owed him. Instead he steered O'Toole into the similarly commercially efficient hands of Hal B. Wallis, the former head of Warners and the slick producer who could claim to have discovered Errol Flynn, Olivia de Havilland, Burt Lancaster, Kirk Douglas and, as a movie star, Elvis Presley. He was also the producer of such classic films as *Little Caesar*, *The Maltese Falcon*, *Casablanca* and *Gunfight at the OK Corral*. O'Toole approved of being put into such skilled care, for he was eager not to trip up on his second important outing. Since *Lawrence* had hitched him up into the stratosphere, he

Peter O'Toole playing the bagpipes in a scene from **Kidnapped**, his first film made in 1959, △ with Peter Finch in the foreground *(Walt Disney)*

O'Toole in Willis Hall's **The Long and the** △ **Short and the Tall** at the Royal Court Theatre in 1959 *(Zoe Dominic)*

As Petruchio in **The Taming of the Shrew** △ at Stratford in 1960 *(Zoe Dominic)*

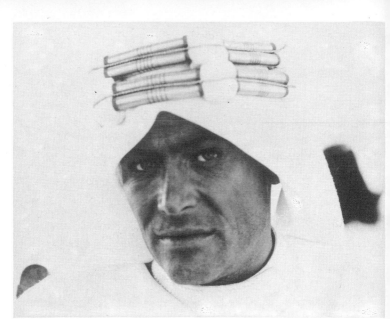

Peter O'Toole as Lawrence of Arabia *(Columbia Pictures)* △

At a rehearsal for **Baal** *(Zoe Dominic)* △

O'Toole in October 1963 *(Zoe Dominic)* △

O'Toole with Daliah Lavi in a scene from **Lord Jim** *(Columbia Pictures)* △

What's New Pussycat (1965) – l. to r. standing – Paula Prentiss, Romy Schneider, Ursula Andress and Capucine. l. to r. sitting – Woody Allen, Peter O'Toole and Peter Sellers *(United Artists)* △

O'Toole with Audrey Hepburn in a scene from **How To Steal a Million** △
*(Twentieth Century Fox)*

Peter O'Toole in his costume as King Henry II during the shooting of **The Lion in Winter** *(Bob Willoughby)* △

Peter O'Toole and Katharine Hepburn. O'Toole's cape reads 'Tiger O'Toole, Paperweight Champ'. Hepburn later changed her sign to 'Tiger O'Toole's Widow'. *(Bob Willoughby)* △

Murphy's War *(Hemdale)* △

O'Toole with Arthur Lowe in **The Ruling Class** *(Keep Films)* △

Peter O'Toole introduces his two daughters to his co-star James Coco, who played Sancho Panza, during the filming of **Man of La Mancha** △ *(United Artists)*

Peter O'Toole with Sophia Loren relaxing on the set of **Man of La Mancha** *(United Artists)* △

O'Toole during the filming of **Caligula** *(GTO Films)* △

In costume for **Macbeth** at the Old Vic in 1980 *(Zoe Dominic)* △

With Lisa Harrow in a scene from **Man and Superman** *(Zoe Dominic)* △

My Favourite Year *(MGM/UA Entertainment Co.)* △

A recent portrait *(Zoe Dominic)* △

was determined that he would not slip. At the same time he wanted to do something honourable, at least of the same intellectual worth as *Lawrence*.

Wallis inevitably wanted O'Toole to follow *Lawrence* with something equally sensational. Under Spiegel's direction, the young barely-known Stratford actor had become the hottest property in the cinema. And Wallis was prepared to use the fact that O'Toole was eager to establish in the public mind that he preferred to be known as an actor rather than a star. There was money to be made in marketing a popular intelligent actor: it would maximise a film's appeal to encourage a popular and serious audience simultaneously. And it was necessary, on Wallis's behalf, to ensure that O'Toole was kept up to the mark. Wallis knew as well as O'Toole that O'Toole's performance in *Lawrence* was largely caused by the impeccable direction and fanatical perfectionism of David Lean. Lean, however, was eager to press on with *Dr Zhivago* for Carlo Ponti and there was no obvious place for O'Toole in that – nor would it have been healthy for Lean or O'Toole to work so closely together again. They did not get on so well that they remained personal friends once shooting ended.

In any case, there would have been an element of gamble involved in pairing the two on another grand project. It would smell too much of a sequel and *Lawrence* was a hard act to follow. So, how to keep O'Toole on his mettle? How to prevent him resting on his well-earned but frail reputation? The most obvious options available to Wallis were to find someone as demanding as Lean to push O'Toole hard again – and there was no one who was in Lean's league – or draw another fine performance from O'Toole by pairing him with a sublime actor, thereby playing on O'Toole's vanity. As Spiegel had learnt from the *Lawrence* auditions, O'Toole acted at his best when competing against others. His best performances came when up-staging others.

There were rumours that O'Toole had signed to play Henry Higgins, the elocutionist role which Rex Harrison had played on stage, in the film musical *My Fair Lady*. He had even been quoted as saying that he was eager to play the part because he needed to play opposite a woman after the exclusively male company he kept in *Lawrence* and that Audrey Hepburn would do very nicely; but he vehemently denied it. He told Kenneth Tynan: 'Never in my life. It's also in print that I'm living with Rudolf Nureyev, and that isn't true either. The simple fact is that someone from Warner Bros approached me about *My Fair Lady* and I said that the only man who could and should play Higgins was Rex Harrison. I did say I wouldn't mind playing Doolittle, but they didn't like that at all.'

And there was a first attempt to get him to follow his haunting portrayal of the loner T. E. Lawrence with a similar role: that of Joseph Conrad's loner, Lord Jim. It was not to be – not yet, at least. 'Richard Brooks asked me to do Lord Jim, but when I asked to see the script he said I should "trust him", so that was the end of that.'

Meanwhile, O'Toole was hankering after a little high culture. He was in a bullish mood and felt he could call the shots. He was damned if he was going to be browbeaten into dropping his standards. He wanted to maintain the reputation he had among the high arts set. For someone with two years of education behind him, his biggest thrill had been to accept the acclaim of the intelligent, the wise and the discerning on the stage of the Shakespeare Memorial Theatre. There he had mixed with the able and talented and he was determined not to be seduced into frivolous, idiotic, money-spinning nonsense. He thereby set about expanding the ambitions of Keep Films, the company he shared with Jules Buck and which Spiegel had employed for his services in *Lawrence*. He decided to translate his passion for Samuel Beckett's play *Waiting for Godot* into a film. The first move was to buy the film rights, which still rested with Beckett. O'Toole went to Paris to see him and spent several hours drinking, chatting and, above all, persuading.

'It took me about eight hours and seven bottles to convince him that *Godot* was never meant to be a stage play at all but was really a film all the time. He's a marvellous man, one of the most striking men I have ever met. I can't say we discussed abstract entities or the truth behind the truth. You know, we just blathered. He is about the best blatherer – second to me – that I know. He gave me all the encouragement I needed by saying he wished he had never given me the rights and saying I could never make a film of it.'

O'Toole defied Beckett. He thought he knew better and, although he guessed that there would not be wide commercial distribution for the film, he imagined that there would be enough money in the art cinema circuit to cover the costs. For his own part, he would accept no money for acting. The idea was a two-week shooting schedule on the west coast of Ireland with a budget of £20,000. Some commercial companies had offered money, hoping to sneak a little of the O'Toole action from under the noses of the big producers. But O'Toole had cast the film already. He was to play Vladimir, the part he played at the Bristol Old Vic. Jose Ferrer, the film actor and director who had worked as an actor and director in the American theatre and appeared in *Lawrence*, was to play Pozzo. Kenneth Griffith would play Estragon and Jackie McGowran, Lucky. It was never made.

By this time, Wallis had made up his mind. He wanted O'Toole to play Henry II in a film of Jean Anouilh's play *Becket* – ironically the play over which the Shakespeare Memorial Theatre took Spiegel to court and lost. In fact, O'Toole had been keen to play the part of Henry II as soon as the filming of *Lawrence* ended and he had made persistent approaches to the Stratford company, asking whether he could take up the original option. After all, the company had sued on the assumption that they really wanted O'Toole to play the part. O'Toole badgered away, hoping to return to Stratford or the Aldwych, but he did not understand the long memories of the Stratford Memorial Theatre administrators. Finally, O'Toole met Peter Hall, who tried to duck away from him. O'Toole pinned him against the wall, one arm either side of Hall, gazing down from his lanky height. 'Well P. Hall, can I or can I not return in *Becket*?' he asked. Hall was embarrassed into giving a clear answer: no.

Wallis doubled the irony by having O'Toole play exactly the part in his film that he was to have played for Peter Hall. He knew that O'Toole would accept. O'Toole had genuinely always wanted the part and the clash of loyalties when he won the part of Lawrence was a real one. O'Toole was happy with the part and Wallis thought that there was money in the project. Anouilh's play about the anguished philosophical arguments between Henry the king and Thomas à Becket, the intellectually honest king's servant, could be sauced up a little without straying from Anouilh's intentions, by expanding on the historically accurate passion that the King had for hunting and wenching.

Wallis's wiles, however, were best displayed in the casting of the pious Archbishop. He had tried and failed to woo the ultimate competition, Olivier, to play 'the meddlesome priest' but, finally, against O'Toole was cast another of the most distinguished British film actors of the time, Richard Burton. O'Toole would have to fight for attention against Burton's effortless acting.

But O'Toole still had a bee in his bonnet about going back to the theatre: 'to get back to the stage is the most obvious thing for me to do, because one of the reasons I love the theatre more than anything else is that it imposes on me a discipline I don't normally possess. If I were a sculptor or a musician or whatever, I would never do a stroke. I am bone idle. In fact I cultivate my idleness. For me, idleness – well, fun – is a very important thing.'

A couple of months before, in New York, he had said: 'What I really want to do is establish a repertory theatre with Kermit Bloomgarden, combining British and American actors – people like Anne Bancroft, Zero Mostel, George C. Scott. We'd do a season of comedy classics from Congreve to Coward and work for a common vocal approach.' It was to remain an unfulfilled dream. His only realistic alternative was to return to the London stage. In his conversations with Samuel Beckett about the filming of *Waiting for Godot* he had suggested also a stage version directed by Beckett himself, but it came to nothing.

All the plans to continue his stage career after *Lawrence* was completed had been aborted because the schedule went on so long. 'I expected to finish this picture in a year at the most. When it was over I was going to play in *Becket* at the Aldwych and *Lear* at Stratford, Ontario. And Larry Olivier wanted me to play for him at Chichester. Well, all that had to go by the board as the Lawrence film dragged on.'

He had a pet project in mind, but the first stop, for a quick draught of the adrenalin which he knew could only be obtained by treading the boards, was to be a play-reading. Not only would he be recharged with the excitement of performing before a live audience instead of the blank gaze of Freddie Young's camera, behind which was the icy regard of David Lean, but he would show that he was not such a big star that he was unapproachable. This was an important thing for O'Toole to demonstrate, not least to himself. He enjoyed the money and thrill of success, of being recognised everywhere, of course, but he disliked the thought that his head had been turned by it. He was bigger than the commercial machine that had turned O'Toole the person into O'Toole the phenomenon.

He did not resent it. To be a celebrity was what had driven him onto the amateur stage in Leeds, to bounce his way into RADA, to work round the clock at the Bristol Old Vic, take Stratford by storm and to hurl everything away – even his old, bent, ugly nose – to win the part of Lawrence. Now he wanted to prove to himself that he was still the ordinary actor, the humble player which he romantically wished to remain. A play-reading was just the thing, a little outing, a humble offering to the public, to say that he was first and foremost a stage actor – and that that is what he would always wish to stay.

The event was a typical O'Toole project, an unrehearsed reading of Sean O'Casey's *Pictures in the Hallway* at the Mermaid Theatre, Bernard Miles's personal hall which he had cajoled the City of London's big businesses to provide for those who must live in London's barren financial section. He shared the stage with Maggie Smith, at that time little known outside the British stage and seven years before *The Prime of Miss Jean Brodie* made her an international star. And they were joined by Marie Kean, Jack MacGowran, Donal Donnelly and Godfrey Quigley. It was a one-off, a dramatised reading of the O'Casey play, given on a quiet Sunday in September. It was no more than an amusement, a pleasant stop gap before his real, substantial return.

Even before the opening of *Lawrence*, O'Toole had decided that the way he was going to return to the stage was in Bertolt Brecht's first play *Baal*, the life story of a sleazy womaniser which had never been granted a professional stage anywhere outside Germany. He had first come across the play when acting in *The Long and the Short and the Tall* at the Royal Court. Oscar Lewenstein had shown him a précis of what the play was about and the sordid nature of the principal character greatly attracted O'Toole's sense of the sensational. Without reading a full script, he and William Gaskill became excited and rushed round to see Oscar Lewenstein who was at the opening night of *Happy Days* at the Royal Court.

By the interval, the whole deal had been fixed. The play had not been performed since 1926 in Berlin and would undoubtedly cause a fuss in the London theatre, which in 1962 was still operating under a much derided form of stuffy censorship directed by the Lord Chamberlain's Office. With O'Toole's reputation flying high, the play seemed an ideal vehicle for his purposes: a high profile re-entry to legitimate, high intellectual theatre in a play which would shock the traditional theatre establishment. In 1962, London had only just begun to evolve into Swinging London.

He explained his motives in great detail to Tom Stoppard:

I want to do *Baal* a) because I love the play. I think Brecht never wrote anything like it afterwards. Its range and attitude is extraordinary. It's pre-Marxist Brecht so it has nothing to sell.

And b), it solves in advance the question of what is going to happen after the première of *Lawrence*. I am going to be very busy in rehearsals so my mind will be occupied. If *Lawrence* is a terrible failure I will have something to work on and look forward to. And if it is a success, the usual immediate pressures will not apply because I am in gainful employment.

And c), it is the only way I know to get back in touch with what I know I am about. That is, the theatre. It is the only way I can measure what I have done for the last two years, how I have grown or changed. It gets me back to the freedom I need as an actor.

Also d), it will be a great skylark. With me, fun is a deep philosophical attitude. Brecht's chances in the West End are one thing. *Baal*'s are another. I think we will get arrested. It makes Jimmy Porter [of *Look Back In Anger*] and *The Ginger Man* look like *Mrs Dale's Diary* [a radio soap opera].

The opening was planned for 7 February 1963. William Gaskill was to direct and the cast was to include Harry Andrews, returning to the stage from film acting, Tim Preece and Marie Kean. Mary Miller and Vivian Pickles were to play the two young girls whom Baal persuades to jump into bed with him, having stripped naked in front of the audience – the part of the play which O'Toole was happy to think would cause the most outrage. Rehearsals began, with final rehearsals on the stage of the Phoenix Theatre in Charing Cross Road. Oscar Lewenstein put up the money and the production was designed by Jocelyn Herbert. It was the first time that O'Toole had worked with Gaskill, although they had known each other for a number of years.

'Bill and I were looking for a play to do. I haven't worked with him but I know him and I like his work and he is the kind of person who would not mind having a crack at something like *Baal* – you know, would not be afraid of it – and we had all sorts of things going around. It was going to be Pirandello's *Henry IV*. Anyway, for one reason and another, that fell through, and *Baal* came to the surface. The character is a guitar-playing poet and philanderer. What do I mean, philanderer! He's a lecher. It's the kind of part I'm often asked to play, I suppose because of my publicity – you know, the wild-man bit. I have been asked to play Rimbaud and Dylan, but the trouble is it sounds great and when you come to read the play it becomes just like a footnote. But *Baal* is not.'

O'Toole had said before *Lawrence* what he would do with the money if the film were a success. He answered that all he wanted was to buy a big house in London, a small cottage in Connemara, set up a trust fund for his daughter Kate and buy a new guitar. He had done the first and the last and irritated Sian a great deal by strumming away idly in his den. At last, as Baal, the guitar-playing would come in handy. 'Actually, the really true reason I'm doing *Baal* is that at least I can get to play a guitar without someone throwing boots at me and saying I'll wake the baby,' he jokingly explained.

O'Toole grew a beard and dyed his hair auburn for the part of Baal. He was very happy. 'It's so relaxed, it's wonderful,' he said in the week of the opening. 'None of that penny-pinching that you get in films, because the people who are in the theatre are in it for love.' The script came back from the Lord Chamberlain and, to everyone's surprise and amusement, the sexual scenes were left intact – even the notorious young girls scene – while all the blasphemy was taken out. 7 February 1963 was opening night.

The production of *Baal*, which in other circumstances and with another lead actor might have been greeted as a fringe production, dominated the theatre reviews in that week. *The Times* theatre critic the next morning gave a rave notice: 'Indifferently performed, Baal's part would be both ludicrous and boring. But in this production, Peter O'Toole stamps it with heroic authority: Baal's actions may appear senseless, but one never questions them. Mr O'Toole delivers the lines with a harsh measured dignity that can make bombast sound like a passage from the Old Testament; and he plays with a fiery depravity that raises the character to Dostoïevskian grandeur.'

And Harold Hobson, the unrivalled principal drama critic of Fleet Street, testified that: 'The famous verses in which Brecht acridly compares life with a privy do really in this version, and as Peter O'Toole sings them, sound like poetry. As again does the tender and terrible song, a prelude to murder and homosexual frenzy, which Mr O'Toole strums in the last act.'

But, for Hobson as for the audience, the production was not the scandalous event which O'Toole had hoped. In 1926 at the original, amateur production in Berlin, during the naked girls scene, according to Martin Esslin, 'people whistled, shrieked, booed, applauded.' Nothing of the like happened at the Phoenix. Hobson reports: 'As the two tiny tots took off their clothes and climbed into bed, one on each side of the drunken but enterprising poet Baal, not a single crack on the jaw could be heard in the entire theatre. Instead, the thousand and ten faces round, behind and in front of me were wreathed in happy smiles.' Hobson reports a damp squib. 'This unforeseen reaction was not criticism of the performance of Mr O'Toole and his juvenile friends: it is not even a criticism of Brecht. The roaring young lion of the Twenties inevitably becomes the indulged pet of the Sixties.'

Two weeks into the run, O'Toole was shaken by news from America. In Los Angeles, he had been nominated for the Academy Award for the best actor. *Lawrence* had picked up no less than ten nominations. To begin work on *Becket*, O'Toole would have to withdraw from *Baal* some time during April. By that time, the Oscars would be announced and he might well begin his second major film as an Oscar-winner.

On 8 April the American Academy Awards gave seven Oscars to *Lawrence*, including one to O'Toole for best actor. This was followed by the British Academy Awards, which also gave O'Toole the best actor prize. It was a great boost to the prospects of *Becket*. The press release announcing the details read: 'Straight from the award winning *Lawrence of Arabia* for which he personally also won the British Academy Award for the Best Actor of the Year, O'Toole goes into a role which gives him a complete switch from his introspective playing as Lawrence. King Henry is a lusty, outgoing monarch – a great lover, soldier and huntsman. That O'Toole is able to play two such totally dissimilar characters in succession confirms the opinion of those who believe that he has the potential to become a legend while still in his thirties.'

This was all getting too much for O'Toole. He needed some time to think, some peace and quiet before beginning the three months shooting schedule at Shepperton Studios for *Becket*. As so often before and since, he took refuge in a life-restoring trip to Ireland for reflection and stock-taking. There was also a practical reason. Sian was pregnant for the second time and O'Toole was determined that, whatever happened, his second child would be born in Ireland, not England. The birth was due seven weeks away – five weeks into the shooting of *Becket* – and he was going to make the hospital arrangements for Sian to have it in Dublin.

It is to the great credit of O'Toole that, years before it was fashionable to do so, he took a keen concern in the circumstances of his wife giving birth. He came from a family and from a neighbourhood where childbirth was considered firmly a woman's business, but that is not the way O'Toole saw it. Some of his interest came from his Irish nationalism – he was determined that his second child should be Irish first and British second – but a great deal came from a respect for Sian. He explained: 'Sian, you know, is Welsh and my first daughter was born in Stratford-on-Avon, poor child, and the second was born in Dublin. There was Sian, who is really Mother Wales – she is the Welsh national heroine, dripping with every honour and degree the Welsh can afford. She had to learn to speak English. But there she was in Ireland.

'They don't have any of this highly sterilised, pampered systems of birth for the mother. None of your painless childbirth. They're not put in glass tanks while some great, moustached lady bullies them into having no pain. There are things like contractions and they say "pain". There's no brute leering at you, telling you to relax. Some old yokel from Connemara stands with the sweaty mother's head in her arms, holding her and wiping off the sweat and saying: "Come on, girl, I know it hurts. I know what it's about. Come on, girl." And when that little thing sticks its head out, they slap a whole bunch of cotton wool soaked with chloroform all over the mother's physogue and out she goes and somebody yanks the damn' baby out.

'Well, Sian was going under the chloroform and the doctor, who had once played rugby for Ireland, was pulling the baby out and Sian suddenly started singing the unofficial Welsh anthem as she was going under. The poor doctor – having played against Wales, where this thing is sung all the time at every game – felt as though he was in a rugby match, pulling a ball out of the scrum. He nearly passed my second one out to the matron. But wasn't this a marvellous unconscious protest against being in Ireland?'

It was a good trip. He had time to unwind, drink a lot of Guinness with old friends, go to the races at Punchestown and have a walk in the countryside. He arrived a celebrity and was welcomed down the aircraft steps by reporters and photographers. He was dressed all in green for the occasion: the triumphant return to his emerald home – green corduroy jacket, green bow tie and, of course, his mandatory green socks. The beard for Baal he was allowing to thicken out for Henry II's beard in *Becket*.

He enjoyed being an Irish hero, answered all the questions politely, had a drink – not forgetting to buy all the press one as he went – then took a limousine into the centre of Dublin. At his hotel he had a few drinks at the bar, explaining about the pessimism of the Irish to anyone who would listen. Then he went to the hospital to make the maternity arrangements, back to the bar for a drink with Siobhan McKenna, Kevin McClory, the theatrical producer, and a bunch of friends from the Abbey Theatre. They drank and bemoaned the English and held each new glass of Guinness or whiskey up in the air and toasted the Republic. At eleven at night they adjourned for dinner, then on to an after-hours drinking club, slipping it down until five in the morning. He was up bright and early the next morning – two Guinnesses and a whiskey for breakfast – before off to the races at Punchestown, an old stomping ground of his father.

It was a regular session for O'Toole, who could always find a friend or five to demolish a few bottles. It is true that O'Toole used to drink a lot. It is one of the best known things about him beyond his films. His public may know nothing of his wife and children, even nothing of his stage work, but they all know of his drinking. O'Toole used to consume a lot of Guinness and a lot of Scotch whisky if he could not get the Irish sort.

Harry Andrews worked many times with O'Toole and came immediately to like him. He, too, could attack the bottle hard if he wanted to, but he was surprised how O'Toole punished himself. But it was not always with quantity, according to Andrews. O'Toole could appear drunk when only a small amount of drink had passed his lips. It was as if the climate of drink, not necessarily drink itself, caused him to become inebriated. There was also a need to drink, to master himself more completely. Even when more drink than was wise had been poured noisily down O'Toole's throat, he was capable of cool conversation and work of a very high standard. Drink was not a prop in the traditional sense for O'Toole. He was not an inadequate who needed a couple to bolster his confidence. The truth was quite the opposite. O'Toole appeared to need drink to slow his brain down, to make his imagination and fevered conversation more ordinary, less outrageous to those about him. He liked drink and he liked those who drank. Given a spare moment, he would sidle off and find a bar and be into his second before he was found again.

He likes the company of those who are happy to let themselves go and float free. Sobriety is uncomfortable for O'Toole. He sees life very clearly without the hindrance of alcohol and it gives him little pleasure. He prefers his own company only when he is not sober. His drinking sessions in Dublin during that visit are typical of O'Toole's off-duty life. He likes a blether and a few yarns and the friendship of those he has known a long time – or those who he has just met at a bar.

There is little doubt that his peculiar digestion system was both particularly prone to alcohol and was soothed by alcohol. That frail stomach and intestines actually prevented him from overindulgence in drink, because it made him vomit profusely and often. His capacity might have appeared larger than it was for this reason. So, although he was consuming a great deal of alcohol, very often only a small amount was being ingested. O'Toole was often in pain from his insides, although he never liked to investigate too closely. He was scared of what he was likely to find out. His insides were to play him up for years and the drink both aggravated and alleviated his condition. There was to come a time, however, when doctors would prevent him from drinking by telling him the truth: that persistent drinking would undoubtedly kill him, although he would not die of drink.

When it came to hard drinking, O'Toole rarely met his match. But he did during the filming of *Becket*. In Richard Burton, O'Toole found an instant soul-mate, someone who would share his mischievous love of booze. At the same time, O'Toole was terrified of Burton simply because they both liked to play the same game. For once O'Toole had someone to measure himself against. They both liked to drink and both thought that drink improved their performances. But which was the best at it? They entered into a friendly rivalry from the very first day, starting with a peculiar truce. They agreed that both should go 'on the wagon' until they had mastered their acting personalities. Once O'Toole had established the character of Henry in his mind and Burton had found how he wanted to play Becket, there were no rules. It proved a heavy-drinking five months – from May to September – for both of them and, for them at least, a gloriously enjoyable romp.

The director who had to cope with two drunks who were playing a perilous game of chicken in front of the rolling cameras was Peter Glenville, the stage director who had directed Laurence Olivier in *Becket* on Broadway in 1961, the version which O'Toole had visited at the expense of the Stratford Memorial Theatre. This was the second time that Glenville had worked with Burton. The first time, Glenville had sacked him from a prominent part in *Adventure Story*, Terence Rattigan's play about Alexander the Great, after three rehearsals. Glenville claimed that Burton looked too young for the part, but others say it was because Burton was upstaging the principal actor, Paul Scofield. Either way, Glenville had done Burton a favour, for he picked up a part in Christopher Fry's *The Lady's not for Burning* in a cast which included John Gielgud.

Gielgud was also in the cast of *Becket*, by chance, taken as a fortuitous stand-in when the unit moved to Newcastle and the actor playing the King of France dropped out. And that, in turn, led both Burton and O'Toole to play Hamlet. The way Burton tells it, he and Elizabeth Taylor went to see Gielgud in the play *The Ides of March* which had brought Gielgud to Newcastle. After a performance, in the bar of the Station Hotel, Gielgud asked what Burton was doing for Shakespeare's quartercentenary the following year. Burton said someone has asked him to play Hamlet in New York, but that he would only play it if Gielgud would direct him. Gielgud, flattered, agreed, hardly believing that the suggestion was serious. It was and the production was a great success.

One way that O'Toole tells it is more colourful. Burton and he were having a Guinness lunch when the news came through that they were not needed for three days. They promptly switched to champagne and they started dreaming up wild schemes for each other to work in. The both decided to return to the theatre after *Becket*. Both agreed to retain the healthy competition which they had been enjoying so much on the set of *Becket* by accepting the same role in the same play for which they would invent separate productions. *Hamlet* was the chosen play and Hamlet, of course, the chosen role. They settled the directors and location by tossing coins. As to directors, Burton won the toss and demanded Gielgud; O'Toole lost and made do with Olivier. And then, as O'Toole explains it: 'I said, "But we can't both do Hamlet on the same side of the Atlantic." We flipped the coin again. I got London, a fact that we duly celebrated. Then Richard had to do his Hamlet in New York, and we toasted that.' And that, according to O'Toole was that: Gielgud and Olivier were delighted.

Their rivalry, however, had serious overtones. O'Toole was very impressed with Burton who was at the height of his notoriety. He had just returned from filming *Cleopatra*, the film in which he had stolen Elizabeth Taylor away from her husband, Eddie Fisher. Half-way through the filming of *Becket*, Burton and Taylor decided to marry – for the first time – and O'Toole realised that, as famous and lauded as he was, there was no comparison between the level of stardom that he had achieved through one major film and that level of showbusiness publicity which surrounded stars like Burton and Taylor. He was, of course, happy to share the limelight and grateful that his sequel to *Lawrence* should have so much publicity going for it. But, at the same time, the pressure of standing up to Burton, with all his Welsh acting guile, his ability to demand attention when remaining absolutely still and his most considerable asset, his voice, was enormous. Even O'Toole, the master of upstaging, was expecting a tough match.

O'Toole and Burton lived very close to each other for three months. Elizabeth Taylor remained for the most part in the Dorchester Hotel in Park Lane while the two of them slugged it out on and off the set of Stage H at Shepperton Studios outside London. They used to drink at the King's Head, one of four pubs on Shepperton village square, where the landlord, Archie, had greeted them with their lunch on their first day: 'Now is the winter of our discontent made glorious summer by this leg of pork.' It became a regular haunt and both soon started calling the landlord's wife 'Mummy'. Elizabeth Taylor sometimes joined them.

Also among the cast – which included Donald Wolfit, before whom O'Toole had once auditioned, Martita Hunt, Pamela Brown and Margaret Furse – was another wife, Sian Phillips, who, after working closely with Burton and Taylor, declared that she had no intention of running a cosy Burton-Taylor acting partnership with *her* husband. 'We loathe working with each other. It's a quick way to the divorce courts. I'm always afraid he's going to dry and he's always waiting for me to do something wrong. We're both so nervy for each other we can't possibly act. The few times we have worked opposite each other have always been due to force of circumstances or it's been an accident. In the film *Becket*, for instance, where I played Pete's wife, they only picked me because they needed someone who could read music, sing Welsh and dredge up a few medieval Welsh words.'

Burton had a lot of respect for O'Toole. He had been working on a gramophone record of *Henry V* with Kenneth Griffith and had first sent, through Griffith, his best wishes and compliments. He might have made fun of his lanky figure, but he had already been beaten by O'Toole for a part he wanted: that of Lawrence. When Burton was considering *Becket*, he at first had wanted to play the King, a wenching, rollicking, hard-drinking rogue, but Elizabeth Taylor persuaded him out of it. 'She said the King was the kind of part I was always playing, and she was right.'

Burton had demanded of Wallis that he would agree to play in this Anouilh play, barely an obvious commercial property, only if he was surrounded by first-class supporting actors – and he was delighted when O'Toole was cast opposite him. Burton remembered how he had first noticed O'Toole: 'I had first seen O'Toole some years ago playing Edmund in *Lear* at the Bristol Old Vic. I had not heard of him before – I went to Bristol to see another actor – and found myself intrigued with O'Toole. He looked like a beautiful, emaciated secretary bird. He was extremely young and his acting was unformed and half-derivative, but his voice had a crack like a whip. And, most important of all, you couldn't take your eyes off him.' Burton was conscious then, and had his judgment confirmed during the filming of *Becket*, that O'Toole's was a special acting talent.

On the set, in front of the plaster replica of the front of Canterbury Cathedral and inside its nave, O'Toole and Burton proved a difficult test for Glenville. After the first ten days without drink, they agreed to start boozing in earnest and were not unnerved by the prospect of wandering on to the set drunk. When Paramount executives came to watch the filming, they were horrified that both of their principal actors appeared to be high. But when the director called for order before a take, both recovered instantly and managed the repetitive acting which makes up film work. Even the scene where the King has to clip a ring on Becket's finger – in which Burton described O'Toole's performance as 'like a man threading a needle wearing boxing gloves' – was perfect despite a surfeit of drink.

When the shooting was over, Burton paid O'Toole this tribute in a piece which he wrote for *Life* magazine: 'Acting is universally regarded as a craft, and I claim it to be nothing more except in the hands of the odd few men and women who, once or twice in a lifetime, elevate it into something odd and mystical and deeply disturbing. I believe Peter O'Toole to have this strange quality.'

O'Toole saw it differently. '*Becket* was a draw between me an' Richie – and I had all the twiddly bits at that.' And O'Toole described the friendship between Burton and himself, which was to bring them together in two further films: 'It simply is a relationship on two levels, professional and personal, which happened to gel. We complete each other in a way, off-scene, too. We get on famously. We had an enormous time doing *Becket*. It was initially written for Gérard Philipe and Daniel Invernel. They had a very similar thing to what Richard and I have.' The gossip writers, who preferred not to report all sweetness and light on the set, liked to picture them as at each other's throats. O'Toole and Burton staged a fight for their benefit before the end of shooting.

O'Toole has described the filming of *Becket* as 'the happiest professional experience I've ever had.' It had been a relief to him to find out that all first-class film work was not as gruelling as *Lawrence*, nor all directors as brutally demanding as Lean. 'We worked like dogs, all of us,' remembered O'Toole, 'Richard, Peter, Gielgud, myself – we laboured like lunatics. I never laughed so much in my life, nor cried so much. I never worked so hard nor enjoyed myself so much. We did it in thirteen weeks, you know. We shot it off the cuff – and it was really something to put me in amongst those pros. We shot the play, really, we didn't change it at all. Anouilh should have got an Academy Award.'

And Burton remembered it this way: 'I think it is essential in any performance (though this is by no means the general opinion among actors) that rapport between players should be absolute. I find it impossible to give my best if I am forced to act with someone I cannot admire and respect. Therefore, and more so than usual because of the nature of this work, it was essential that the man playing Becket and the man playing King Henry should at least get on well. I give you my word, they got on very well. They may have failed but they got on very well.'

And he remembered the drinking truce: 'Initially, Peter and I were apprehensive about that spark that was so needed between us if our roles as Becket and the King were to come off properly. For that reason, we both decided to drink absolutely nothing for the first few days of the production. We had the reputation – ill-deserved, I must say – for terrible wildness. So our colleagues were quite surprised to see us holding nothing but tea-cups for ten days. When it became clear that the two of us did have on-camera rapport, I put on my best Irish accent and said: "Peter, me boy. I think we deserve a little snifter." Then we drank for two nights and one day.'

The critics were kind to them both, although the film's direction was thought generally to be rather flat. Dilys Powell, the *grande dame* of British film criticism, wrote: 'Coming out of the cinema, a friend gave all his praise to the Henry of Peter O'Toole, none to Burton's Becket: and since I don't like arguing until I have cleared my mind – and since I find it doesn't clear until I come to write – I was noncommittal. In fact the two players seem to me excellently matched – O'Toole with his rage and bravado broken down to wild pleading when he realises that the Becket whom he loved is now his implacable opponent; Burton as the servant turned master, his calculating habit transformed by the sense of purpose to calm resolve.'

The Americans were less reserved and went overboard about it, for it not only coupled the two most talked-about actors of the time, but Burton had just married Elizabeth Taylor and, even if it was slow, the photography in *Becket* of an idyllic England was staggeringly beautiful. O'Toole couldn't believe his luck. 'You'd be surprised at the people who told me I should never have done *Becket* after *Lawrence*. A costume drama would be death, they said. They wanted me to get into a teeshirt, stubbing out cigarettes on a woman's thigh.' And with Olivier's *Hamlet* to look forward to, everything looked rosy and his reputation seemed more secure than ever.

# 6   Opening the National

THERE WAS a lot riding on Sir Laurence Olivier's production of *Hamlet*. O'Toole adulated Olivier and welcomed the chance to work for him. More than that, he was very relieved that it was proving so easy to alternate between top-flight films in which he was allowed to act properly, without compromises, and first-class theatre. Olivier was the master of being able to mix cinema and theatre successfully and O'Toole hoped to achieve a similar position. But more than that, this production of *Hamlet* was laden with expectations. It was the first play to be produced by Olivier's newly formed National Theatre Company, which had recently been set up by Act of Parliament to establish a company of fine British actors working as a single unit, performing plays of English and distinguished foreign literature permanently. Until a new theatre complex was built to accommodate the company, it would work out of the historic Old Vic Theatre in Waterloo Road and the National Theatre administration would operate from four rows of prefabricated huts on a bomb site nearby.

There had been no contest as to who should run the company. Of all the beknighted actors, Laurence Olivier took precedence over Sir Ralph Richardson and Sir John Gielgud as the actor/director most likely to make a success of the venture and bring to the company an immediate distinction and international reputation. However, Olivier was quickly criticised for the direction he was taking. He ignored the traditional acting homes of Shakespeare – at Stratford and the Aldwych – and the more established actors in favour of young and more progressive elements of the London stage.

'I am not interested in using the National to institutionalise the comfortable but often money-losing ways of the past in this country,' he explained. 'If this is going to work, we will need new ideas, blood, new approaches. We will do our share of classics, but the National is for everyone in England. It is especially for new writers as well as old, for new actors as well as old, for new directors as well as old.'

This radical philosophy opened the way for O'Toole, who was given the awkward and heavily loaded task of opening the new company's line-up with *Hamlet* and proving that Olivier's guiding principles made sense. He was chosen to represent the new generation of actors and to show that Olivier's National Theatre would work.

Kenneth Tynan asked O'Toole whether there was any jealousy that Olivier displayed toward O'Toole, for Olivier, after all, was used to the attention falling on him. O'Toole thought not. 'If he was sending out waves like that, I wasn't aware of them, and in any case, it wouldn't have affected me; after all, he asked me to play the bloody thing. He came to the house and asked me a lot of oblique questions about the part, and finally I said to him: 'Look, it doesn't matter what theories I've got about *Hamlet*. All that matters is what comes through in the performance.'

This is not the way Olivier remembered it. For a start, it was O'Toole who asked him whether he could play Hamlet and not *vice versa*. 'Early that autumn [1961], I was sitting in my London office in Hamilton Place,' Olivier wrote in his autobiography, 'when I was brought word that Peter O'Toole wanted to see me. In came Peter at the appointed hour and brought his agent in with him. He told me that he wished very much to play Hamlet for a short season in the West End, some time in the following year, and would I direct him in it? I said no, I wasn't available for the West End just then, but if he would like his Hamlet to be the opening number for the National Theatre in October I could fix that; so we shook hands on it.'

And Olivier remembers that, far from being delighted at the deal, the two young directors Olivier had chosen to help him in shaping the National, William Gaskill, who had directed O'Toole in *Baal*, and John Dexter, were very disappointed. It is clear that O'Toole barely understood how important he was to be to Olivier's plan and reputation. On this opening would hang the rest of Olivier's ability to mould the National Theatre as he wanted it and to cast O'Toole, particularly considering his reputation for drinking and bad behaviour, was a large gamble for Olivier to take.

Like all other actors, O'Toole had a deep respect for Olivier's work and had watched his career closely. He claims to have seen Olivier on the stage at least three times by the time he came to act Hamlet under his direction: the 1944 Old Vic Company production of *Richard III* at the New Theatre, London – 'The relish of it – that was what impressed me, although I was only a child – the way he seemed to savour everything Richard said, with a nagging, almost pedantic delight'; the 1955 Shakespeare Memorial Theatre, Stratford, production of *Titus Andronicus*, with Vivien Leigh; and the 1959 Stratford production of *Coriolanus* – 'where he came on like a boy, with that wonky, juvenile gait'. And he had seen the 1948 J. Arthur Rank film of *Hamlet,* produced, directed and starring Olivier. But most of all,

O'Toole was haunted by the memory of Olivier's 1937 Old Vic production of *Hamlet* which made history and brought an avalanche of praise upon him. It was a myth of the theatre, this production which O'Toole had not seen and which gained stature as memories of it faded. And O'Toole was to tread out on the same boards and match Olivier – that was what Olivier was defying him to do.

O'Toole recognised this personal challenge, even if the wider dimension of National Theatre politics was lost upon him, and Olivier would not let him forget it. Olivier's style of direction was similar to that of David Lean: one of pouring disdain upon the struggling actor who will strain and stretch through the normal barriers of competence in order to evoke a favourable response from the greatest living actor. It was the act of a bully, but it produced extraordinary results. And the key to his method was his victims' eagerness to please. O'Toole was no exception.

'I've worshipped at Larry's shrine for years,' he confessed. 'Nothing has ever been done, or ever will be done, like his Richard III at the Old Vic in 1944. I'm hooked on Larry Olivier. I mean, he's done it; he's sat on the top of Everest and waved down at the Sherpas. He speaks from Olympian authority, and I think he bridles that authority admirably. I know lesser farts in bigger organisations who brandish their puny accomplishments like a club.'

Like all the others, O'Toole fell happily under Olivier's spell, although he often claimed that he was untouched by the thin layer of charm spread over a silent intimidating directing style. Olivier was asking a lot. First, he was demanding that the full version of *Hamlet* be played, not the cut down version which he had played in 1937 and which O'Toole had used at the Bristol Old Vic. And he was demanding a punishing schedule which ran *Hamlet* non-stop, every night except Sundays, with two afternoons of matinées. O'Toole would need to remember all the tricks about conserving stamina that he learnt in the desert.

The rehearsals were very hard work, encounter sessions across the proscenium arch, with Olivier being very sparing of praise. It was not going as well as it ought. Olivier had demanded so much that he would get an interesting production, but one which could easily stumble at any stage. It was very ambitious – as the opening of the first British National Theatre ought to be – but it was turning out to be so ambitious as to be impossible for those who were meant to realise Olivier's intention. And at the centre of that deficiency was O'Toole, falling short of what Olivier was expecting, what he was hoping for.

While a new generation of theatre directors in Britain – among them Peter Brook, Peter Hall and John Barton – had established a successful and critically favoured trend of reinterpreting Shakespeare, thereby introducing fresh assessments of his lesser known plays – or revealing assaults on the standard works – Olivier had hoped in O'Toole's *Hamlet* to set a permanent trend at the new National which would prove just as revealing to the audience. He wished to refreshen well-worn Shakespeare plays by the sheer power of acting, by the energy and excitement which could be generated on stage, just as he himself had done so often on the stage and on the screen by his own powerful acting presence.

His choice of O'Toole to lead the assault on convention – both of traditional theatre and the new convention of reinterpretation – was inspired, but either O'Toole could not be stretched as far as Olivier wanted him to be stretched, or Olivier was asking too much of him. Either way, O'Toole did not break through and fulfil Olivier's expectations. 'I'd learned nothing from the first time and had forgotten everything. I have said goodbye to it now, you bet. I said goodbye to it on the first night. I asked myself: "What the hell are you doing?" '

The rapport between Olivier and O'Toole was never established, partly because O'Toole was so capable of remaining cool and arrogantly unaffected by the power of others. O'Toole remembers: 'I found him perhaps the least terrifying man I've ever met in the theatre – because at first glance I could see through him and he could see through me, and he knew that I knew that he knew. Look, love, I've been bullied all my life by bigger experts than Larry Olivier, I can assure you, and he's just got to get in line. He turned me to stone a couple of times with that grey-eyed, myopic gaze of his, but a couple of times he made me very happy. After one rehearsal he said to the company: "Ladies and gentlemen, for the first time in living memory we have seen the real Hamlet." When the greatest actor on two stalks says a thing like that, what can you do? Of course, I felt I was being watched every minute.'

At the same time he fell under Olivier's spell. 'Have you ever tried to argue with Olivier? He's the most charming, persuasive bastard ever to draw breath. I said "No", but then I said "Yes". Then I said I wanted to play it in a cut version – "I'll only do two and a half hours," I told Larry. A week later I was doing the uncut version which takes five hours. Then I wanted to play it with a beard because I said why should I be the only man in Elsinore with a razor blade. Three weeks later I'm standing on stage clean-shaven in a Peter Pan suit with my hair dyed white. Such is the power of Olivier.'

The opening night of the National Theatre, with O'Toole as Hamlet, was an important milestone in the history of British theatre, but it was hardly a glittering occasion. No royalty attended. The most dazzling figure in the audience was the Chancellor of the Exchequer, Selwyn Lloyd – an ironic chance, in the light of theatre's subsequent financial troubles so often blamed upon the meanness of the Treasury. Evening dress was not required. Because the full-length *Hamlet* was being staged, the audience had to arrive for curtain-up at 6.30 p.m. – in full daylight.

O'Toole had been very relaxed in rehearsals, keen to play practical jokes. Max Adrian remembered him putting ice in the shower of the star dressing-room, which Olivier had lent him, and that he had tried to ply Adrian with 'green whiskey' to make the performance pass more quickly. O'Toole was alone in his ability to control his nerves. 'The star dressing-room became a sort of oasis of relaxation while he was there,' remembered Adrian. But by the afternoon of the first night, even O'Toole was feeling nervous. He stomped around backstage, dressed in a red dressing-gown, shadow fencing around Sean Kenny's set. There were last minute panics, such as the trap-door which provided the grave which stuck closed. But, by 6.30, everything was sorted out and the performance went through without incident.

Soon into the run, the strain on O'Toole of repeated long performances began to show. One night, at the end of the evening performance which followed a matinée, O'Toole had been on the stage for nearly nine hours with only a short break between the end of one and the beginning of the next performance. At the final words 'The rest is silence', he gave a hysterical laugh. The exhaustion finally broke through and he saw the irony of the line. The audience thought it was O'Toole misbehaving.

The strain upset his sleep pattern. Never one to spend long in bed, he found that, for almost the first time in his life, he was physically exhausted. Yet still he persisted in staying up late and drinking. One time this nearly led to disaster – and did lead to an unnerving experience with drugs. 'I had spent a night talking, as I often do, and I had to play the Moody One next day – Hamlet, his melancholy nibs. I felt a bit dreary, so a lady in the company gave me a little green pill out of a silver Victorian pillbox. I was on the ceiling for forty-eight hours. I was cuckooing and crowing from chimneys, hurtling about and gamboling and skipping – and I never stopped talking. I wept at weather forecasts.'

The critical verdict was that the production was misconceived and that O'Toole was overstretched, a lightweight given a heavyweight job to do, although some, among them Harold Hobson, the *Sunday Times* drama critic, whose opinion was the most valued and respected by the acting profession, was reservedly enthusiastic: 'When the curtain rose on the National Theatre's *Hamlet* and I saw the mounting curves of Sean Kenny's dangerous rocks and the poised figures of the sentinels against the sky, I had a great and delicious emotion of peril, as of one venturing into realms of threatening ambush: that on looking at Desmond Heeley's rich gold brocades and jewels I felt that I had my hand upon the royalty of an age of high romance, and that when in his very first speech Peter O'Toole's grieved Hamlet spoke of "customary suits of solemn black" I felt in my throat that catch, down my spine that shiver which Housman says is the reward and the aim of the highest poetry.' And he singled O'Toole out for the highest praise: 'Especially the manly, richly spoken Hamlet of Mr O'Toole matches Sir Laurence's conception. It is a joy to hear the words of Shakespeare so universally given their just weight and colour and measure.'

The review in *The Times* was worse, pointing out what everyone in the theatre world was thinking: 'It bears the stamp of having been put on as a means of exhibiting a number of big names in the most famous and popular work in the classical repertory. And even with the cuts restored, is a tried and routine performance.' And O'Toole's Hamlet was considered ordinary, 'his features twisted . . . into an introspective melancholy.' O'Toole and Olivier were relieved that the notices had not been worse. There had been an unspoken agreement among the critics not to be too tough on the National – at least on its birthday.

The common wisdom among theatre people was more harsh. Olivier had blown the launch of the National Theatre and, by casting a highly idiosyncratic film star instead of a solid, reliable stage actor, a great chance was missed. Stories came out of the Old Vic of O'Toole's antics back-stage. During one matinée, having mugged up his lines between scenes, he re-emerged onto the stage with his glasses on, causing a snigger throughout the audience. O'Toole was a crowd-grabber, at least, and the production played to packed houses. But the decision was made early on to end the run after only twenty-seven performances.

As the run wore on, only the portrayal of Claudius as a villain by Sir Michael Redgrave brought consistent kind words. It was a bad opening for such a significant and important event in the British theatre and Olivier would pay highly for such a poor start. The sniping at *Hamlet* began a persistent assault upon Olivier's capacity to act, direct and administer simultaneously. The commonly held point of view was the one expressed by O'Toole himself: 'I'm not sure he ought to be running the National Theatre. Larry's business is acting; he belongs in the stable, as head stallion. I don't think he's got a great deal to contribute as a director. In *Hamlet* I wandered amazed among scenic flyovers and trumpets; I didn't know where I was. I only did it because I was flattered out of my trousers to be invited.'

O'Toole puts the blame for the mediocre performance he gave on Olivier and his impossible demands, particularly the decision to attempt the full version of the play. 'You have to cut *Hamlet* to suit your performance,' said O'Toole. 'I'd done it three years before, very successfully, using the cut version John Barrymore used, and that Larry had used in his film.'

At the same time, he admits falling under Olivier's spell and bending his preferred acting techniques to please his most demanding director. 'I was the loudest Hamlet of the century. Disaster. Too influenced by Larry Olivier. Far too influenced. I mean, really in-awe department. He's been something I've admired all my life and still do. When he said he wanted to direct me in Hamlet – National Theatre opening and all that – I conned myself. I thought we could really pull something special out of the old hat. But Larry beguiled me into every bloody trick: blond wigs, short skirts and the uncut version. Five and three-quarter hours on stage! Of course, I think it is the worst play ever written. Every actor does it out of vanity.'

O'Toole saw his Hamlet as a defeat – and it had been a long time since he had so publicly failed. Since his season at Stratford as the youngest leading man ever, he had become used to praise. He resented the fact that Olivier's ambitions had embroiled him in a humiliation. This *Hamlet* acted as a spur to future actions. He was determined to prove that he *was* a major actor, capable of performing the principal roles of Shakespeare – the great roles of Hamlet, Lear and Macbeth – and he vowed that he would return to the Old Vic and make up for the mess of Olivier's *Hamlet*. The next time he appeared on the Old Vic stage was to be as Macbeth in 1980.

O'Toole, who had been given an easy ride by the press so far, found with *Hamlet* that there was nothing they liked so much as a successful person on the run from harsh criticism. He had been warned. 'Before I did Hamlet in 1963 Larry said: "Are you ready?" "For what?" I said. "For them," he said. "They're out there with their machine-guns. It's your turn, son." ' Olivier was right. From *Hamlet* on, O'Toole would no longer enjoy the generous coverage, sympathetic interviews and warm critical notices which he had become used to. The press, which like to indulge newcomers and shower upon them publicity – the only gift of patronage that they have – had finally turned on O'Toole. Now that he was well-known and an international star, the stories were better if he was in trouble, caught brawling, fighting in the Rome streets, embarrassing his wife. Hamlet was the turning point and the next target for their scavenging attentions was O'Toole's next project – Richard Brooks's film of Joseph Conrad's *Lord Jim*.

Conrad's book had been filmed before, in 1927, a silent American film starring Percy Marmont. Richard Brooks was eager to remake the film as lavishly as he thought the story deserved, and once again O'Toole would be photographed by Freddie Young, the cinematographer on *Lawrence*. A writer himself, Brooks admired Conrad's style and thought he would be able to translate the spirit of the prose. Even for a writer-director like Brooks, who had begun Hollywood work as a screenwriter, then begun writing and directing [such] films [as *The Brothers Karamazov* and *Cat on a Hot Tin Roof*] the prospect was a difficult one.

O'Toole was tempted by the prospect of Conrad's hero. The role satisfied the two demands which he now made of a part: that it should be an intellectually worthwhile project with a literate script; and that it should offer him the chance to expand his range as an actor. If he had thought more carefully he might have anticipated the disappointing outcome – that the character of Lord Jim was one of an introverted, almost silent hero, stranded in an alien world but living in the only terrain in which he could be happy, and that it was a character too similar to that of T. E. Lawrence and would inevitably attract comparisons and criticisms for repeating a familiar type.

Did he not see the pitfall? Was he not conscious that he was allowing himself to be typecast? He had even given interviews saying he was getting tired of playing martyred types in the desert. How did he see it? 'Let's go through the list. Lawrence of Arabia? Yes, I suppose he was a martyr of sorts. Henry II in Becket? Well, he ended up being whipped for his sins, but he didn't enjoy it. He accepted it because it was politically expedient, and he loathed every second of it. As for Lord Jim, he certainly chose to die, but I played him not for that reason but because it was the only chance I'd ever had of doing a Western – or an Eastern, if you like. He was a simple, silent, guilt-ridden fellow who rides into town like Shane; I just fancied the idea.'

O'Toole thought the part would be noticeably different. He trusted the judgment and skill of Richard Brooks, who had an enviable record of success behind him. Brooks had begun work as a radio-writer; had progressed to film screenwriting, including the script of *Key Largo* for John Huston; then writing and directing films such as *Elmer Gantry*, for which he had won an Oscar, which had given Burt Lancaster such an extraordinary acting opportunity as the evangelical preacher; and he had made a film of Tennessee Williams's play *Cat on a Hot Tin Roof*, with Elizabeth Taylor and Paul Newman. He had just finished shooting another Tennessee Williams play, *Sweet Bird of Youth* with Newman, Geraldine Page and an Oscar-winning performance from Ed Begley. O'Toole was impressed with Brooks's credentials and was happy to entrust the next section of his career to him.

He was encouraged by the ambitious nature of the project. Brooks was producing the film of *Lord Jim* himself and he was planning an epic blockbuster which would last three hours. The rest of the cast was also encouraging. It included James Mason and Curt Jurgens and Sian had been offered a part. And there would be extensive location shooting in Cambodia, Hongkong and Singapore before studio work in London. After *Becket*, which was mostly shot in the studio and did not stray outside Britain, O'Toole welcomed the prospect of a long, serious project which would take him to exotic locations. Not because he particularly wanted to travel. He hoped that he might, through hard location work, recover some of the magic that he felt during the shooting of *Lawrence*.

The shooting turned out to be far more gruelling even than that for *Lawrence*. After a session at Shepperton, they worked in tropical jungle, surrounded by insects. It was not a happy set. O'Toole quickly became irritable and impatient with the local people. A great amount of the filming was dangerous, floating on barges and manoeuvring boats. After shooting afloat in Hongkong, in Kowloon and Aberdeen harbours, a team of one hundred actors and technicians set off for Angkor Wat, near Siemreap in Cambodia, where a whole set was built. Schoolhouses, shops, a hall, a stockade, a tribal palace and straw huts on stilts were constructed.

Conditions were the worst so far. And the political stability of Cambodia was fragile. 'It was very rough,' said O'Toole. 'There was a pulse of political violence beating just below the surface. In fact, we got out just in time. They burned down the British and American embassies the day after we left.' He was also indiscreet to an American reporter from *Life* magazine who quoted O'Toole saying that he had found a live snake in his soup. Prince Sihanouk, the Cambodian Prime Minister, promptly blacklisted O'Toole from the country – the unit had already left. 'That is the sort of thing that tends to make tourists nervous,' said the Prince. O'Toole was indignant. 'The Prime Minister, Prince Sihanouk, denounced me over the national radio after we had left, do you know that? They exploited the company and charged double for everything and took just about everything that wasn't nailed down and then they get on the bloody radio and denounce us all as Western capitalist invaders.'

Acting Lord Jim depended upon interpreting a very sparse script, often giving O'Toole no more than two sentences at a time. During the shooting, O'Toole found this a great challenge and one which he enjoyed. 'Jim's an inarticulate. It's great fun playing an inarticulate. It's a challenge, a real challenge. Jim never talks unless he absolutely has to.' By the time the filming was over, O'Toole had changed his mind. 'I was so wrong for the picture. I can't play inarticulates, I find. When I play reflective types I tend to reflect myself right off the screen.'

Before long he realised that he had taken the most important role, but not the one which would do him the most good. He believed that the role that James Mason was given, that of the nineteenth century buccaneer, Gentleman Brown, would have been better for him. To have taken the role of Lord Jim had been 'an error of judgment'. 'I think one of the faults it had,' O'Toole explained, 'was that it lost simplicity. I don't know who was responsible, but at one point it was a very simple narrative yarn, but it got rather overstated. I don't know how it happened.' Certainly the forbidding jungle of Cambodia had helped no one. 'How much I hated it you can judge from the fact that in three months I didn't learn one word of the language, whereas after nine months in the desert I was speaking Arabic well.'

In March 1964, on the way home from Cambodia, O'Toole and Sian made a lightning tour of Japan. From there they flew non-stop to the East Coast of America to attend the US première of *Becket* and do a couple of chat-shows. They should have rested first. They were staying at the St Regis Hotel in New York and O'Toole was booked to appear on Johnny Carson's 'Tonight' show and the 'Ed Sullivan Show', both networked programmes which would have greatly assisted the boosting of *Becket* and *Lord Jim*. O'Toole was genuinely tired and, after three minutes with Carson, excused himself and walked off the set. The effect was sensational. No one had been known to do such a thing before. O'Toole then backed out of the Sullivan show and another interview programme, 'Password'.

O'Toole collapsed twice before reaching the hotel. 'The time I fell over in New York was something special,' he explained. 'I'd just finished *Lord Jim* in Cambodia. The natives were burning down embassies and Sian and I had hid in lavatories; it was very unpleasant. We went to Japan for a holiday and then flew to New York. That's a frightening flight; I hate aeroplanes anyway; I can't believe all that tonnage can float in the air. Anyway, we stopped at Anchorage, Alaska, where I bought a pair of cuff links and a bowl of chili con carne and as soon as we left, the place fell apart in an earthquake, which shook me up. By the time we got to New York I hadn't slept for thirty-six hours. There was the usual bloody circus of journalism and television, which I subscribed to, but my reserves were getting low. Then I went on Channel 13 for an hour, and the interviewer dug very deep and I was moved both to laughter and to tears. By now I hadn't slept for sixty hours, but I thought I could do the Tonight show, and I went on it and suddenly I fell over, crunch, broke my dark glasses and came home in a box.' And on top of all that, he was suffering from fleabites. 'I was running alive when we left Cambodia. Fleas as big as your fist.'

'Lord Jim' was chosen for the Royal Film Performance, but, despite a fair public response, the critics did not like it. O'Toole was as imperfect as he had guessed. One called his performance 'inexcusably indulgent'. Another wrote. 'He ingratiates himself with his audience in the most shameless matinée idol manner. O'Toole was upset, but hardly surprised. He did not bother to see the completed version of the film when it was released, but he took the lessons of it most seriously.

He had clearly misjudged the part he had to play and the worth of the film. After a poor, conspicuously wobbly Hamlet and a poor performance in the moderate Lord Jim, he was anxious to recover his old form. He decided to make a clean break and find projects which removed him from the inevitable, easy comparisons with Lawrence. He was thinking clearly and described his dilemma at the time. 'I was in danger of becoming known as a tall, blond, thin dramatic actor, always self-tortured and in doubt and looking off painfully into the horizon. What I am doing now is consciously to change gear. Really I suppose it was the film Lord Jim, which brought me to the decision. Lord Jim, in which I was tall, blond, tortured and the rest of it, was my come-uppance. It was a mistake and I made the mistake because I was conservative and played safe. And that way lies failure. I should have taken the challenge of another part – the General perhaps – but not Jim, who looked at times too much like Lawrence. It was a juvenile lead part and I've decided now at thirty-three that I'll never become another ageing juvenile. You know the sort of actor. His face is so carefully made up and clean of lines and he looks off into the distance and it is only when you get up close to him that you see that what is behind the juvenile face is something old and nothing to do with being a juvenile at all.'

Despite the disappointing release of Lord Jim, O'Toole was still a hot property and people were queuing up to ask him to work for them. And he still owed Sam Spiegel work from his original Lawrence contract. One studio bought the screen rights of the New York stage hit Dylan, about the life of the Welsh poet Dylan Thomas, for £90,000, in the hope that O'Toole would agree to star in it. O'Toole's response was: 'I really think it's Richard Burton's part. But I'll do it if they twist my arm to, say, a king's ransom.' In fact he had already made up his mind about his next three projects: each one of them quite different from the other and, most importantly, a radical departure from the blond-haired, haunted characters.

He explained: 'Really what I am is a character actor who looks like a star. After I played *Lawrence of Arabia*, Hollywood saw me that way and no other. Now, deliberately, I am out to surprise people. First, in *What's New Pussycat*, then the play *Ride a Cock Horse* and next, God in *The Bible*. I'm not going to get set in any pattern. Look at Cary Grant: they'll let him play light comedy for ever, but never anything else. *Lord Jim* taught me to avoid that pattern.' The other person who taught him this lesson in avoiding typecasting was his wife, Sian Phillips, who had been taking an increasing concern in the direction of his career at the expense of her own.

They were now living very comfortably in their publicly private Georgian house in Hampstead, with their two bespectacled daughters, who had inherited O'Toole's poor eyesight. An odd combination of an ordinary family life, with ordinary family values, ran side by side with the flash extravagances that stardom, notoriety and a large income had brought them. They now were driven by a chauffeur in a midnight blue Rolls Royce. They were having the garden of their house landscaped by Ian Mylles, one of the most talented, fashionable and sought-after garden designers in Britain. Their home was stashed with art and precious objects, many of them bought from the countries where he and Sian were filming.

It was their system to buy a single good thing, instead of a number of smaller, inferior objects, from each place they visited. O'Toole enjoyed collecting things and was none-too scrupulous about how he got them home. He told Dorothy Willoughby, the wife of Bob Willoughby, the location photographer, that, during the filming of *Lawrence* he smuggled some precious Greek earrings through customs by hiding them in his foreskin – an act of daring which caused him pain for weeks after. Noh masks fought for space in Heath Street with pre-Columbian sculptures. And O'Toole, a shambles around the house, liked to drink a good deal, have his friends drop in and sleep very little.

He was kept in order – and his career was maintained in a like manner – by Sian, with a little help from her Welsh mother, who moved in with them. O'Toole knew Sian's worth. He said of her at the time: 'Stardom is not really so bad. Look, when it hits some people they bounce around like corks because they have no middle of themselves to measure from. And I have a very definite middle. My centrepiece is Sian and the kids. I measure everything from there. Without Sian I could never have made it at all. Not this far, not this fast. I would have been removed under the Litter Act. She got a grip on a pretty wild, roaring Irishman and pointed him in the right direction.'

His first attempt to deliberately break the typecasting which he rightly felt was narrowing his range – and diminishing his career – was that of a hooded, cloaked figure with a staff, trudging across the desert: a trio of angels in John Huston's film of Genesis for Dino de Laurentiis, *The Bible . . . In the Beginning*. The filming took place in the Laurentiis studio in Rome, a city which O'Toole came to hate. The film was shot in episodes and O'Toole was to play the three angels of God who visit Abraham, played by a hard-drinking George C. Scott, and his wife Sarah, with Ava Gardner made to look similar to Elizabeth Taylor in *Cleopatra*. Because *The Bible* was directed by Huston and starred O'Toole and Richard Harris, also an Irishman, O'Toole joked that it ought to be retitled *Sodom and Begorrah* or *The Gospel According to Mick*.

'When I arrived in Rome to start work,' explains O'Toole, 'they gave me the usual first Communion nightie and a pair of wings, because they obviously hadn't read the Old Testament. So John Huston asked me how I visualised God, and I said it would be more like a Hittite statue, and so that's how we did it. It's anthropomorphic with a vengeance, because we played it for a lot of fun. What else can you do? "Sarah was reproved," it says rather sternly in the Bible, after she's spent a perfectly innocent night with Abimelech. How can Sarah be reproved? She's one hundred and twenty-seven years old.'

The shooting for O'Toole's principal scene was in the Abruzzi Mountains. 'I played the Author,' he said. 'As a matter of fact, there are three of me in the film. Huston had this marvellous idea about the three strangers who appear to Abraham in Chapter 18 of Genesis. He thinks they're a pre-echo of the Trinity, so I play all three of them, and one of them is God. I use three different voices, ranging from senile Scunthorpe to juvenile Scunthorpe.'

There was a good deal of irony in O'Toole appearing as God. His image at the time – and one confirmed by his actions – was that of a hell-raiser, but his amusement at playing a holy man does not come over in the film; nor, for that matter, does the Scunthorpe accent. The three hooded figures stand hunched outside Abraham's tent and O'Toole's face pops in and out of each darkened cavity like a ghost.

The screenplay was written by Christopher Fry, the author of *The Lady's Not for Burning*, and this satisfied the serious side of both O'Toole and Scott, who were notoriously sniffy about the intellectual standard of the projects they appeared in. O'Toole was happy with his part. 'He's the full anthropomorphic God. He's the troubled old fellow who comes down and has to decide whether or not to blow up Sodom and Gomorrah. And he has the first recorded Levantine argument with Abraham about how many righteous people make a town worth saving – fifty, thirty, ten: they really bargain with each other.'

Strangely, O'Toole's Roman Catholic upbringing fully equipped him for such a film – a serious-minded attempt to tell the story of the Bible in Hollywood terms for the benefit of a mass audience. Although Huston's film was a misnomer – it stops half-way through Genesis – it was the beginning of a project which was intended to end with Revelation. O'Toole had no qualms about taking part, although he was barely religious.

O'Toole had not thrown his Catholicism away lightly. He reasoned each of the issues out before deciding that the Church line was untenable. 'When I was a Catholic – and I really went all the way, I had a bad case of handmaiden's knee – I remember a frightening debate going on about the sin of being cremated. Intelligent people were shrieking against it from the pulpits. Nowadays cremation has been given the blessing, but I can remember real terror; people hiding their heads if they'd had a relative cremated. I thought at the time that unless they allow cremation and birth control shortly, there's going to be a mountain of dead bodies with a pyramid of newborn babies on top, and that's all there'll be on sea or land or in space.'

And he had, with a little soul-searching, sorted out his attitude to birth control. 'It's lovely. I adore making love, I really do, but I don't want babies at the end of every sweet hour. I can't see how anyone could make it controversial. The whole argument is based on a wonky interpretation of a wonky bit of Genesis about Onan being slain by the Lord because he spilled his seed on the ground. Seeing that everyone in that part of the Bible is rushing around seducing their sisters at the age of about eight hundred and fifty, it seems a mad point to dwell on. Unless birth control is sanctioned, the world is going to be in terrible trouble. I haven't the faintest idea why the Church should promote the strangulation of early seed by the rhythm method rather than by bouncing it against a piece of rubber. Somebody once asked me to suggest another name for the rhythm method and I said it ought to be called "parenthood".'

Although O'Toole's appearance as the angelic trio looked remarkably like his playing of Lawrence, Huston was very pleased with it. 'One of the best scenes in *The Bible*, to my mind,' said Huston, 'was never really remarked on by the critics. This was where the three angels appeared to Abraham and revealed that Sarah – in her old age – was going to have a child. Sarah's laugh when she overheard this prediction was beautifully done by Ava Gardner. I had Peter O'Toole play all three angels, because what do angels look like if not alike? To have had three different individuals would have been disturbing to me – anthropomorphising the angelic species, so to speak. And, finally, George C. Scott was magnificent as Abraham bargaining with God in an effort to save the city of Sodom and its people. I may not like Scott as a private person, although my admiration for him as an actor is unbounded. Christopher Fry had given Ava, Peter and Scott very fine dialogue, and all the performances were outstanding.'

While everyone was perfect, devout and angelic on the set, as soon as they were off, all hell broke loose. As Huston describes it: 'Scott professed to be madly in love with Ava. He put on shows of jealousy, was extremely demanding of Ava's time and attention, and he became violent when they were not forthcoming. This very intensity turned her off, and pretty soon she started avoiding him. Scott was an on-and-off drinker, and he was on at the time. Although it didn't actively interfere with the shooting, it did make life rather difficult on occasion. While we were filming in Abruzzi, the whole company stayed in a small hotel in Avezzano. One night Scott got very drunk in the bar and threatened Ava physically when she entered. In the process of trying to slow him down before he hurt someone, I climbed on his back. He's very strong and he carried me around the room, bumping into things. He couldn't see where he was going because I had my arms wrapped around his head. Ava was persuaded to leave, and we finally got Scott calmed down.'

Life wasn't much quieter in Rome. At three one morning, in the Via Veneto, O'Toole came out of the Café de Paris with Barbara Steele, the Liverpudlian actress who was a big star in Italy, Albert Finney and ex-champion boxer Dave Crowley. The *paparazzi* descended like vultures, among them Lino Barillari, who preceded them, backwards, down the street, clicking and flashing as he went. Someone hit him square in the face and he fell over backwards, sprawled on the pavement. As the crowd gathered, the accusation flew at O'Toole. Barillari was taken off to hospital for five stitches in a gash on the head and O'Toole and Barbara Steele were taken by plainclothed police to a police station, where they were questioned for two hours.

'I had been warned about the *paparazzi*,' explained O'Toole, 'but they were even worse than I feared, always lying in wait, trying to catch me out. You can't imagine what these photographers are like. One night Peter Perkins [his stunt man and friend, now a dog-breeder in Ireland] and I were sitting in my suite when the door burst open and a blonde fell at our feet. I shot into the next room just as two photographers came in. One night one called me a name and I slugged him. The police came. It became a big thing.'

The next day the police returned to O'Toole's hotel. They were going to press charges and were anxious that he did not do a bunk before the trial began. 'The day the bogeys came to my hotel to confiscate my luggage and passport I was being smuggled out the back. Peter Perkins put on my cap and spectacles and went out the front door as a decoy. It worked fine. I was still wearing my beard for God and nobody spotted me.' O'Toole vowed never to work in Rome again and founded a loose group of actors who agreed to refuse to work in Rome until the *paparazzi* problem had been cleared up. O'Toole recruited Albert Finney, Richard Burton, Elizabeth Taylor, Ava Gardner and her close friend Frank Sinatra: all had suffered at the hands of the plague of street photographers in Rome.

And O'Toole quickly set about putting his economic sanctions into effect. His next project was the Woody Allen farce, *What's New Pussycat?*, and he held a significant stake in the capital. 'I was directly responsible for moving away a three million dollar film production from Rome to Paris,' he boasted. But O'Toole was to encounter similar trouble there and more trouble with the police. As he explained: 'Violence comes to me. I have given up looking for it.'

# 7   Exit the Golden Boy

'*WHAT'S NEW, PUSSYCAT?*' was about as different from the *Lawrence* tradition as any part could be. It was a comedy, written in the main by Woody Allen, about a man who is irresistible to women. 'There were lots of birds in it,' O'Toole remembers. 'Hundreds of pretty girls. Usually in a movie I'm in love with the Truth, or Richard Burton or a camel.' The film demanded a co-star of equal weight to play the perplexed psychiatrist who tries to alleviate his most awkward problem. The producer, Charles Feldman, made an inspired – but, for the project, dangerous – choice of co-star for O'Toole in Peter Sellers.

Sellers was an extraordinary liability. He had just recovered from a series of heart attacks which he survived after months of intensive care. After technically dying eight times, it was very rash to hinge an expensive film upon him. To lose a leading actor would mean reshooting from the start. No insurance company would take on a film with Sellers at this time, but Feldman was so eager to have him that he put up the money himself and calculated exactly how much he would stand to lose if Sellers were to become indisposed. To minimise the risk, Seller's shooting schedule was trimmed to sixteen days. O'Toole was simultaneously delighted and rather frightened. 'It was lovely to do a farce with Peter Sellers, though I was nervous of him at first. Here I'd been dying to do a comedy and then I had to go and pick one with the funniest man alive.'

O'Toole had first met Sellers in the company of Kenneth Griffith after a performance at the Vaudeville Theatre. Sellers was in the audience and O'Toole and Griffith were meant to meet him in the foyer after the curtain came down. To pass the time until the performance ended, O'Toole and Griffith drank in a bar opposite the theatre, where they were entertained by one of London's best known buskers at that time – a man pushing a pram with a gramophone inside and a dog sat like a baby, a skit on the His Master's Voice record label. Griffith remembers O'Toole saying, softly: 'Look, Griffith. I'll bet that dog is nailed down. Look carefully at its paws. Can you see the nails?' And when they went for their rendezvous with Sellers, he was not to be found. They went into the empty auditorium and, on their hands and knees, searched the rows of seats, shouting: 'Come out, Peter.' Sellers finally turned up and they went, late, to a dinner à trois in a restaurant in Chelsea. Sellers supervised the cooking over a brazier on the table.

O'Toole took his preparation for Pussycat very seriously, deliberately trying to steal some of the W. C. Fields magic by running as many Fields films as he could lay his hands on, looking carefully at his technique. O'Toole considered himself to be rather good at comedy. He thought that his comic stage appearances were among his best, particularly Dogberry in Much Ado About Nothing and Doolittle in Pygmalion. But it was stiff competition to be put next to Sellers, a chameleon of a comic actor whose reputation was daunting.

From his beginning in British films, particularly in the Ealing comedies such as The Lady Killers and I'm All Right, Jack, Sellers had taken off on an impressive international career, working with directors like Stanley Kubrick in Lolita and Dr Strangelove, often doubling up on parts and stealing scenes from under others' noses. He had already made two films as the daft French police inspector, Clouseau. To act next to Sellers was as intimidating and liable to produce the best from O'Toole as was casting Richard Burton opposite him in Becket.

From the start, O'Toole and Sellers got on well with each other. The first thing that the two of them decided, amicably, was who should top the credits. Although technically the two parts were of equal weight – although Sellers was the senior actor, he did not outrank the expensive O'Toole – one or other would have to take top billing. They decided by tossing a coin and O'Toole lost. O'Toole could see why it would be good for him to appear above Sellers on the credits, but he was entirely happy with the verdict.

O'Toole, who was arrogant, brash, loud and generally self-serving, found in Sellers someone to respect. He certainly envied Sellers' acting ability, but also he envied Sellers' humility and nervousness, which were quite opposite of O'Toole's natural, bragging, confident exterior. O'Toole found Sellers willing to make friends and he was flattered and even humbled a little when Sellers took him into his confidence. They were honest with each other and O'Toole respected the rare friendship which Sellers had dared to extend to a person so opposite in almost every way.

'I knew Pete,' explained O'Toole,' and I think he knew about me. We were totally comfortable together – not cosy, it was far from cosy, it was sometimes downright edgy but it was the sharp edginess of stimulation and exploration. I found myself completely eaten up by Pete's personality. I took far more from him that he took from me –

yes, I was hugely influenced by him when we were together. I found myself listening more than I did with most people. I even found myself imitating him.'

On the set, it was O'Toole and Sellers who dominated the action, O'Toole as a magazine proprietor smitten with an embarrassing knack of attracting girls; Sellers as his psychotic psychiatrist who tries to solve his problem – 'You call that a problem?' A third force was in the small form of Woody Allen, whose conception the film was. He had also written the script and was going to act as O'Toole's best friend and sidekick in the film. Allen was squeezed out and ignored. He hated how the film, under the direction of Clive Donner, was turning out and became more and more desperate.

O'Toole describes what happened: 'We began with a brilliant, sketchy, Perelmanesque script by Woody Allen, who is a genius. Then things got a little neurotic, with lots of politics and infighting and general treachery and finally – with the ghost of W. C. Fields hovering over our heads – we improvised the whole thing from start to finish. There were areas in the script that were undeveloped, which is the norm with most films: you cast first and write afterwards. I actually wrote with my own fair hand about three-fifths of the script. When I say "wrote" I mean that we'd meet at ten in the morning – Sellers and I and Clive Donner, the director – and sit around talking and hoping. Sellers had the ideas, I did the words and Clive was the arbitrator. We jotted things down on the back of contraceptives and off we went. I play a fashion journalist and Sellers is my analyst. We took it on the wing every day, grabbed an idea and built it from there.'

This is an example of the extemporised script.

*O'Toole*: In England we have a national therapy. It is called cricket.
*Sellers*: Is there any sex in it?
*O'Toole*: Oh, no. It is a game played by gentlemen for gentlemen.
*Sellers*: It is sick, sick.

Woody Allen, who had an ego and a talent equal to both O'Toole and Sellers, resented being pushed out of the way. He had worked hard on what he considered a creditable script, his first feature-film screenplay after an arduous apprenticeship as a stand-up comic on New York night club stages. The producer of *What's New, Pussycat?* had spotted him in the Blue Angel club in New York when with Shirley MacLaine and had asked him to write a comic screenplay for him. When it came to filming, he found that his big chance was being squandered by two anarchic actors. Allen remembered: 'They would say: "That scene between you and Peter Sellers or you and Peter

O'Toole. We're going to let the two Peters do it!" ' He thought it bad mannered and unprofessional to ignore his work.

O'Toole learnt from Sellers and Allen and from writing and acting gags how difficult comedy was. 'What I now understand,' he said, 'is why comics are so introverted. Why they go *Brr-brr-brr* all the time. What a strain it is having to be funny – even with someone else's material. Farce is really tragedy without trousers. Shoot a man in the stomach and it is drama. Shoot him in the backside and it is comic. When you are doing a storm scene from *King Lear*, everything is riding for you. The audience cannot look away. But in farce, if you mistime a move or a line you are lost. This part is much more difficult than Lawrence. Not the acting, but the balancing of the personality. It is balletic and timing as well as finding the right focus and point of view. I mean, here is a man who wants to get married and just can't keep his eyes off other women. Wherever he turns there are beautiful women all ready for him; why, Ursula Andress even parachutes out of the sky into his open car. His situation is desperate and like Hamlet's. And it is to be played in dead earnest and without any winking.'

O'Toole came to understand what Sellers had told him about the loneliness of comedians. Sellers was at a new chapter of his life; he was having to rethink his career in the light of his multiple heart-attacks. He could not be strenuous and, always a vulnerable man, he felt even more vulnerable having been debilitated by ill-health. O'Toole bolstered him as best he could. He told him, for instance, how actors and punters in London had greeted the news of how close Sellers was to death in Hollywood. O'Toole, Sian Phillips and Jules Buck were in Claridge's. On their way through the main lobby, a porter handed them a piece of news wire-service tape which said that Sellers had had a serious heart attack and that he had been taken to the Cedars of Lebanon heart clinic. They were due to go on to a cocktail party.

'We were all pretty badly shaken,' O'Toole remembers. 'We went straight to the cocktail party, and don't forget we'd just got the news red-hot off the tape-machine, and already everybody was talking about Sellers.' After the party they went on to a restaurant in Soho, the Trattoria Terrazza. 'Nobody was talking about anything else. The news was beating us all the way through town, right down the line. It reminded me of Raimu's death, the great French actor-clown. He died during the war in Marseilles, I think it was, and apparently within fifteen minutes of his death every bistro along the whole coast was mourning him.'

In telling the story, O'Toole emphasised to Sellers how significant it was that the news travelled fast. Sellers had been given a unique chance to discover how his death would be received by the world, for he had technically died eight times on that Hollywood operating theatre table and his admirers were not to know that it was a dress rehearsal. O'Toole told him. 'Look, love, you must understand, they weren't talking about the layers, they were talking about the centre. You. Not the myth, not the legend, but the man. Because you do bloody well exist, you know. He said something noncommittal like "Really?" or "I didn't know that." I don't know whether it did any good or not, my telling him that story. I got the feeling he didn't believe me.'

Sellers was subdued and little fun off-camera. He had to take it easy. But O'Toole discovered, to his delight, that on the adjacent set, Richard Burton and Elizabeth Taylor were filming *The Sandpiper*. O'Toole decided to lay a prank on his old drinking-mate. During one of Burton's love scenes, there were two walk-on parts for actors to play drunks who slightly disturb the amorous couple. O'Toole did a deal with one of the actors and smuggled himself onto the set. As the cameras rolled, O'Toole exploded in bad Welsh, cursing the terror-ised Burton. 'I'm charging one hundred dollars for crowd work,' O'Toole joked.

But Burton had his revenge. He demanded equal time and a scene was swiftly written for him to walk through *Pussycat*. He is not in the credits and his appearance lasts a matter of seconds. O'Toole is in a crowded bar, pushing past people in search of someone. He bumps into Burton, who asks him: 'Haven't you seen me somewhere before?' to which O'Toole replied: 'Give my regards to what's-her-name.' It was one of the many in-jokes which the critics were to latch onto when the film was released accusing O'Toole and Sellers of gross self-indulgence.

Paris was good for partying. But whenever the drink flowed, O'Toole was prone to trouble-making. 'I am violently pacifist,' he said. 'I think I understand violence. Perhaps that's why I hate it. Although I'm a great blatherer, when the talking stops the simple answer always adds up to a punch on the nose. It's part of the human make-up, I'm afraid.'

In one night club, O'Toole was happy to indulge in a little violence against the police; but, he claims, in a just end. As he was going into his hotel, he saw two policemen tackling a prostitute who had been soliciting from her car. They were being violent, which upset O'Toole's natural sense of justice. 'The door of the car was wrenched open and one of the cops had the girl by the hair,' he remembered, 'while the other whacked her with his truncheon. My instinct was to rush at them and break up the shindig. But experience prevailed. I ran all right, but back to my hotel.'

The memory of the incident stayed with him and, his sense of moral indignation aroused, he determined to take his revenge on the Parisian police, one way or another. His chance came in a night club dancing a new dance called the Bostella. 'It's a giggle,' he said. 'You weave around the dance floor clapping your hands above your head and screaming all your happy thoughts. Then the music dies, the lights fade, and you fall down and roll around the floor, shrieking all your unhappy thoughts. The dancers fall on top of each other and simply yell for ages.

'Well, every night the club is visited by a permanent joke known as the Dancing Policeman. He's a real cop, but he comes into the club to be plied with brandy till it's running out of his ears. Then he weaves around the dance floor while everyone jeers at him. Watching this clown, I suddenly thought of the two cops who had beaten up the hooker outside my hotel. Here was this bogey who, ten minutes later, would be outside patrolling his area with his truncheon. So I got them to start up the Bostella and as the music got to the part where everyone starts falling to the floor I moved over to where the Dancing Policeman was weaving about and jumped him, knocking him down hard and "accidentally" roughing him up on the floor. By the time I'd finished with him I don't think he was in any condition to whack any poor old whore around the head for a night or two.'

Even by the time he had become very wealthy, a respected actor, a worldwide film star and celebrity, O'Toole still harboured grudges against authority: even those agents of authority who were there to protect him and his sort. In revenge for the treatment of the French whore, O'Toole took the law into his own hands and thumped an innocent man. O'Toole's pompous, self-deluded judgment on the Bostella incident was: 'I hate violence. But most of all I hate judicial violence. It's so cold blooded.' The arrogance which had helped him become one of the world's highest paid actors also had this dislikeable, bullheaded side. With liquid courage he could right the wrongs of the world; but, even more chilling, in the sober light of day he could justify his actions. A lasting grudge against authority and a bullying nature gave him a reputation for being difficult which caused many actors and film directors to discount him from their plans.

After *Pussycat*, O'Toole wanted to return to the theatre but still keep up the momentum of breaking new ground. Coming out of different holes was not just advice for film work; it applied to the theatre, too. He was offered the prospect of a gruelling part in David Mercer's new play *Ride a Cock Horse*. This was a decent change from the classics. O'Toole wanted to make a few things clear: that he was a capable actor, not a lightweight who was only of use to film makers;

that he could withstand the rough and tumble of a long major part, to answer accusations that he was not physically capable of the exhausting, uncut role of Hamlet; to break into something of contemporary relevance, to show his range; and to prove himself in the commercial theatre.

The part of Peter in David Mercer's play suited all these demands. Mercer was at the top of his profession and he was well respected for the intellectual weight of his writing. Harold Hobson, the *Sunday Times* critic, wrote of *Ride a Cock Horse*: 'Not only were the words the right words but that there was the right number of them, for you cannot build high except on a broad base. Mr Mercer builds very high indeed, and his building does not topple.' And strangely, the central part, which demanded that O'Toole appear on the stage non-stop for three hours – all but the full length of the play – echoed O'Toole's life. It was eerily autobiographical.

The hero was a young man, Peter, from Yorkshire, who becomes an overnight success as a novelist and moves with his wife to London and a home in Hampstead. Peter likes to drink, to whore and to blather. He is not entirely happy in London and yearns for his romantic notions of Yorkshire. But he dare not return, even though his parents and his wife encourage him to go back and live a happier life. Success has upset and spoilt the simple, sincere Peter. To make things even more poignant, Sian Phillips was cast as Peter's mistress. His wife in the play, Nan, is going through a rough patch and cannot achieve sexual satisfaction with the wayward Peter. One of the dissimilar aspects of the play is that the couple had a great unsatisfied wish to have children.

O'Toole commented on working once again closely to Sian: 'You know the old saying that the easiest way for a man to get a divorce is to teach his wife to drive. Well, it can be as dangerous as that when you act with your wife. Neither Sian nor I want to become a jet-age Lunt and Fontanne [the American acting husband and wife]. It takes too much out of us. Before I start work on a film or a play I walk around like a ghost not talking to anyone. Now at home there are two of us. And one of us is likely to wake up at three in the morning, nudge the other and say: "You know when you make that move. . . ." When we are rehearsing on stage we are apt to address the other through the director. So I don't think either of us will want to go on as a professional married couple on stage.'

*Ride a Cock Horse* opened for previews in Nottingham. O'Toole had decided to accept no fee for his acting until the production costs had been met. By the time it reached the Piccadilly Theatre in London, it was plainly going to make a lot of money. Harold Hobson's verdict on the London opening night was: 'Mr O'Toole has an enormous part. He is on the stage for three hours in a play that lasts for three hours and twenty seconds. He never wearies either himself or us. Some of his intonations and inflections are of extraordinary pathos, of the most touching resignation, and he delivers three unconventional prayers with great beauty. He is particularly impressive in the second of these, when, half mockingly, he imagines the way in which his and Nan's parents in the north talk of their children's life in London, their tender and complacent assumption of success. We have seen what the real truth is, and there is in Mr O'Toole's recital a serene poignancy that pierces the marrow.'

Other critics were not so gentle. One called the play: 'a heavy-handed bore'. And another: 'it flounders in a bog of verbiage'. The first night had brought boos from the auditorium. But the proof was in the size of the audiences that O'Toole was pulling. Bookings broke the theatre record. O'Toole declared: 'Look at this play. It's the biggest straight hit in town. The other night we took £1,233 and the theatre capacity is only £1,200. Don't ask me how. They must have been swinging from the chandeliers.'

He ignored the harsh criticism that dismissed him as a cinema matinée idol. 'It's quite simple,' he said. 'It's my turn. I've been the golden boy for too long, so now I've got to be slapped down. The critics always feel: We made you, we can break you. All right, fine. I've no complaints. Some people love to see you fall from grace. But I must be forgiven if I don't take any notice of what they say.' And he described David Mercer as 'a magical voice in the theatre, yet look what they said about him – these same people who made such twits of themselves when they first wrote about Pinter, Osborne and Bolt.' O'Toole was arrogant, on top of the world, and ready for a fight.

He was determined to use the power that fame had brought him. He was eager to wield some clout, to make his presence felt. And, at the time that *Ride a Cock Horse* was previewing in Nottingham, an issue arrived that he felt passionate about and which allowed him to take a strong stand against established authority. John Fernald, the Principal of the Royal Academy of Dramatic Art, O'Toole's old acting school, resigned after ten years in the post, amid speculation that he had been elbowed out by a board of governors who did not appreciate his radical approach to theatre.

O'Toole was indignant and promptly took Fernald's side. He was willing to fight for Fernald and use all the instruments of the publicity machine with which his success had armed him. He organised a letter to the *Sunday Times*, protesting at Fernald's ousting, and got his wife Sian, Sarah Miles, Sean Curry, Barbara Sykes and others to sign it. 'We know he has been forced into resigning because of backward-thinking council policies,' they wrote, 'and are very concerned that if he leaves, the progressive work he has done will be destroyed in a single blow. We strongly urge the council to reconsider its policy and to allow Mr Fernald to continue as principal. Over the past ten years he has achieved a great deal for students who nowadays are able to play before worldwide audiences. Last year, for instance, they were able to tour both the United States and Europe. This would have been impossible before Mr Fernald came to the RADA. He has earned the respect of the entire theatrical profession — and, more important, he has earned his students' respect.'

O'Toole went further: 'Mr Fernald cannot say that he's being elbowed out by a lot of fogies — but I can. I think there's a faction trying to move Fernald out because of his policy of keeping strong connections with the living theatre.'

Fernald started fighting back. 'I was forced to resign,' he said. 'They wanted someone more docile. You can say that I was an uncomfortable person to have around.' He offered to withdraw his resignation, but the RADA council refused his suggestion. After the London opening of *Ride a Cock Horse*, O'Toole and his band attended a private meeting of the Academy. A policeman stood outside, expecting trouble. O'Toole and Richard Briers called on the twenty members of the council to resign on grounds that twelve of them had been illegally elected, thereby breaking the terms of the Academy's Royal Charter. Sir Felix Aylmer, the Academy's vice-president, hesitated: 'The Academy has been running for many years on rather loose lines, and I would agree that the legal formalities have not always been strictly observed. But we're going to get ourselves on the straight and level.'

The next day, Sir Felix fought back, announcing an investigation not only into the election of the council — but also into the election of the 184 associate members of the Academy, which included O'Toole and Briers. O'Toole riposted with a threat to withdraw a scholarship for two young actors that he had donated if Fernald was not reinstated. O'Toole admitted feeling 'sick and sad over the whole affair', not least because one of the twelve not elected according to the rules was his close friend Lord Snowdon and, more amusingly, Lord Cobbold, the Lord Chamberlain, who was given the power to censor plays. However, Fernald was a lost cause. The establishment closed ranks and would not allow him back in. O'Toole's only compensation was the bad publicity awarded to those he disliked.

Three hours a night on stage and a full-scale political battle in his time off was proving a physical strain for O'Toole. He caught a chest infection and had to duck out of two performances. The Piccadilly Theatre was full every night and O'Toole, who had never missed a performance through ill-health before, was heartily sick of himself. He went on stage each night with agonising pain and dizzy spells which he tried to disguise from the audience. He was receiving daily visits to Heath Street from his doctor.

By the beginning of August, after six weeks of the run and with two weeks still to go, O'Toole bowed to his wife's advice and decided to leave the production. O'Toole was angry with himself. 'It's the first time anything like this has happened,' he said, 'and it's doubly wretched to leave such a red-hot hit.' It was decided to close the show altogether. Wendy Craig, one of O'Toole's three leading ladies in the play, expressed her feelings with the most generous compliment to O'Toole: 'I would not want to finish the run with any other actor. He is the greatest professional I have ever worked with.'

O'Toole left for a nursing home to recuperate, to rest and make plans for the future. *Pussycat* had been released to mixed reviews. One critic called it: 'Vulgar, absurd, sick and tedious.' Another said O'Toole showed 'absolutely no flair' for comedy. But, like *Ride a Cock Horse*, the public had a different view. In less than two months it took over a million dollars and United Artists thought it could be one of their greatest hits ever. O'Toole had a stake in the profits. He was asked what he was spending his money on. 'Oh, I've bought some art. And horses, of course; don't forget my horses. There's Eric, a three thousand guinea yearling bought last year. He won his first race at Ascot before the Queen. And then there's Mr Fierce, my favourite. He never runs, though. He just turns and bites the starter. It's all a hell of a giggle.'

His next film was to be shot in Paris and starred Audrey Hepburn, whom he had hoped to act with ever since the rumours about his joining the cast of *My Fair Lady*. It was a deliberate attempt to break the horsehair image that had dogged him since *Lawrence*. *How to Steal a Million Dollars and Live Happily Ever After* was a romantic comedy, what O'Toole called 'a touch of the Cary Grants', which demanded that he look debonair and elegant. 'It's one of those sophisticated comedies. Every morning you can see a long, thin figure slipping into Savile Row to be measured. Imagine me, well-dressed.' He also spent his time running old Cary Grant films, not so much to copy him but to register his technique.

At the same time as *How to Steal a Million* he was in negotiation with Sam Spiegel to deliver a film he owed him from his *Lawrence* contract. They were toying with the idea of a screenplay called *The Night of the Generals*. He was also eager to make a film of the life of Will Adams, the British sailor who insinuated his way into the Shogun's court in Japan in the seventeenth century. Although never made, the preparations for the film became well advanced. He and Jules Buck were going to produce it through Keep Films. John Huston had been approached to direct. Dalton Trumbo had written a screenplay, which O'Toole thought was 'the finest script that ever breathed' and Toshiro Mifune was to appear in the cast. O'Toole had stumbled across the story of Will Adams when making a fleeting visit to Japan between the filming of *Lord Jim* and the opening of *Becket* in New York. He had visited the Golden Pavilion in Kyoto and contemplated the Zen garden of stones and gravel there.

'Just five rocks and a load of pebbles – but the use of space,' he remembered. 'I sat there and I contemplated peace. Japanese poets have been describing it for centuries, but for me it was like a huge ocean, with little bits of life appearing and being very beautiful. Anyway, that was where I met this actor, who told me that Adams was still revered as a Buddhist saint, with a shrine of his own and all that. I listened with my mouth wide open, came home and looked up the records and got thoroughly hooked. Will Adams was the first Englishman to go to Japan. He's the unknown Elizabethan. He made a much greater contribution than Raleigh or Drake, but he committed two grievous crimes: he was born in the lower classes; and he didn't come home to share the goodies.

'He was a shipbuilder's apprentice who fought against the Armada and went off with a Dutch trading fleet to open up the East Indian market. He was wrecked on the shores of Japan, where the Jesuits grabbed him – the Portuguese Jesuits, whose main contributions to Japanese civilization were Christianity and the gun. He was sentenced to be crucified – as you've already spotted, the cross occurs and recurs in my speech – when the Emperor met him and liked him. He taught the Emperor mathematics, built his first ship for him and became his most powerful adviser, the first and last white samurai. I don't want to raise any monuments, but Adams was about the only one of Elizabeth's great globetrotters who didn't go to plunder.'

And he was keen to act in a film of *King Lear*. As he told Kenneth Tynan: 'I'm going to make it. One of the marvellous things about having a few shillings is that I'm in a position to call the shots. And I hope the director will be Kurosawa, the man who made *Rashomon*. I think he knows *Lear* in his bones – that monolithic, feudal thing.'

The filming of *How to Steal a Million* went without incident. William Wyler, who had recently completed *The Collector*, directed. It was a daring robbery adventure along the lines of *Topkapi* and O'Toole dyed his hair blond and played an insurance agent, a lightweight character. It was a fair film, well crafted by Wyler, but it was hardly O'Toole's picture. The attention of the audience was too divided between Audrey Hepburn, Eli Wallach, Charles Boyer and Hugh Griffith.

The film is most memorable, as far as O'Toole is concerned, by the fact that during the filming a French Count made a complaint to the police about him. Leaving a Paris night club a little the worse for wear, O'Toole became embroiled in a fracas with a Frenchman who turned out to be Count Philippe de la Fayette, a man with a strong sense of aristocratic honour. Short of challenging O'Toole to a duel, the Count lodged a complaint with the police, accusing O'Toole of wilful assault – a charge which O'Toole shrugged off.

O'Toole had been eager to develop a light comic style, but was irritated by the emptiness of *How to Steal a Million*. He wanted to get his teeth into a good part. In Feburary 1966, a project appeared on the horizon which looked ideal. Richard Burton, newly arrived in Rome to begin filming *The Taming of the Shrew* with Elizabeth Taylor, finally agreed to play Napoleon in a film of the Battle of Waterloo. O'Toole was being sought to play the Duke of Wellington. John Huston, whom O'Toole hoped would make *Will Adams*, was to direct the Waterloo film.

O'Toole was delighted. The shooting schedule would begin at the start of 1967. In the event, like so many other projects which Huston has tried to build around O'Toole – like a film of Rudyard Kipling's *Kim* and another of Kipling's *Man Who Would Be King*, eventually made with Michael Caine and Sean Connery rather than O'Toole and Burton – it never got off the ground. *Waterloo* was finally made by Sergei Bondarchuck and starred Rod Steiger as Napoleon and Christopher Plummer as Wellington.

With *Will Adams* shelved indefinitely, he returned to the staring-eyed character which he had forsaken since *Lord Jim* and played General Tanz, a former Nazi general who represses the memory of the prostitutes he had murdered during the war. O'Toole was delighted to get back to some strong meat, some real acting, after the fripperies of light comedy.

And the chance to play Tanz came from an unlikely person: Sam Spiegel. O'Toole still owed him a film and there had been many disagreements about which project Spiegel's credit would be spent on. The inability to find a compromise led to an angry exchange of solicitors' letters. Spiegel, who had so happily tramped across the Shakespeare Memorial Theatre's plans to use O'Toole when he needed the actor for *Lawrence*, found himself in the other court, considering suing O'Toole for breach of contract.

The film Spiegel had in mind was *The Chase*, about sex and sin in a small Texas town, to be directed by Arthur Penn, with a cast including Jane Fonda, Robert Redford, E. G. Marshall and Angie Dickinson. If O'Toole refused the main part – which finally went to Marlon Brando – Spiegel would sue for five million dollars. *The Night of the Generals* allowed them to reach agreement. As O'Toole said: 'We're friends again. We were suing each other. He wanted me to play a Texan. Me, a Yorkshire-Irishman! I thought it was ridiculous, like asking President Johnson to play Sam Weller. So I said No. I defied the bold Sam. And the lawyers got busy. Finally I rang up and said: "Let's settle this amicably," and we did. It's all right now. The lawyers were terribly disappointed.'

And with *The Night of the Generals*, which was to be the first western film made in Warsaw since 1945, O'Toole thought he had broken new ground. 'I've finally left him behind,' he said, 'the romantic twit. In this film they're paying me to be an actor.' His hair was cut short and again dyed blond. 'It is a hell of a part. Mind you, I made a great sacrifice to play it. I had to shave off three miles of eyebrow to look right. They're selling them down the Champs-Elysées, I shouldn't wonder; souvenir Irish eyebrows. But it seems to be working. I'll stand by this part. Though I don't so much act in the film as bloody well haunt it, strutting about all strapped up in my German uniform. It makes you feel like a tank, that uniform. No wonder the Germans were always stepping on people.' Anatole Litvak was directing for Spiegel. O'Toole was reunited with Omar Sharif, and Christopher Plummer, who the previous year had completed *The Sound of Music*, was also in the cast.

Nothing emphasised more his joy at being back in robust, meaty parts than his having to slip back to redo some lines from *How To Steal a Million*. Not used to seeing rushes, he was taken by surprise. His mind was far away from *How To Steal a Million*. 'There's a line in it where I say: "Ring out wild bells," but apparently you don't hear it because of the bloody bells. So I turned up to do the lines and looked up at myself on the screen and for the first time I thought: who's that? There I was, deep in the role of old jackboots here, and up on the screen was this great blond nit wafting about, all light and gay and lovely. It threw me. I couldn't even remember the voice to use. That's never happened before!'

A change was coming over him. He was becoming more and more disenchanted with the film world and film makers. He explained: 'Direction is something very odd and recent. It's an innovation of the twentieth century, invented to protect the author from the vagaries of the actor-manager. I think it's time there was an innovation to protect the author and the actor and the public from the vagaries of the director. Given a good play and a good team and a decent set, you could chain a blue-arsed baboon in the stalls and get what is known as a production.'

He found that with *The Night of the Generals* a good screenplay was being spoilt by changes made by Sam Spiegel and Litvak while filming was going on. He was being messed about as Woody Allen had been messed about by him. And he blames that interference for the failure of the finished film: 'I find that the moment changes start coming in, when people start taking them seriously, it's all going to fall apart. The producers have influence. It does happen. *The Night of the Generals* could have been a smashing movie, but, once again, I adhered faithfully to what had been the original material and everybody else was in a different movie. Unless you have conviction in your material, how do you start?'

And seeing himself in *How to Steal a Million* brought on the same sensations. 'It's all part of my dislike for the film world, I suppose. How would you like a bloody great camera crawling all over you from morning to night? And all that tycoon stuff – breakfast conferences, things like that – just impossible. Someone asked me round for breakfast the other day to discuss something. I told him I only ever had a fingernail and a Gauloise for breakfast. I only make films for money. And I don't care who knows it. The rest of it is a lot of old rubbish. Fame? What's fame except a few bob and an entrée. I look at other actors with their cars and agents and seething masses of secretaries and I wonder what it's all about. What have I got? A bulldog with in-growing eyelashes. Poor Scoby. He's just had an operation for it. Never be the same again.'

After filming *Night of the Generals*, O'Toole took the chance when in London to work briefly with Peter Sellers on a film of Ian Fleming's *Casino Royale*, an absurd part work, shared between different directors, which was filmed on a closed set with the identity of James Bond kept a secret. The Bond film had been making a mint with Sean Connery and the rights for this one had slipped past the clutches of Cubby Broccoli.

The Fleming plot was quickly thrown out of the window and the film was set up to be a complete farce. O'Toole's appearance, like many of the actor guests who passed through the studio, lasts only thirty seconds. 'It was done for a joke,' explained O'Toole, 'a St Patrick's Day spoof. It wasn't meant to be in the film at all. I heard that P. Sellers and U. Andress were cavorting about the set with a hundred pipers and all, so I decided to make it a hundred and one. After all, I do play the pipes. But it should never have been included in the film.'

Before settling down, ever more reluctantly, to film work again, O'Toole arranged to do some work in the theatre in Dublin. Sean O'Casey's *Juno and the Paycock* was an Irish Civil War tragi-comedy which Laurence Olivier had revived for his new National Theatre. Olivier played down the comic elements, to allow the tragedy to come through and his production flushed out new interest in Dublin.

Peter O'Toole agreed to join Denis Carey's production at the Gaiety Theatre in August 1966. He was always happy working in Dublin. The beer was good, the bars were friendly and there were always drinking mates to be had. And the acting – particularly this time – was a test.

O'Toole's wish to be a good Irishman meant holding his own against those who had lived all their life there. To act in Dublin was an act of faith for O'Toole, an essential purchase of Irish credentials to match his romantic fondness for his father's country. And *Juno and the Paycock* provided specific Irish tests. The 1926 production was immensely memorable to Irish theatre people and O'Toole and the rest of the cast would work in the shadow of the 1926 cast of Sara Allgood, Barry Fitzgerald and F. J. McCormick. The 1966 cast was impressive enough: Siobham McKenna as Juno; O'Toole as her husband, Captain Boyle; and Jackie McGowran as the Captain's disloyal sidekick, Joxer Daly.

It was important for O'Toole's Irish aspirations that his perform- ance was first-class. O'Casey's play was a crucial testament to a most important chapter of Irish history, and the test – and O'Casey's memory – were held in awe. O'Toole, wearing a red moustache and a shaggy wig, pulled all the stops out and romped to universally good notices. J. W. Lambert of the *Sunday Times* described his Captain Boyle as 'by far the best performance I have ever seen him give' and Sean Day-Lewis of the *Daily Telegraph* agreed; 'Peter O'Toole gives his best stage performance for years, more than simply powerful. He has a nervous struggle with the accent, at times his vowels get no further west than Liverpool, but he is truly involved with the Captain and the aggressive bluster of his delivery is most effective.'

Once more, after the two-week run, O'Toole confirmed to himself that he was really happiest working in the theatre and that film making was a lucrative drudge. He decided that control was essen- tial to turn film work into the joy that theatre was for him and he therefore decided to directly concern himself with the business side of his next picture.

O'Toole's frustration with the film industry was only heightened by his attempts to master it. He and Jules Buck decided to co- produce *Great Catherine*, a film version of George Bernard Shaw's one-act play *Whom Glory Still Adores*. O'Toole cast himself in the lead role and surrounded himself with those he preferred. It was to be a truly actors' film. Jeanne Moreau was Catherine; Zero Mostel stole the film from everyone; Kenneth Griffith was there; and Jack Hawkins, whom O'Toole had taken to a brothel during the filming of *Lawrence*, made his first appearance in films since an operation for cancer of the throat removed his voice box.

To ease his return to films, Hawkins – whom everyone knew affectionately as The Hawk – was given only four speeches. Hawkins could no longer speak without extraordinary effort and, without a voice box, he had to burp while moving his lips. During filming he mouthed all the words he was given and formed the words in a recording studio later, where all the belches were removed and the sentences made to sound fluent. O'Toole had given Hawkins four speeches of which the script demanded that he only finish one: 'Yes, you'll like the Prince. He's a charming fellow.' It was an act of affection, of loyalty to an old stage actor and colleague on *Lawrence*, that O'Toole made room for Jack Hawkins to appear in front of the camera again.

It was a weird, wild film, which confirmed O'Toole in his worst beliefs about the misery of the mechanics of making films. 'I have high hopes for *Great Catherine*,' he said. 'I think it is good – but I'll never produce and star in a film again. Our first director, Elliott Silverstein, quit. We couldn't agree, so he went. "I didn't want to be a star's lackey," he said – and I quote exactly. So we began in chaos. It's not easy making pictures. The dollar is the new sacrament and the money-changers are in charge and they've all got wives and secretaries with opinions. And none of them trusts the people who're actually making pictures. My heart just dribbles out of the bottom of my toes when I think how this industry works. "Get me the director of *Divorce Italian Style* and we'll make a story proving Rommel was a woman and is now in hiding in South America." That's how it starts. But I'm not going to have anyone messing with our film. Nobody's going to work on it with a knife and fork. If it's going to be wrong, I want it wrong my way.'

The making of *Great Catherine* was an experiment which O'Toole never wished to repeat. To co-produce your own film gave absolute power over the end product, to an extent, but it distracted from the acting – the most important thing as far as O'Toole was concerned. So *Great Catherine* was a lesson in disillusionment. And not only in the business side of film making, which he always expected to include a large number of messy, wasteful, exhausting setbacks. O'Toole was disillusioned by both a good friend and a great actor, Zero Mostel.

Mostel was a close pal and family friend, who had visited his Hampstead home. He was a roly-poly actor, once on the Hollywood blacklist for his left wing beliefs, and a great comedian, both on and off the stage. O'Toole was very fond of him. By the end of shooting for *Great Catherine*, Mostel had worked two days longer than his stipulated contract. He was owed two days overtime, he said. O'Toole could not believe that Mostel, of all people, should demand his pound of flesh – particularly for a film made by a friend with high hopes for breaking the mould of film making in favour of actors. Mostel suggested an alternative. If O'Toole would appear without fee on Mostel's imminent American television special, Mostel would waive the overtime due. O'Toole agreed in principle, but when it came to it, did not arrive for the television recording. Mostel therefore asked for – and got – two more days' pay. O'Toole could not believe a friend and fellow actor could behave in such a mercenary way.

# 8    Tilting at Windmills

BY THE time of *The Lion in Winter*, at the end of 1966, O'Toole knew his way around the film world a lot better. He had seen it from all sides and come to the conclusion that the only way to safeguard a performance was thoroughly to plan the rest of the picture. With *The Lion in Winter* he did just that, and, at the end of filming in May 1967, was able to say with confidence: 'If this one doesn't come off, then I shall hang up my jockstrap and retire.' O'Toole checked and double-checked everything to his satisfaction. The producer Joseph E. Levine had hired O'Toole for a film called *The Ski Bum*, but there was an insurmountable delay because the stage snow and foliage were not ready. To cut his losses, Levine bought the rights to a current Broadway hit, *The Lion in Winter* by James Goldman, and Goldman was asked to prepare a screenplay. A budget of four million dollars was fixed.

It was a project which immediately excited O'Toole. The play was a witty, literate, modern appreciation of the intrigues and bitchery between King Henry II, his wife, Eleanor of Aquitaine, and their three sons, each of whom is set to inherit his father's kingdom. For O'Toole, it was as near as you could get to a stage-piece while working in films. There was plenty of proper acting to be done. He was also amused by the chance to play Henry II again. He had played the character in *Becket* and this would give an unusual opportunity to develop a character with which he was already familiar, a King who has grown older and even more politically efficient since, in his youth, he had had Archbishop Becket murdered at Canterbury.

As O'Toole explained: 'It was marvellous, because they were somehow extensions of each other. It may of course be something I projected on to it, but I'll tell you this, unless I'd played Anouilh's Henry, I couldn't have played Jimmy Goldman's Henry the way I did, 'cause the sense of the loss of Becket filled everything I did in that play, everything. The reason I was practical, bluffing, the reason I was political – they were all things that I was taught by Becket in the Anouilh play. So when I blundered in *The Lion in Winter*, it was because Becket wasn't there. When I played that later Henry, I was bereaved. I don't know if this came across, this central vacant space in the character. I hope that the lack of Thomas Becket in that play was apparent.'

Because the production was quickly dreamed up by Levine, there were few expectations or prior commitments. There were simply O'Toole, Levine and Goldman. The casting had to be established and a director chosen. O'Toole was eager to use his influence. For the part of Eleanor – a tough-speaking, strong part for an older woman – he favoured Katharine Hepburn, the woman who had, nine years before, burst into his dressing room at the Royal Court Theatre, after one performance of *The Long and the Short and the Tall* and told him: 'You're absolutely first class.' O'Toole was very impressed by Hepburn, who was twenty-three years older than he.

She was unpersuadable on the telephone and O'Toole set out to Hollywood to woo her under the pseudonym J. P. Morgan, the name of the American steel and railway millionaire and art collector. She finally agreed, imagining that the work would encourage her out of the gloom she had fallen into since the death of Spencer Tracy earlier in the year. She had not worked since *Guess Who's Coming for Dinner* the year before, which was Tracy's last film and marked the final chapter in their lifetime's partnership on and off the screen. She was not going to dribble into any project simply to pull herself out of it, but thought *The Lion in Winter* read well as a play. And, like the lesson O'Toole had just mastered, she wanted to clear every major casting and artistic appointment before she became too involved.

Both O'Toole and Levine were keen to use as director the British film maker Anthony Harvey, who was just celebrating a *succès d'estime* with *Dutchman*, his first film. O'Toole was first introduced to Harvey by Kenneth Griffith, who had come across him editing films for the Boulting Brothers. Griffith had recommended Harvey to O'Toole as a potential director for the aborted *Godot* film. When *The Lion in Winter* was being planned, O'Toole telephoned Griffith to ask whether he thought Harvey would be the man to direct. Griffith warned that Harvey was good but tough, and that he was the son of the actor Morris Harvey. O'Toole was delighted that acting was in his blood. 'I knew there was something right about him!' O'Toole shouted to Griffith.

Katharine Hepburn was willing to be persuaded of Harvey's virtues, but she had missed *Dutchman*, which had been a critical success but was not granted very wide distribution in America. She said that she would not decide until she had seen it. The difficulty was that it was only playing the midnight-matinée slot in small cinemas and drive-ins – hardly the place to take a senior and twice-Oscar-winning actress. O'Toole located a cinema and took her to see Harvey's film and they seemed to be the only couple in the audience who were there for that purpose. O'Toole reports that the rest were either necking violently or smoking marijuana. They did not prove a distraction to Hepburn, whom O'Toole calls 'this lovely New England puritan': she agreed immediately to the choice of director and confirmed her willingness to join the company.

She still, however, demanded a hand in choosing the cast. A list of established actors was provided, but she turned it away. 'The trouble with most actors today,' she told O'Toole, 'is that they're either skeletons or eccentrics.' O'Toole suggested a solution which would also benefit his interests. He would trawl the young British acting talent in the British provincial theatres and introduce them to film work. This film, he was determined, would be a theatre people's film and acting would come before anything else.

A young British cast was found, among them Anthony Hopkins, John Castle, Nigel Terry and Timothy Dalton. Hopkins remembers the care with which O'Toole handled the auditions and the generous advice, without patronising, which O'Toole gave to all the young actors. One of the texts O'Toole used for the auditions was *Country Dance*, a play he much admired by his friend James Kennaway. When Hopkins, on the set, moaned about O'Toole, Kenneth Griffith took him aside and reminded him that, if it had not been for O'Toole, Hopkins would not have been cast and that O'Toole had fought Laurence Olivier to release Hopkins from his National Theatre contract.

Again, O'Toole used competition as a spur. 'All that crap about never looking behind you because somebody is always gaining on you. It doesn't worry me at all. I love it. Love it. The more the merrier.' And he actively encouraged it on the set. 'I told them at the beginning of the film: the rules are simple. The gloves are off. I'm out to steal every scene. Stop me if you can.' The presence of those young actors, however, made him realise for the first time that he could no longer consider himself a bright young thing, the youngest lead at Stratford, the young star of *Lawrence of Arabia*. Time was moving on and a new generation was coming up quickly behind him.

'It really wasn't until I was doing *The Lion in Winter* with Katie Hepburn,' he remembers, 'that I suddenly realised where I'd got to. There are three brilliant young actors in that film. It never occurred to me that I wasn't their contemporary until one of them came to me for advice on a sex problem. In the middle of the natter, I suddenly realised he was talking to me as though I were his father.' To some extent it was a relief to have grown up a little. On the first morning, he turned to Griffith and said: 'Thank God the pretty boy has gone.' Lawrence had at last been buried.

Before filming began in France, Wales and at the Ardmore Studios at Kilbride, Ireland, the cast spent two weeks rehearsing on the stage of the Haymarket Theatre in London, a process which O'Toole believes to be essential for good film acting. Then filming started and O'Toole had the problem of finding the old Henry of *Becket*, trying him on for size, seeing if he would be the basis of the Henry of *The Lion in Winter*, then ageing the character for the new film. 'I try to do my homework,' he said. 'I've now played Henry II twice and I reckon I can hold my own on the subject with most history scholars. The last time I played Henry, I was searching round for the right voice and suddenly came across a description by one of his contemporaries who said that his voice was like the sound of someone rubbing his heel against glass: again, that gave me the vital clue. I also dropped my voice by an octave. What I did was to buy every Paul Robeson record I could find and then spend an hour each morning accompanying them – it was a sort of "sing along with Paul".'

The main reason for the success of the film, however, for which Katharine Hepburn shared the best actress Oscar, was the special relationship between her and O'Toole. She was, according to O'Toole, 'sent by some dark fate to nag and destroy me'. She and O'Toole developed a haranguing friendship. She called him 'Pig' and he called her 'Nags'. O'Toole used to abuse her quite openly, in the friendliest possible way. 'That bloody female impersonator,' he said. 'You've never seen anything like it. She took me over completely.' He enjoyed every minute of their encounters: 'I just adore her, even if she does hit me. "I only hit people I love," she'd say. "Then for Heaven's sake hate me a little," I'd beg. Working opposite her was extraordinary. With her you have to be one hundred per cent or forget it. She's like a bloody poultice: she pulls a performance out of you.' She made fun of his poorly-received films. ' "You're not a good picker, Pig," she said. "I'm not that bad," I said. "Only one flop since I started." "Don't argue, Pig," she said. "In future send all your scripts to me for approval." So I now appear by kind permission of Old Nags.'

Hepburn was a lively intelligence whose passion was acting and she and O'Toole had rustled up a funny, flirtatious, mutually-admiring friendship. 'Marvellous Kate. Marvellous Kate,' he explained. 'She's perfect. Incapable of being disloyal or telling a lie. I love her. A few years ago, Spencer Tracy wouldn't have stood a chance. I would have chopped his head off. Or broken his fingers. All of them, one at a time.'

Katie Hepburn had also left a deep impression on Sian Phillips, who admired her independence both from other people, since the death of Tracy, and from everyday conventions. 'Kate goes her own way,' said Sian. 'She's given up clothes, just wears trousers and an old jacket, and she doesn't bother with possessions. I think she's got the right idea. In fact I'm gradually working up to it myself.'

Griffith's warnings about Anthony Harvey's toughness turned out to be true. Harvey continually stood up to O'Toole's hectoring manner and would hide in other people's hotel rooms to avoid O'Toole's wrath, as he stomped around trying to get him to change the direction of the film. Although Harvey was nervous and often discourteous to technicians on the set, he was not awe-struck by the presence of O'Toole and Hepburn. When the final print was completed, O'Toole was dissatisfied and angry. He took Griffith and his chauffeur to Harvey's home in Chelsea and thumped on the door with his hands, cursing at Harvey for a particular grievance. Griffith was never told the exact nature of O'Toole's furious complaint against Harvey.

By the time that *The Lion in Winter* was released, O'Toole was thirty-six and felt, somehow, that he had crossed the border into middle-age. Working so closely with young actors – and feeling so close to Katie Hepburn – O'Toole felt part of an older generation. The young actors treated his achievements with respect. Of them all, Anthony Hopkins watched the closest, learning tricks which he would later use in his own film career. The young actors were, O'Toole remembered indignantly, 'looking to me for advice, for bloody guidance'. At one stage, when they decided to swim the River Rhône, he had to step in like a schoolmaster in charge of a school trip. 'That mother is about as wide as the Orinoco in parts and just as treacherous. I had to throw the book at them. The problem was keeping a straight face. I'd done exactly the same thing when I was their age. Playing *Man and Superman* in Switzerland, I'd swum across one of the lakes. In evening dress, as I remember.'

Ironically, it was a schoolmaster that O'Toole was to play next and one that would emphasise growing old: he would age, in five years, until he appeared a decrepit old man. He was riding high. *The Lion in Winter* had been a great personal success – and the public and critics agreed with him. The film won three Oscars: for Hepburn's performance, for John Barry's music and for Goldman's screenplay. Although O'Toole was disappointed that he was not on the roll of honour, he took great pride in the fact that he had carefully prepared every element of the film to his satisfaction and the Oscars reflected his competence as well as their individual efforts.

He accepted another acting change of gear next: a remake of the old 1938 Sam Wood film, *Goodbye Mr Chips*, based upon James Hilton's story of a soft-hearted school-master. O'Toole was to play the part for which Robert Donat is best remembered and which won

Donat his only Oscar. Taking the Greer Garson part was Petula Clark, and playing the headmaster was Sir Michael Redgrave. The new version, to be directed by a new director, Herbert Ross, formerly a choreographer on *Funny Girl* and *Dr Doolittle*, was to be radically different from the original monochrome film.

The producer, Arthur P. Jacobs, had given Ross a budget of two and a half million and it was to be a lavish musical, filmed on location in the ruins of Pompeii and other picturesque locations. The original story told of Mr Chipping's love affair with a woman, Katherine, whom he met on holiday in the Austrian Tyrol in the 1870s. Early in the film, she dies in childbirth. Ross's film was to be set in the 1920s and Chipping first meets Katherine when she is starring in a mediocre London West End Revue called *Hi there, Harry!* Chips meets her again in Pompeii, then Positano and Paestum, before taking her back to his school at Brookfield, much to the chagrin of the stuffy staff who consider her, as a stage singer, little better than a tramp. And she dies, not through childbirth but, while entertaining the troops in a German rocket attack.

O'Toole, wearing round horn-rimmed glasses and a broad moustache – and, according to the studio press release, weighing twelve stone six pounds – was glad to be in new territory and amused to be in a musical. The last time he had sung professionally in public – he had sung many times in public bars, for nothing – was in his Shaftesbury Avenue debut in *Oh My Papa*. But he admired the Sam Wood original. 'I saw the original film with Robert Donat when I was about eight and loved every second of it,' he said, 'but at first the thought of its being done again as a musical filled me with horror. The only thing that cause me to read it was the fact that the script was by Terry Rattigan. Now Terry isn't an oil-painter so much as a line drawer and he's written a beautiful script for the film, elegant down to the last detail.'

There was some high-powered opposition to O'Toole taking the part of Chips, led by a thundering attack from, of all people, Lord Fisher, the former Archbishop of Canterbury who was also a former headmaster of Repton. Perhaps he thought that the man who had on the screen killed Becket inside Canterbury Cathedral should not taint the fond memories of the kindly Robert Donat as Chips. Fisher bellowed: 'No, no, no, Mr O'Toole. I have a very firm idea of the sort of man that Mr Chips was, and you can't possibly play the part.' O'Toole was careful in the wording of his reply. 'If I was good enough to play *three* angels in John Huston's film of *The Bible*,' he said, 'I don't deserve the black ball now.' Fisher gave his nervous blessing.

O'Toole found the character of Chips – 'Incidentally, my Mr

Chips is a fairly dreadful teacher' – in an unlikely source. 'If I'm doing a part that's well-written,' he explained, 'then I know that all I have to do is start digging about and something will happen. With Chips, for instance, I was looking around and suddenly came across a photo of the Irish protest leader, "Potash" Pearce: at once I knew that was exactly how Chips should look.' He also combed his hair off-centre, copying the style of Sean O'Casey.

The return to singing did not cause much trouble. Ross was innovative about musical techniques and wanted to avoid the un-fashionable musical traditions of the 1950s and the original great Hollywood wave of musicals in the 1930s. 'We don't intend to stop the action while Peter or Pet warble their way through a song,' he said. 'That's the way they did it in *Broadway Melody of 1933*. We've updated our technique a bit since then. The songs will come in naturally or there will be one or two dream sequences or memory flash-backs to bring them in unobtrusively.'

This new method suited O'Toole perfectly. He would have found the usual conventions of musicals very trying. 'It's not the sort of screen musical where everything stops for five minutes while some bloke yells the place down. Most of the songs are sung off-screen and are done completely in character. I mean, if I had to sing in my own normal voice, I'd recommend the audience to leave the building right away. In fact, I do my songs in the slightly cracked voice of an ageing schoolmaster, a voice full of chalk and reflections.'

The shooting of *Chips* went well and smoothly, except for the ill-health of Terence Rattigan who was struck with chronic appendi-citis shortly after he arrived on the set. He was rushed to a hospital in Naples, where the conditions were abysmal. The appendix burst and went gangrenous and only the intervention of a British doctor, who ordered that Rattigan be removed immediately from the unhygienic conditions and treated properly, saved his life.

For O'Toole, however, there was little trouble, even though he was back working in Italy and the *paparazzi* were again out in force, hoping to catch him out or tempt him into a brawl. O'Toole had two-fold protection: there was Dave Crowley, proprietor of a bar called Dave's Dive on the Via Veneto, who acted as O'Toole's bare-fisted bodyguard; and there was the blameless company of O'Toole's adviser on public school protocol and etiquette, Robert Powell, Headmaster of Sherborne. There was a great deal of location work at Sherborne and the boys were from the school, paid as film extras in their holidays. And Powell accompanied the cast and crew to Italy, to answer the steady stream of queries about English old-fashioned manners from Ross, an American, and from O'Toole, whose two years of education was at St Anne's, 'an

Irish-Catholic roughhouse elementary at Hunslet, Leeds', not at one of Britain's tradition-tangled public schools.

The *paparazzi*, hoping to catch O'Toole in an indiscreet pose with Petula Clark, kept stumbling across O'Toole and Powell, deep in conversation about English history and literature. Still, the persistent presence of the photographers niggled O'Toole, who was becoming increasingly jealous of his privacy. During a thunder and lightning storm on the set in Pompeii, O'Toole quipped: 'Sacrifice a *paparazzi* to the angry gods.' And O'Toole's behaviour was comparatively moderate. He had announced that he would give up drinking for the duration of the filming and, when in Italy, pretended to keep only to Dom Perignon champagne, which he did not count as alcohol. In fact, he was doing no such thing, swigging away at the hard stuff, as usual.

Technically, however, *Chips* was straightforward and O'Toole managed to obtain the system of working at post-synchronisation that he had instituted in *The Lion in Winter*; working through the rushes in the early evening, laying down the sound while the memories of the day's acting were clear in the mind. O'Toole insisted upon this method to avoid the change of interpretation allowed by overdubbing days or weeks later. O'Toole, in his dedication to acting, tried to keep the voice and the vision paired as it was originally intended on the set. It was yet another attempt to make the wasteful, slipshod, inaccurate process of film making conform to the standards of the theatre.

Although O'Toole was becoming very disillusioned with film work, he was a perfect technician, able to turn on and off as the cameras rolled, able to repeat and identically duplicate a performance until all the elements of the take were to the director's liking. Max Caulfield visited the *Chips* set at Pompeii and gave this verdict: 'Only when the clapperboard bangs and the action begins again does one appreciate why O'Toole appeared so much at ease. He instantly becomes a stooped, celluloid-collared, floppy-hatted, baggy-kneed, crumpled and creased semi-myopic. The flat Leeds tones atomise into the crisp cadences of decent public school English. He takes the scene by the scruff of the neck and pulverises it immaculately.' His make-up was a considerable feat and, when an old man, he was easily able to fool the waiter at a nearby restaurant. But the disguise did not trick Sian, who walked straight up to him and told him how good he would look when he was old and gray.

O'Toole was also helped by the quiet professionalism of Pet Clark, who admitted to being terrified of acting with him, but found him, instead of bullying, to be 'desperately kind and really helpful'. O'Toole and Pet Clark did not have much in common except for their professionalism. Their backgrounds were totally different; her life on the stage since childhood gave her a blinkered view of ordinary life, whereas O'Toole was perpetually conscious of what life outside acting was like. And they maintained a cool, professional relationship, rarely slipping into familiarity. 'Come in out of that sun, or you'll turn into a fig,' was about as close as O'Toole was to come on the public set. And O'Toole did not want for female company.

*Chips* allowed a little time to be spent with Sian. She, too, was in the cast and, when filming in Dorset, they rented a house. It was the nearest thing they had had to a holiday in three years. Success was all very well, but it ate into family life. The response to success was to try to cut themselves off. They were having a house built in Connemara, simply as a place to get away from it all. Until that was built, their holidays were mostly browsing around beautiful cities. 'I don't really like holidays,' Sian explained. 'Work *is* a holiday. Anyway, neither of us likes the hot weather, probably because we were brought up in wet climates. We go to Venice as often as we can – always in the off season when it's raining – and we trudge round, just walking. Pete visits the museums because he collects archaeological pieces. When people know he's a collector they bring things to sell. It worries me because there are so many phonies. Often I think, gawd, there's a year's salary gone on that, but he's never made a mistake yet.'

O'Toole brought a great number of pots and historical objects back from the area around Pompeii, taking advice from the local museum curator and from Bob Willoughby, the publicity photographer who had a keen and sound eye for a good artistic piece. O'Toole would lean heavily upon Willoughby's eye and his knowledge when buying things. Willoughby was able to smell out a fake much more readily than O'Toole, because he had done a great deal of reading and, as a consequence, amassed a large and valuable collection in his home in California. O'Toole had the instinct for a good piece and the intelligence to spot a piece of good art and realise its worth, but he had never acquired the knowledge to match his enthusiasm.

Hunting for pieces in Naples, O'Toole and Willoughby stuck close together. It reached a stage where Willoughby would let O'Toole take first choice and browse for as long as he liked as long as Willoughby was left to keep the pieces which he picked. O'Toole packed up a large number of ceramic objects to take home, even sending one large, precious and very valuable second century Apulian pot to travel in the back of a chauffeur-driven car, to take the less vulnerable route across Europe to London, but disaster struck. When the car suddenly braked, the pot was smashed.

Next on O'Toole's agenda was a film about a Scottish laird,

*Country Dance* (known in the United States as *Brotherly Love*), to be filmed in Ireland by J. Lee Thompson. The part of Sir Charles Henry Arbuthnot Pinkerton Ferguson, commonly known simply as 'Pink', was not far from the Lawrence/Lord Jim/General Tanz/Henry II composite. He is an upper-class, socially reckless, amorous reactionary who rails against progress as much as his own past and was the creation of James Kennaway, a close friend of O'Toole's, who died in a car crash in December 1968 as he drove away from O'Toole's home.

O'Toole was very keen on making *Country Dance* in order to preserve the memory of Kennaway. It was based upon the play of the same name which Kennaway had adapted from his novel, *Household Ghosts*. Kennaway's first novel, *Jock*, had been turned into a successful film, *Tunes of Glory*, starring Alec Guinness and John Mills. The stage play, *Country Dance*, opened at the Hampstead Theatre, very close to O'Toole's home in Heath Street, and O'Toole had seen it and enjoyed it very much, particularly the main role, taken at Hampstead by Edward Fox, of Pink, the wayward Scottish aristocrat who had developed an over-close relationship with his sister. O'Toole had liked it so much that he had used the script, with its rich, dense language, as a test piece for the young actors he found for *The Lion in Winter*. Kennaway had taken seven years to write the play and had had a distant cousin, Susannah York, in mind when writing the part of Pink's sister.

O'Toole and Kennaway had become fast friends. They shared similar personality characteristics: both were loud, thoughtful, romping, larger than life characters. Kennaway had sent O'Toole a provisional screenplay for *Country Dance* when he was filming *Goodbye Mr Chips* and O'Toole was keen to film it. Indeed it was after one of a number of screenplay revision sessions at O'Toole's Hampstead home that Kennaway died, driving home on the M4 to Gloucestershire. O'Toole took it very badly. 'He had not been drinking, although I don't suppose anyone will believe it,' he said. O'Toole was determined that the film should be made, as a tribute to Kennaway, and as Kennaway had intended it – with Susannah York in the part written for her.

It provided a chance to return to work at the Ardmore Studios, outside Dublin, with location work at St Bridget's, Enniskerry. But O'Toole was far from happy during the shooting. The technicians remember him as being very rude to everyone except Susannah York, who was playing opposite him and with whom he established a firm and close friendship. The bad feeling during the shooting became well known throughout the film business. One of the crew who worked with O'Toole on his next project, *Murphy's War*, explained: 'Peter gets paranoiac about people for the first three weeks on a film, then he settles down and he's great, though on *Country Dance* I hear he was unapproachable.'

The film certainly has an atmosphere of gloom over it, even though half of it was filmed on Irish locations and reunited him with many he had worked with before, among them Harry Andrews. From early on, however, it felt as if it was going wrong. O'Toole was at his most manic; the screenplay, which had O'Toole's seal of approval, was disappointing; and the cast and crew were riven with personality clashes.

O'Toole pointed the director, J. Lee Thompson, in the direction of his relatives when looking for a bar as a location. A scene was needed of a pub in a market town on a market day and the bar chosen was the Harbour Bar at Bray, run by O'Toole's uncle, a former Irish Member of Parliament. And it was managed by O'Toole's cousins, Des and Paul O'Toole. It fitted Thompson's bill exactly, an atmospheric bar, crammed with trophies and souvenirs, including a lion's head, which Peter O'Toole had given to them after filming *The Lion in Winter* at Ardmore, and the head of an elk, also given by O'Toole. It also boasts an enormous gravestone, given by Laurence Harvey, when filming *Of Human Bondage*. The film crew took the bar for the day for filming, on condition that the other half of the bar was kept open. O'Toole was not in the scene and took the day off for fishing.

O'Toole was, however, to get into trouble drinking in Dublin. He was staying at the Shelbourne Hotel, one of Dublin's most plush hotels and a meeting place for Dubliners. Drinks there one evening were followed by a tour of Dublin bars, with O'Toole leading a small band of film technicians, actors and hangers-on. By three-thirty in the morning, they had reached The Last Post, a restaurant on Ellis Quay owned and run by Richard Markowski. Before long an argument broke out and Markowski encouraged the O'Toole party to leave. When they did not, he fetched his Alsatian dog, which promptly bit O'Toole and ripped his trousers. O'Toole left the bar with his drinking companions and, when the door was shut, started kicking it. Markowski came outside and confronted O'Toole, who knocked him to the ground.

Unfortunately for O'Toole, the whole incident had been watched by an Irish policeman, one Terence J. Hurson, who arrested O'Toole and testified to what had happened in the Dublin district court. Markowski, the next morning, went to the police station and said that he did not want to pursue the case, but the matter had gone too far. The magistrate hearing the case, Mr Justice Farrell, said that he understood the restaurateur's concern. 'It is understandable that this other party does not want to prosecute,' he said. 'It would not be popular.' O'Toole was in the court and heard the magistrate declare that he would not impose a prison sentence upon him in view of his good character. All the same, he fined O'Toole £30.

And O'Toole was to disrupt shooting with his drinking. Monday morning shooting schedules were arranged without O'Toole because it was known that he would not have returned from the session he had started the previous Friday night. Bob Willoughby remembers one particular bar crawl in Ireland when O'Toole decided to invite a number of the crew to his cottage in Clifden in Connemara. They stopped at a succession of bars, each of which identified themselves as regular stopping-off places for O'Toole because of a signed photograph of himself on the wall. At one bar the critical moment in the journey had been reached when the driver had become so friendly with O'Toole – and so happy from drink – that O'Toole included him in his party and another driver was hired to take them on the rest of the journey.

When they reached O'Toole's cottage, it was pitch black. O'Toole wanted to show them the view and he took them to the edge of the grass, which, during daylight, would look across to the sea and the small islands off Clifden. O'Toole pointed and asked them if the view was not a splendid one. The drinking party gazed into the blackness and, after a little hesitation agreed – indeed, the view was marvellous.

They returned to a bar in Galway, which had remained open behind closed doors even though it was well past closing time. O'Toole delighted in the drama of drinking illegally and made the driver park a great distance from the bar, then, leading the others, he ran across to the wall, pinned himself flat against it, crept up to the door surreptitiously, knocked and slyly entered. As soon as he was in, the others strode boldly across the road into the bar. In the Irish countryside, such play-acting is unnecessary to drink after hours.

It was on this same lost weekend, that O'Toole and his party made a spontaneous impromptu visit on the home of John Huston. Huston was not entirely pleased to see a scruffy group of half-cut film men led by O'Toole. When they arrived at his splendid Irish castle, St Clerans, in Galway, he was having dinner and could be clearly seen through the dining-room window. He glanced towards them but made no acknowledgement. He was, in fact, entertaining a young lady. A butler opened the door and the O'Toole party were invited to enter the drawing-room. Huston left them to stew for a long time as he finished his meal, then showed them round his art-laden mansion. But they never did get to see who the woman was.

The cast and crew of *Country Dance* eventually moved to Scotland, to stay at the Gleneagles Hotel, filming in the area where Kennaway grew up, the real location for all the action in *Country Dance*. O'Toole made a point of visiting Kennaway's parents. However, the gloom in which O'Toole found himself, painfully exorcising the memory of Kennaway, came through into the film, deadening the impact of the performance.

It was given its world première at the Edinburgh Film Festival in 1970, but failed to ignite critical or public attention. O'Toole's personal involvement in the project was widely misinterpreted, as in the pasting given to the film by *Time* magazine: 'Often a good actor and sometimes a great one, Peter O'Toole nevertheless has little talent for concealing his boredom in film projects that seem unworthy of his skills. There is always one sure sign of his desperation: O'Toole begins to twitch. His right eyebrow arches, his mouth creases, one shoulder appears to rise several inches above the other, and his neck bobs back and forth as if a series of tiny explosions were occurring at the top of his spinal column. This invariably happens at moments of great stress, when the actor, not the character, has come to the end of his rope. *Brotherly Love* is so bad a movie that O'Toole appears to be in almost continual spasm from beginning to end.'

After *Country Dance*, O'Toole and Susannah York had the chance to work closely with each other again when, at the end of filming, Eamonn Andrews invited them to play in Shaw's *Man and Superman* at the Gaiety Theatre, Dublin, the idea being that O'Toole would stay for a restorative production of *Waiting for Godot* at the Abbey Theatre, Dublin, before taking it to the Nottingham Playhouse. He was soon back in front of the cameras in *Murphy's War*, to be directed by Peter Yates.

After the disappointing reception given to *Country Dance*, the prospect of working with Yates – the director of the much-acclaimed and highly profitable *Bullitt* – was encouraging. The plot of *Murphy's War* was similar to that of John Huston's *African Queen*, about revenge on the German enemy by one man in a tin-pot boat. O'Toole was to play an Irishman, the sole survivor of a British merchant ship sunk by a German U-boat during World War II, who takes it upon himself to sink the submarine on behalf of his drowned companions. It was another tough, exotic location, like *Lord Jim*. The bulk of the shooting was to be in Venezuela; Sian also had a part; Philippe Noiret, the French actor, was in the cast; and O'Toole's fee was a quarter of a million dollars – the same as that of Peter Yates.

O'Toole had come across the script by chance. It had been sent to Sian and she read it and spotted the part of Murphy and saw it as one to take him out of the doldrums in his career. He asked the producer, Michael Deeley, who was working for the impresario Dmitri de

Grunwald, whether the part had gone and found that Warren Beatty, Lee Marvin and Robert Redford had been offered the role and had each turned it down. Deely offered the part to O'Toole and he happily agreed. Yates, fresh from the success of *Bullitt*, was working with a big budget and O'Toole saw in the part of Murphy a gruelling, physically destructive, thoroughly engrossing character that he hoped would rekindle the magic which had inspired him in the making of *Lawrence*.

Yates, however, was no David Lean and was nervous of O'Toole – so nervous that his ability to guide him through the filming was seriously impaired. O'Toole, for his part, was trying to reclaim some of the masculinity he thought he had lost in the quiet, family pictures he had been doing. 'I was going soft,' he explained. 'That's why I took this part on. I thought I needed toughening up.' He was about to endure the most gruelling, the most mind-stretching experience he had had since the assault course of *Lawrence of Arabia*.

The filming, which began at the end of February 1970, was plagued with bad luck. O'Toole, who knew a thing or two about superstition, thought the answer lay in the title. 'I warned them,' he said. 'You cannot make a picture called *Murphy's War* and not get clobbered. It's all down to Murphy's Law: nothing is as easy as it looks; everything takes longer than you expect; if anything can go wrong, it will and at the worst possible moment. They wouldn't believe their old uncle.' And things certainly went wrong.

The filming, on location on the Orinoco River, riddled with piranha fish, was delayed an expensive ten days because no one had packed the film stock. Delays meant that a pier, specially constructed on the river bank twenty-seven miles from Puerto Ordaz, was submerged by the fast-rising river, swollen by rain in the mountains. The £30,000 jetty had to be rebuilt from scratch above the waterline. A script-girl, who fell off the jetty, was flown back to London but died in hospital of her injuries. Delays also meant that the lease ran out on the battered old tug which Murphy drives insanely towards the German submarine. Negotiations with the wily Venezuelan tug-owner went badly, with the film crew guarding the tug lest it was reclaimed. Meanwhile the owner confiscated an essential part of a crane which was also needed for shooting.

O'Toole was in an odd mood. He and the rest of the cast were irritated by having to live for seven weeks on a former Belfast ferry, the *Odysseus*, steaming up and down the Orinoco delta. He smelt that the filming was going badly and that he would once again be involved with a stinker. He retreated to his expensive air conditioned caravan which was guarded by three armed bodyguards. There had been terrorist activity in the area and a number of foreigners had been kidnapped by the guerrillas. The government of the Orinoco Delta sent seventy-five soldiers to surround the set because it was thought that international film stars would be an obvious target for a kidnapping to draw worldwide attention to the terrorists' cause.

O'Toole was further irritated by this constriction on his freedom and sank into an uncommunicative, glowering temper. He would only talk to Sian and Philippe Noiret. It was generally thought by the technicians and production workers on the set that O'Toole was a first-class pain. René Dupont, the production controller, put it like this: 'I like actors, but I don't like some of the things they ask for. I knew O'Toole would go mad if he didn't get a caravan and air conditioning. I know him from Cambodia and *Lord Jim* days, remember. Actors, like hams, are better when fresh.'

O'Toole, in his turn, could not find a good thing to say about anyone in the film industry. 'One is in the hands of absolute lunatics,' he said. 'Today the film business is run by twopenny-halfpenny bird-brain morons. They excuse their own failure by spreading the propaganda that actors cost too much. That is one of the most delightful pieces of pulp fiction I have ever heard.'

He also started hitting the bottle pretty hard, knocking back spirits from early in the morning. One member of the crew described the mood on the set as 'picnicking on Vesuvius'. Every now and then, O'Toole would arrive from his self-imposed solitary confinement and greet people with warm smiles and cheerily play a game of impromptu cricket, after which he would collapse in a sweaty heap, saying: 'I'm feeling my age now. Daddy's getting old.' He would also go drinking with the crew in a nearby restaurant and end up singing Irish songs. But his moods were always near breaking point. When someone asked why he did not record songs and make a lot of money (Richard Harris had reached the hit parade on both sides of the Atlantic at the time) he became very angry and shouted: 'Never. They are private. Private. For my friends. For me.'

O'Toole, frightened that success would leave him forever, had grown introverted. Sian Phillips said at the time: 'He has a more intense inner life than he used to have. He spends more time alone than ever before.' And O'Toole himself admitted that his inability to find the right sort of material to suit his special talents was beginning to wear him down. 'Success brings prizes,' he said. 'But most of them are consolation prizes. Mostly success has taught me to expect the right hand. Only now I know where to put my guard, because, believe me, it's coming, that right hand, and it's going to hurt. The trick is getting off the floor.' And he was feeling time slipping away. He was growing older. 'What, am I older? Yes. Am I more profound? Not at all. All experience, in my experience, corrupts. You learn too many tricks. Tell me any experience that you've had that has ennobled you?'

Worst of all, O'Toole was becoming disillusioned with acting. 'It's sheer hell. I live it for three months, and every day is agony. I can never hang a part on a peg when I go home. I've been in this game too long to be fooled by it any more. I've never had any illusions. It's got no enchantment for me. But then something clicks, then it's great. Then I love it.'

He was seriously considering one option which would try to claw some of his most enjoyable experiences and recapture some of his old energy: a return to the Bristol Old Vic, his old *alma mater*. He thought he might return to his roots and relive the early excitement of working in a repertory theatre again.

Miles away from the set, O'Toole did enjoy himself. He, Sian and Bob Willoughby set out in the unit helicopter, piloted by the Frenchman, Gilbert Chomat, to explore the Venezuelan jungle. 'Peter has a great sense of adventure,' said Sian. 'He decided we should find the source of the Orinoco River. That's 1,600 miles of river. Well, I have a latent sense of adventure. If it was left to me I would never have gone.'

O'Toole had already been up to Jungle Rudy's Lodge, a small guesthouse made up of a huddle of wooden shacks and a bar where the Rios Churun and Caroni meet. It is an end-of-the-line staging post for the ritzy travellers who make their way out from Caracas to take a five-day trek to the Angel Falls, the highest waterfall in the world, which spills off the top of a flat-topped mountain. It was named after an American bush pilot who once dodged the clouds which smother the view of the falls and landed on top of the flat-topped tepui. His plane got bogged in and he and his passenger – his wife – spent weeks trekking back to civilisation.

It was O'Toole's plan to arrive at the very top of the falls in the unit helicopter, an Alouette 2 – something which no one else had ever done. The four set out and headed for the falls, a breathtaking journey over miles of virgin green forest, spattered with odd luminous trees in yellow and red, then following the wall of stone of the mountain. The map said the falls were 3,212 feet high, but the altimeter read 5,500 feet when they landed on what looked like a single boulder perched just above where the water shot out of the mountain.

O'Toole wanted to see over the edge and, against Sian's advice, crept and crawled so that he was stretched flat out on the rock, peering down. Sian, meanwhile, picked wild flowers unlike any she had seen before. Chomat kept a careful eye on the clouds. If they fell quickly, it would be dangerous to take off, flying blind off the cliff edge. As the clouds moved in, Chomat said: 'I think we must do something.' O'Toole and the other two rushed back to the helicopter and they set off back to Jungle Rudy's. A mile away from their destination, a red light on the dashboard of the Alouette lit up. They were out of petrol. O'Toole thought his Irish luck was up and, when they finally landed, he kissed the ground in thanks.

The thrill of the Angel Falls trip excited O'Toole's appetite for an even more thrilling prospect: the chance to visit the Waika tribe, a primitive people who live deep in the Amazon rain forest, touched only by the hesitant western presence of anthropologists such as Dr Inga Goetz, who had been studying and visiting them for ten years. As soon as O'Toole heard of the Waika, he wanted to see them, but it was not straightforward. The Waika are protected by the laws of Venezuela and can only be approached with the prior consent of the Venezuelan Department of the Interior.

Bob Willoughby arranged a meeting between Dr Goetz whom he knew from the University of California, Los Angeles, and O'Toole and convinced her that O'Toole was genuinely interested in anthropology. Permission was granted for O'Toole, Sian Phillips and Willoughby to make the journey to the Upper Orinoco, on condition that they would not betray where the Waika village was. They set out with Dr Goetz and a pilot in a twin-engined Piper aeroplane to a small mission station, then on by dugout canoe for four hours up the Orinoco. Both O'Toole and Sian Phillips used their acting skills to learn from Dr Goetz as many Waika words as possible, including 'shori noje', meaning 'good friends'.

They were greated at the Waika village with astonished looks. No one had seen anyone as tall as O'Toole, whom they quickly nicknamed 'High Mountain'. And they were fascinated by Sian, whom they explored all over with their hands, groping her body and her breasts. 'They had never seen white people before,' said Sian. 'They tried to pull my clothes off to see if we were the same all over.'

At first, only the women and children came forward to meet the party, the men staying behind. But gradually the males, their penises strapped upwards by a string around their waists, advanced to make friends. They showed O'Toole how to fire their longbows, which were almost twice as tall as them and a little taller than O'Toole. And they showed him how to sniff the drug *ebena*, a hallucinogenic substance which one Waika blows up the nose of another using a long bamboo blowpipe. He saw wapu fruit being ground and turned into bread. In return for a sheath knife, O'Toole was given a bow and some arrows and a woven basket.

The visit to the Waika village was unlike any experience which O'Toole had had and encouraged him to explore other remote parts of the world when he had the chance. It was after this that he became fond of Mexico; accepted odd but potentially interesting invitations like one from President Marcos of the Phillipines; and was inspired to go on safari in Africa. And, while in South America, he and the Willoughbies went to Machu Picchu, the old Inca fortress.

When *Murphy's War* was released at the Radio City Music Hall, New York, in July 1971, and at a royal charity première attended by Princess Alexandra in London in January 1971, the scale of the disaster was clear. O'Toole had been right to be depressed. Although made on a huge scale, Yates came up with none of the skills which had lifted *Bullitt* from a humdrum crime thriller to one of the most exciting films of the 1960s. O'Toole was all over the place and his accent followed him, flitting from Irish to cockney to Liverpudlian, although he had based it upon that of a Dublin-born technician on location. Only Sian Phillips comes out of the film with distinction. Her part, as a hospital doctor who tends Murphy's wounds, stands out from a rash of mediocrity.

Of all the American reviews, only a couple were favourable and the vast majority were negative. Gary Arnold of the *Washington Post* wrote: 'Evidently O'Toole is playing an Irishman for the first time on screen, and considering how he overdoes it, one rather hopes it's the last time.' And Charles Champlin, from the *Los Angeles Times*, was just as unflattering: 'Peter O'Toole's performance is all flash mannerisms and unintelligibly gargled accents. He conveys only an airy disbelief in everything that is happening.' The film which the producers boasted before the American première would put into reverse the fashion for films like *Easy Rider* and *Midnight Cowboy*, seemed feeble stuff. O'Toole's final verdict on *Murphy's War* is this: 'It was just a good, uncomplicated funny adventure story. I loved doing it. And it didn't attempt profundity. That's why we did it.'

O'Toole tried to recover his confidence in himself by finalising the arrangements to film a project which he and Richard Burton had dreamed up on the set of *Becket* – a film of Dylan Thomas's 'play for voices', *Under Milk Wood*. A clash of filming schedules had repeatedly delayed their start on the film, as had Burton's elaborate tax-dodging itinerary. To avoid a large British tax bill, Burton – unlike O'Toole – rationed the amount of time that he spent in Britain. In 1971, his schedule allowed him some spare days in Britain and he agreed to spend them in Fishguard, West Wales and London with O'Toole filming *Under Milk Wood*. Elizabeth Taylor was also going to take part and none of them would accept a fee, merely £10,000 each for 'expenses', although, if the film made an unexpected profit, all three would benefit. Burton and Taylor had made a similar high-art, low commercial potential film in *Dr Faustus* for Dr Nevil Coghill at Oxford.

O'Toole appeared as Captain Cat, Burton as First Narrator and Taylor as Rosie Probert. O'Toole grew a moustache and beard, which were dyed grey, and he wore a grey wig and a false nose. Andrew Sinclair directed from his own script, the film was co-produced by Jules Buck and Hugh French with a budget of £300,000 provided two-thirds by the British National Film Finance Corporation, one third by Hill Samuel, the British merchant bank. A simultaneous sound record was produced.

Burton's verdict on the film was: 'It's quite remarkable how Elizabeth has got the Welsh accent. And O'Toole is absolutely marvellous.' But Paul Ferris, who has written biographies of both Dylan Thomas and Richard Burton, was more critical: 'The film they made was no better or worse than might have been expected of a well-meaning attempt to find ways of illustrating Thomas's "play for voices". There was much scenery and demented frolicking.'

Certainly the small scale of the production brought many rewards. O'Toole did his five days filming in Wales, wearing milky coloured double contact lenses, which were agony to wear. He had suggested them himself as far more convincing than black glasses. By the end of the first day he could only bear to have them on for a half an hour at a time and later found that everything had to be done in five-minute takes before he was forced to take them off. This meant that he had to be word perfect each time; a feat he was proud to achieve. For his last four shots, which were each quite long, he could bear the lenses no further and Sinclair had to film either from behind or with O'Toole's eyes shut.

Sian Phillips had a part, wearing her own wedding ring and her engagement ring back to front and O'Toole, who, like Burton, had known Dylan Thomas well, was delighted to be performing such a fiercely Welsh piece. 'I have a Welsh wife, a Welsh mother-in-law and two half-Welsh children,' he explained. 'I had to learn Welsh to speak with my family. And that is more than Dylan Thomas can say. He couldn't speak a single word of Welsh.'

The intimacy of the set in Wales also helped life away from the camera. O'Toole was immensely relaxed, as was Burton, mainly because Elizabeth Taylor had decided to do all her filming for the picture in a London studio. One night, O'Toole led all the male members of the crew in a game of the cuckoo song, in which all of them standing in a circle had to drop their trousers while O'Toole told a ludicrous tale. Anyone who dared smile, giggle or laugh was deemed out.

There was also a neat demonstration, when the filming had

returned to London, of the flagrant double-standard which both Burton and O'Toole indulged in. They loved – and still love – to curse the press for invading their privacy, while liking to take advantage of the publicity and resulting increased fees that it can provide.

One lunchtime, Burton took the actress with whom, in the film, he romped naked, to a small, quiet restaurant near the Lee Studios at Shepherd's Bush, London. Burton asked her to arrange for them to sit at a quiet table in the corner, so that he would not be disturbed by celebrity-spotters. O'Toole was to come and join them later. The table was arranged and they took their places. No one recognised Burton, who sat quietly in the corner. Then O'Toole burst in. As he did so, Burton leapt onto a table and sang a verse of a song in Gaelic. O'Toole leapt to another and sang the second verse, and so on. The 'quiet lunch', which Burton had insisted upon, became a publicity stunt, with both actors bawling at each other and attracting a large crowd who came in off the street to see what all the fuss was about.

For all his anxiety that he should avoid being type cast, O'Toole had, whether he liked it or not, become clearly indentified in the public mind with a certain sort of aristocratic, eloquent lunatic: a type he willingly embraced in his next film project, *The Ruling Class*.

Peter Barnes had taken two years to write this black comedy about a mad earl, which was given a first performance at the Nottingham Playhouse. It was well received and transferred to the Piccadilly Theatre. As soon as O'Toole saw it, he thought that the part of the 14th Earl of Gurney, originally played by Derek Godfrey, was just the sort of expansive part he needed after the small-scale theatrical performances he had been giving. And there were advantages to taking a theatre play and transforming it into a film. O'Toole's boast that he was the authors' advocate was not idle. He much preferred a close collaboration between the author and the actor, leaving the director to look after the lighting and the sets. Having convinced Jules Buck that *The Ruling Class* was a suitable project and brought in Jack Hawkins as co-producer, O'Toole bought the film rights from Barnes for £55,000, plus a percentage of the profits of a film if there was one. Barnes was also commissioned to write the screenplay and Peter Medak was hired as director.

O'Toole saw the 14th Earl as a part tailormade for him, although the very eccentricity of the part he conceded made it extremely difficult to play. He relished the prospect of saying such lines as, when asked why the lord is so certain he is God: 'Simple. When I pray to Him, I find I'm talking to myself.' O'Toole described it as a 'comedy with tragic relief' and, although he thought Barnes 'a funny little misanthropist who shuts himself up in the British Museum all day', he liked his fascination with film facts. 'If you want to know who made Buster Keaton's jock-strap in 1928, he'll tell you.'

Filming began in May at Twickenham Studios, then on a variety of locations. At Twickenham they built the interior of Gurney Manor, stocked with armoury from Bapty and paintings from one of the principal locations, Harlaxton Hall. On the second day of shooting at Harlaxton, so many members of the crew were getting lost in its rooms and corridors, that each of them was issued with a map of the building. A replica of the interior of the House of Lords was built at Twickenham, the old earl's farewell speech was delivered in the banqueting hall of the Worshipful Company of Stationers and Newspaper Makers and exterior shots of Gurney Manor were filmed at Cliveden, once home of the Astor family. The Gurney estate village was filmed at Shere.

Although O'Toole was delighted to surround himself with first-class English actors, such as Alastair Sim, Arthur Lowe – whom the critics thought stole the film – Harry Andrews and Michael Bryant, he was well aware that he was running the risk of being upstaged. 'I've gathered these lunatics just to ruin me,' he said. 'I stand no chance. First Arthur Lowe steals the scene, then Sim. I'm just the feed. They're all pissing on my grave.'

O'Toole was delighted to be working with such a cast, but had become gloomy about the way cinema was going. He was guessing that the trends towards more sex and more violence would leave him washed up. He told David Lewin: 'There is too much sex. I have bawled and brawled my way around and I am no prude, but sex is something to be enjoyed, not sniggered over or gaped at. That is why I was so anxious to make *The Ruling Class*, because it has no violence and the sex is light and frolicsome and gay. What it attacks is the closed heart and the closed mind: they are the dangers today.'

The completed print of *The Ruling Class* turned out to be immensely long – so long that United Artists, who owned the North American rights, wanted to make substantial cuts. O'Toole was indignant and said the film was uncuttable and that it must run the full 154 minutes. United Artists were adamant that the length would adversely affect their ability to make money on it and passed on the rights to Avco Embassy, who at first agreed not to cut the film, but ultimately, still with opposition from O'Toole and Buck, cut six minutes. The film was chosen to be the official British entry at the Cannes Film Festival 1972. (When released in France, it was known as *Dieu et Mon Droit*.)

The American reception of the film was middling, the general view being that even if Peter Barnes's attack on the British aristocracy was tiresome, the film was worth watching for O'Toole's performance.

Much was made of O'Toole's dyed blond hair. Vincent Canby, of the *New York Times*, wrote that O'Toole's make-up was 'like Barbara Stanwyck in *Double Indemnity*.' *Time* magazine's Jay Cocks was one of the most generous to O'Toole. He wrote that the 'film will be remembered for Peter O'Toole's Jack, a performance of such intensity that it may trouble sleep as surely as it will haunt memory – funny, disturbing, finally devastating, O'Toole finds his way into the workings of madness, revealing the anger and consuming anguish at the source.'

Although relatively happy about his performance in *The Ruling Class*, O'Toole was generally more pessimistic about life. He was openly questioning how long he would be able to keep up the pace he had set himself. In the September of 1971, before *The Ruling Class* was released, he went to Connemara on holiday with Robert Shaw and his family, who owned a house nearby. He had talked to Shaw many times about starting a small theatre in Ireland together. He had recently planned to convert a disused railway station at Clifden, County Galway, into a theatre, but, unable to face the administration involved in starting such a venture, he abandoned the idea. He was toying with the idea of finding a theatre where he could put on a season of plays – three plays under one roof, played in repertory, and a return to the Bristol Old Vic was once again in his mind.

After the holiday in Ireland, his next film project was already lined up and under way – a musical, which he had never seen, *The Man of La Mancha*, for which Sophia Loren had already started singing lessons. His songs were to be more demanding than those in *Goodbye Mr Chips* and this time it seemed likely that someone else's voice would be used. Nevertheless, during November and December 1971, he began voice training, and during that time he began to learn as much as he could about Don Quixote and his creator. By the beginning of shooting, the director, Arthur Hiller, was impressed by his knowledge: 'There isn't a thing Peter doesn't know about Cervantes.'

The film of *The Man of La Mancha* had had an odd history. It began as an American stage musical based on Cervantes' *Don Quixote* in November 1965 and was directed by Albert Marre. By December 1969, the stage show was to be made into a film musical, also to be directed by Albert Marre. Later, Marre stood down and Peter Glenville, who had directed *Becket*, was asked to direct, make various major casting decisions and also do a film treatment. Glenville signed O'Toole as Don Quixote and delivered a screenplay based more upon the original Cervantes story than on the stage musical.

The producers were incensed. They had paid a fortune for the film rights to the musical and Glenville had had the cheek to deliver them a script based on the original book, which was in the public domain. In July 1971, Glenville was replaced by Arthur Hiller, the film director who had made, among others, *Love Story*, a most successful weepie starring Ryan O'Neal and Ali McGraw. Hiller was well known as a trouble-shooting director who could rescue any large scale project from impending disaster. His technique was to master the logistics of the business side, keeping the film on schedule, while allowing the actors to look after the artistic side. Inevitably, this encouraged a lack of respect for Hiller from the actors.

Filming began at Dinocitta, the studio outside Rome formerly owned by Dino de Laurentiis and where O'Toole had filmed *The Bible* with John Huston in January 1972. All except the windmill jousting scenes were to be filmed there. O'Toole constantly referred to Hiller as 'Little Arthur' – 'not "little" because I am putting Arthur down. God forbid.' However, he got on terribly well with Sophia Loren. He nick-named her 'Scilicone' from the first rehearsal and, according to O'Toole, she 'just cracked and fell around the room'. O'Toole became a great admirer of Loren's guile. 'My first impression was of a well turned out, extremely skillful piece of machinery. It was much later, when we began to work together, that I could see her for what she was. No crap, no artifice – just an extraordinary, sexually attractive lady.'

And he admired her professionalism, making sure that she stole the scenes. 'She has this absolutely unstoppable clockwork professional mechanism put together over the years that tick-tocks, tick-tocks on and on.' O'Toole was hardly equipped for a fair fight. His make-up took two hours to prepare and he was then dressed in plastic armour and set up on high heels. Loren suffered no such handicap. 'They tried to deglamorise her for the role. Failure. The less glossy she is, the more attractive she becomes, especially in the legs apart, blouse ripped, eyes flashing posture. I also discovered she has a favourite profile and she arranged things accordingly. To make sure of it her contortions were magnificent. Her lightning legwork, ducking and weaving, would shame Mohammad Ali. And she was absolutely open and unblushing about the whole thing. I just trotted along on my high heels, poking my head into the lens when I could, mouthing those miserable lyrics and hoping for the best.'

When it came to it, O'Toole's voice did not come up to the standard that Hiller expected. Arthur Hiller explained: 'Peter's got a lot of very difficult songs. That "Impossible Dream". Oh, if it were a matter of just putting in the high notes with some other voice – we've done that many times. Fortunately Peter's not on an ego trip like a lot of actors, at least as far as his voice is concerned. He'll be happy if we can use him; if not, well, he understands.' O'Toole understood. Where his singing did not make the standard – which was for most of it – his voice was dubbed by Simon Gilbert. Even so, six songs were recorded but not used in the film's final cut.

It was a happy set and O'Toole was untroubled by the *paparazzi*. Between scenes, Sophia Loren, James Coco, who played Sancho Panza, as he had done in the stage version, and O'Toole played a lot of poker. 'Scilicone swung from cool reserve to a scratching, gesticulating, cursing Neapolitan,' according to O'Toole, whereas he did 'nothing, I swear, except a little simple bullying and cheating. True, we ganged up on Coco by concealing deuces and aces in my boots and her tits, but I will say this for him and her – they have genuine mirth. So bloody rare.' He got on with Loren much as he got on with Katharine Hepburn and most other women with a strong character: 'Magnificently! I love that cow!'

Loren's professionalism was also generous – as O'Toole described when telling of his death scene: 'I was lying there on the floor, apparently dead, and holding my breath as long as I could. But it isn't easy, mate. And holding your breath after loudly singing a ditty isn't any easier. Anyway, the good Sophia saw my predicament and was superb. She bunched my nightie so I could catch breath. She slyly covered a visibly thudding vein in my neck with her hand. She hid the folds in my false forehead with the hem of her dress. She made me look what I was – dead.'

And O'Toole got close to her in a way that few others except her husband, Carlo Ponti, have managed. One night she phoned O'Toole from her villa to tell him that she was pregnant. Carlo Ponti was away, her sister, Basilio, was in Nice and she had to tell someone. So O'Toole became the first to know that she was expecting a baby. At the end of the film, and the four-and-a-half month shooting schedule, they exchanged presents. She gave O'Toole a bronze replica of a Sicilian warrior, complete with drawn sword. He gave her a line of sharks teeth strung as a necklace. And they continued writing to each other when filming was over. Her next project was *The Journey* with Richard Burton. O'Toole could not resist writing, from Connemara: 'The news is all over Ireland that I am spitting blood at the moon, aghast because you have abandoned me for a bandy-legged pockmarked little Welshman.'

The completed film was badly received. Only one senior American critic found anything good to say about the whole production. Once again, however, O'Toole came in for some good notices amid bad reviews for the film overall. His choice of project, rather than his acting, was at fault. Pauline Kael, of the *New Yorker*, described him as 'like an elongated Alec Guinness'. And: 'He has the staring, unseeing eyes of a harmless madman, and a facial tic – a rattled shake of disbelief. His woefulness is so deeply silly that he turns into a holy fool, and, with the barber's basin on his head, a Christ figure – yet funny.'

David Robinson, of *The Times*, felt he had seen it all before: 'He has become a very strange performer, spitting and mouthing his lines with the excessive vowels of a twenties stage juvenile, and stubbornly keeping all his acting forward of his welling, stretched-open eyes. We have seen too many great Quixotes – Chaliapin in Pabst's film and Cherkassor in Kosintzev's – to feel much indulgence for this one.' But Arthur Knight, of the *Saturday Review*, was more indulgent: 'Peter O'Toole plays Cervantes' hero with extraordinary delicacy and restraint and makes the Don delightfully daft and yet affectingly moral and courageous. It is, after far too long a period of self-indulgence, his finest work since *Lawrence of Arabia*.'

But the compliment came too late for O'Toole to take into account when planning his withdrawal from acting. He was forty in August 1972 and it was a watershed date which he was determined to mark with a reassessment of his life. He was, first, fed up with the film industry. 'There aren't any real movie-makers any more,' he said. 'The business is run by the cornflakes men. And they're only in it for the girls. You used to join amateur dramatics to get at the crackling. These men buy up studios to achieve the same end. You see them flying around in their private jets with birds we used to hide under the table fifteen years ago. It's insane. Crackling should be an added bonus, not an end in itself.'

But, most of all, he was exhausted – his ill-health had returned and it slowed him down – and that exhaustion made him fed up with himself. He started thinking about taking some time off – what others would call a sabbatical, although he did not like to think of it as such. 'I don't go along with the phrase about "recharging the batteries" which is rather grand for a mummer, but I've been at it for twenty years now and I've got to the stage where I dread having to go to work in the morning, even though there is no work at this minute for me to go to. It is bad enough to dread having to go to work when you are in work – but to dread it when you are not is worse. So maybe I will just rest and write a bit and see what happens.' And that is what he did. Still sporting the pointed beard he had grown for Don Quixote, he set off to Connemara for a long rest, which was to last over a year.

# 9   The Rogue Male

'I'M VERY tired, really I am. Genuinely tired. Fed up with acting and the cinema and the theatre. I've done too much. Twenty years of it in one uninterrupted lump.' Thus O'Toole began his self-imposed exile to his house in Connemara, County Galway, his bolthole away from it all. For years he had used it as a private health farm, to drain away the tensions of the hectic, crazy life of learning lines, repeating them endlessly, clashing with egos like his own and, worse, having to jump through hoops for those for whom he had no respect. O'Toole had had enough and had decided to do something about it by breaking away from his career and going it alone.

He was building a new home on the west coast of Ireland and wanted to become involved, build himself a new jetty, spend some time in his boat, dig the drains for his new house. The ten years since *Lawrence of Arabia* had been good years for O'Toole, never mind that the critics and often the public did not agree. He had worked almost without stopping and had a healthy bank balance which allowed him some independence. 'I know a lot of people in my game who are fed up or disenchanted or whatever,' he explained, 'but they carry on because they're professionals. Well, I could do that, but I don't have to. I don't think I've the temperament to just turn up and turn in conservative, well-rehearsed, sort of blueprint performances. I may be forced to, of course. I don't have a limitless supply of money. I'd rather focus on something else for a while – read, dig the garden, see the cottage go together, get the boat ready.'

O'Toole took time off for regeneration, but what he was to return to in a year's time was a theatrical and cinematic world that he did not recognise, that had passed him by. From this quiet year onwards, his work would be more slight, more uninteresting than ever. And it was not only his work that would go downhill in the decade from 1972. He would break up from his wife; he would suffer the most debilitating illness; his name would become a laughing stock in the world of theatre.

O'Toole, however, thought that a year away from the work which obsessed him would change his career for the better. Indeed, he was immensely openminded about the type of work he might return to. One idea he clearly had in his mind was to begin writing in earnest, although he was nervous about even mentioning it. 'I don't think I'm a writer,' he said in the month before he left Britain for a year. 'Well, not a *writer* writer. I don't fancy even trying to lock myself in a study and believe people in a novel. It's hard enough trying to be one. But journalism is attractive. It always has been. And the halls of academe beckon a little. I've no formal education and wouldn't mind studying for a year – for no end. Then, of course, I dabble with archaeology and that fascinates me. But I don't know. I really don't know.'

And so he took a year off. From the end of 1972 to October 1973 he lived a quiet life with his wife and daughters and, most importantly, with himself. He quietened down. He began to sleep more than he had ever managed before. He entertained a very small number of people – the closest of close friends – to kitchen suppers in his glorious cottage which he was finishing with his own hands. It is a short distance outside the village of Clifden, a one street piece of haphazard ribbon development with a stone, steepled church at either end. Out of the village and along the coast road, you come across O'Toole's home, a larger house than all the rest, built two stories high of local stone. The house is surrounded by a stone-built terrace which looks out to sea. O'Toole planted all the trees, shrubs and flowers himself, although the harsh Atlantic wind has meant regular replacement.

Inside the door, off the gravel driveway, the hall is a crowded muddle of family coats and shoes. Country clothes take up space and there are hats of all sorts, brogue shoes and green Wellington boots. The drawing-room, built by O'Toole to his own specifications, has two large windows which look straight out to sea and some small, low exposed islands. It is a grand room for such an ostensibly modest dwelling. There is a high ceiling, the walls are covered in wood panelling and there is a large stone fireplace on which O'Toole burns peat. In front of the fire is a wide, deep, comfortable modern sofa. And against one wall is a large Irish dresser, a sideboard with shelves, which holds the ugly bits and pieces of modern stereo equipment.

And it was here that O'Toole sat out his year, making a home of a shell with the help of an unlikely book called *Bungalow Bliss* – 'No one should be without it. I became fascinated by sewers, I don't mind telling you: a real drain brain,' – and of his architect, Leo Mansfield.

At that time there was no electricity at his part of Clifden. He drove his car or rode a horse around the countryside, near the rock erected to celebrate the arrival of Alcock and Brown in the first ever Transatlantic flight by aeroplane from Newfoundland. And he explored the history of the countryside, littered with historical and archaeological treasures, such as the fairy ring nearby and the marking stone on top of an island within sight of his drawing-room window. O'Toole amused himself, making regular visits to Frank Murphy's bar in Clifden, becoming a regular in his local, as much an uncelebrity as a world-famous actor can be in so small a community. He did some rough shooting, mostly at crows. He read. He listened to music. He walked and tramped across the fields, up the mountains and along the shore. He fished for fun. But most of all he had nothing to do with films or the theatre.

The nearest he came to it was to try to purge the memory of his ridiculous adventures in the film world in a piece of extended writing, entirely autobiographical, which he hoped might someday become a book, with the provisional title *Loitering With Intent*, which he thought summed up his life. Five years later this manuscript was sent to Jonathan Cape, the London publishers, who were very encouraging about it, even though it had been sent anonymously through a third party. They wanted the book to be finished, but O'Toole would or could not oblige.

And he learnt other useful skills. Some workmen helping him with his drains taught him how to divine water with a twig – or at least encouraged him to discover if he could. He discovered, too, that his mother and his daughter Kate also had the knack, although Sian and daughter Pat could not. He was also able to divine water with three eggs, one which spins between the other two when water is under-foot. He lost himself in the country life, so much so that when Katharine Hepburn arrived, unexpectedly, to see how he was, she asked him whether he thought he was escaping from civilisation. 'Hell, no!' he told her. 'This *is* civilisation.' But as his promised year off drew to an end, he was really no clearer in his mind about what he wanted to do simultaneously to revive his career and, more impor-tantly, to avoid it becoming a drudge once more. He decided to extend the joys of discovering his roots in Ireland by exploring the roots of his own career, which meant an approach to the Bristol Old Vic, to see if they wanted him back.

The city of Bristol holds a very important key to O'Toole's life and the small eighteenth century auditorium of the Bristol Old Vic is precious to him. 'In Bristol it all happened,' he explained. 'I fell apart, and found my own little pieces and put them together again. My own private jigsaw puzzle, as it were.' It was a place which, irrationally, he would return to for reassurance. 'Bristol became my home; I was accepted there, and it's where I became *me*. You see, when I left Bristol, I was famous, and the city haunted me.' In September 1973, it was announced that O'Toole would be returning to the Bristol Old Vic, a theatre which had, apart from the main auditorium, been drastically modernised into a modern arts complex, complete with Siddons Bar and Buttery.

He was to begin with the title role in Chekhov's *Uncle Vanya* at the beginning of October; then continue with the role of D'Arcy Tuck in Ben Travers's farce *Plunder*, at the end of October; and also play King Magnus in Bernard Shaw's *The Apple Cart* at the end of November. The first six weeks he found hard work, rehearsing one play during the day and acting in another at night. But he enjoyed hard work and, in as much as Val May, the Bristol Old Vic's artistic director, could arrange it, no special fuss was made of him. At O'Toole's insistence, he was allowed to be simply another member of the repertory cast.

Kenneth Griffith visited him there and they walked the haunted streets together. And he had two old friends from his first Bristol incarnation to ease him back into theatrical work: Nat Brenner, the principal of the Bristol Old Vic Theatre School, directed *Plunder*, and Edward Hardwicke, an actor who used to share a dressing room with him, returned for *Uncle Vanya*. Brenner, in particular, was a help and a guide, even a confidant, and he respected O'Toole as an old-fashioned actor: 'When he came here first, he and Finney were being talked about as the new type. But he's old-fashioned in the sense that his emphasis is on techniques and skills and working in a first-class company. And he has this terrific admiration for the qualities of other actors. He makes special journeys to see them.'

O'Toole was particularly keen about playing in *Plunder*, for he was envious of actors like Cary Grant who could slip so easily into farce, with absolute conviction. He opened to packed houses – his name was still box-office magic – but the press and London critics gave him a quiet re-entry. O'Toole was grateful for this muted reaction. After all, he had wanted a modest return to acting. But he was also wary. The quietness disturbed him.

The hard evidence of his decline in appeal came from the luke-warm offers he was getting. Of all the scripts being shown to him, nothing was coming up to the standard he thought he deserved. He even stumbled upon a leading role by default when, signed for a small part in Otto Preminger's adventure film, *Rosebud*, he was quickly promoted into the principal part when Preminger and Robert Mitchum, in the starring role, fell out amid accusations that Mitchum had been drinking too much. O'Toole had nothing better to do when, only four days into the shooting, he was telephoned in London by Preminger and summoned to Corsica. It was hardly the calibre of project O'Toole had been used to. It was a sloppy and mildly sensational screenplay based upon a novel by Joan Hemingway, grand daughter of Ernest, about a quintet of rich girls, each the daughter of a western magnate, who were kidnapped by Black September terrorists.

Mitchum, then O'Toole, played a *Newsweek* journalist who was also a CIA agent, deputed to track them down. There was no chance of O'Toole following the style of Mitchum, and Preminger allowed him to improvise. There was a fair-to-good cast including Richard Attenborough, Peter Lawford, Isabelle Huppert and Lalla Ward, but for the rest of them it was no more than a routine picture to make a little money. For O'Toole it was an important return to the cinema and he was unhappy that it should happen in such a haphazard way. There was a two million pound budget, location work in Corsica, Paris, Hamburg, Berlin, Tel Aviv, Jerusalem and Haifa, which sounded all right, but O'Toole was aware that Preminger was way past his best.

O'Toole tried hard to make it more than a routine thriller and those who worked near him were impressed at the way he gradually injected a little life and humour into an otherwise lifeless part. A French film historian, allowed to sit in on the filming, described the gradual change in the O'Toole character, noting that he had made the journalist 'a sort of dandy, a little neurotic, precious, perhaps secretly ill . . .'. O'Toole was playing the part to his own specifications and, apparently, basing his assumed role on his own character. Still he was nervous and certainly not up to a severe test of his sense of humour arranged by Kenneth Tynan.

In Paris the crew were filming in the flat of Tom Curtis, an American friend of Tynan's and a *Herald-Tribune* journalist. Tynan remembered: 'I left a letter, written in the most exaggerated terms, accusing O'Toole of being a renegade Irishman and a traitor to true IRA terrorists. I warned him that a dangerous explosive device would be detonated on the set.'

Preminger remembers it this way: 'The apartment was located on the second floor of the Tour d'Argent building. Curtis moved to a flat on the fifth floor that belonged to a friend of his. When I arrived with the crew at seven in the morning to prepare for the first day's shooting, we found a letter addressed: *Peter O'Toole, Personal and Confidential*. O'Toole's call was for eleven o'clock. Upon arrival he opened the letter. It contained a note advising that the writing was reversed and could only be read by holding it up to a mirror. It was a vicious letter berating O'Toole for acting in a film against the Palestinians, who were in the same boat as the Irish. It threatened to stop the production with violence, starting with a bomb that would explode at noon and tear the building apart. We cleared the building at once.'

Noting that Curtis had not left the building, Preminger challenged him for an explanation. Curtis replied: 'It's just a joke. I had a few friends here for dinner last night, among them Kenneth Tynan. He wrote it as a prank.' Preminger telephoned Tynan and swore at him. 'I felt that particularly at a time when bombs explode daily and kill innocent people, his "prank" was cruel, stupid and vicious.'

When they resumed filming, O'Toole was missing. He had found out Tynan's flat, arrived with two beefy members of the crew and set about him. Tynan, already suffering from bronchial trouble and a hernia, sent a letter by hand to Preminger after the incident, complaining of O'Toole's behaviour. He wrote:

'Dear Mr Preminger, Today one of your employees, Peter O'Toole, has very capably beaten me up, I presume not on your instructions or with your knowledge. From his point of view the dispute has been – very audibly – settled by physical force. Like any competent secret policeman, he took care not to draw blood and aimed nearly all his blows beneath the belt. This was very unfortunate because (as I thought he knew) I have a fairly notorious hernia and the effect of having my balls repeatedly punched was to send me straight to a doctor. That I have a clear case of assault against Peter is beyond doubt.'

Tynan explained that his letter was written as a joke, like an applepie bed, and that he had intended to give O'Toole 'a start and a laugh'. He continued: 'Nobody, (I thought) could possibly have taken it for anything other than a parody' and, after apologising, added: 'I suppose O'Toole could be said to have demonstrated his machismo (His steel-blue eyes glinting, Sheriff O'Toole kicked his cowering Apache in the gut . . .) I am not a pugilist; in my physical condition it wouldn't pay. If O'Toole had tried to con *me*, I would have riposted in kind, and probably beaten him at his own game, because I am just conceivably cleverer.' It was an unfortunate end to their never very warm friendship.

*Rosebud* was released at the end of March in London, and David Robinson, of *The Times*, dismissed it, poking particular fun at O'Toole for his 'consonants aspirated somewhere between the manners of Charles Laughton and Bette Davis'. Dilys Powell, however, was glad to see the return of O'Toole: '*Rosebud* has, however, one discovery. Peter O'Toole as the CIA man plays with a lackadaisical composure dead right for the infallible agents of spy fiction. One hopes to see him again in a role of the same sort.' Sadly for O'Toole, roles of the same sort were the only ones available.

O'Toole's final memory of *Rosebud* is: 'It was very odd. In Germany, Otto stumbled along in a sort of mad apoplexy most of the time, saying: "Ze real Nazis are Austrians. I know, I am an Austrian!" One scene he directed from a car. He just rolled down the window: "Action! Cut!" We got on. Off the set he's the most civilised and civilising man. On the set he's unbelievable.' In *Rosebud* they had had a single, very minor tiff, which O'Toole thought was good going.

Next for O'Toole came two films in Mexico, a country that he came to love so much that he bought and still owns a house in Puerta Vallerta, a town made famous for *The Night of the Iguana* filmed there, and because Richard Burton and Elizabeth Taylor had also bought a house there. To rescue O'Toole from the doldrums, Jules Buck and Gerald Green produced a film version of Daniel Defoe's *Robinson Crusoe*, updated as an anti-imperial, anti-racist political allegory with a screenplay by Adrian Mitchell. In *Man Friday*, which was to be directed by the British film maker Jack Gold, O'Toole was to play Crusoe and the American black actor, Richard Roundtree, was to play Friday. O'Toole had thought of the film himself, having seen a production of Mitchell's play.

Filming began in December 1974 and it went almost without incident. O'Toole went to sleep in an ant farm and gave himself a throat infection and Roundtree had a fever for three days and took to his bed. O'Toole was surrounded by technicians he regularly works with; Roy Everson, his stand-in for five years; Bill Lodge, the make-up artist who painted his face red to give it the British well-fed look; and Michael Murchan, the head rigger. Jack Gold had, to O'Toole's delight, held two weeks of rehearsals before going out to Mexico and the five week schedule passed quickly and smoothly. It was so painless, in fact, that it came as something of a surprise that the finished film, which looks as relaxed as it was to film, was chosen as the official British entry to the Cannes Film Festival for 1975.

The critics were less keen. It was released in both the United States and Britain in 1975, its release in America speeded up in a vain attempt for it to qualify for an Academy Award nomination. As soon as the notices were published, it was clear that the film stood no chance, even though six minutes had been trimmed from the Cannes print, including the end sequence where O'Toole shoots himself by pressing his toe on his musket trigger.

Once again, O'Toole was praised while the film was slated. Vincent Canby of the *New York Times* wrote: 'Peter O'Toole looks and sounds right, and he might have made a fine Crusoe in a film of fewer pretensions.' Katrine Ames of *Newsweek* was similarly encouraging: 'O'Toole almost manages to triumph over his travesty. In the film's one lively scene, when Crusoe and Friday stage a makeshift Olympics, swimming, running and playing soccer on the sand, he is wonderfully comic as a poor loser. None is better than playing contained madness than O'Toole (as he did to perfection in *Lawrence of Arabia*), but once he lets it out he turns into a ham.' *Man*

*Friday* was given a restricted release and was not a commercial success.

The second Mexican film for O'Toole was *Foxtrot*, for the Roger Corman outfit, New World Pictures, a company which specialises in cheap, often trashy exploitation pictures. To have fallen into their hands is notorious in the film industry as a sign of falling prestige, as O'Toole was only too aware. But there was little choice. He quite liked the script, which was far from the usual low-budget drivel that Corman encouraged; there was a good cast, including Charlotte Rampling and Max Von Sydow; and it would allow him to continue working in Puerta Vallerta, where he had begun a romantic attachment to a local woman, Malinche Verdugo, more than twenty years younger than he.

It was at this time that the marriage between O'Toole and Sian Phillips began to unstick, although they agreed to keep it quiet for as long as possible. Until then, their life together had been warm and affectionate, although always stormy. O'Toole boasted about their capacity to get along with each other while maintaining their independence. He believed she had been the centre of his success. And O'Toole was not easy to live with. He was reasonably modern, but he was no feminist. It was his career which came first and Sian was expected to bring up the children and see to the house.

O'Toole would put extraordinary demands upon her, turning up at the end of the evening having drunk himself into a state of incoherence, accompanied by a clutch of actors, old friends and new acquaintances. Sian was expected to provide an instant supper for them. When O'Toole was on the road, Sian was a constant companion, always sitting in the corner, guarding him from the parade of press and photographers tramping through the hotel room. But O'Toole took her for granted. To the embarrassment of his friends he was known, when drunk, to ask the chauffeur to stop his Rolls Royce and tell his wife to leave the car. She would leave quietly, amid protests from his friends in the car. 'Don't worry,' she would tell them. 'I'll find my own way home.' And she called a passing taxi to take her home.

The constant travelling abroad for work upset Sian Phillips, whose career was predominantly domestic. And O'Toole's behaviour at home could be just as erratic. She issued him with a box of ping-pong balls to throw at the television after he had, in a fit of rage at something he had been watching, picked up a portable television and hurled it through the colour set. 'She didn't mind my heaving the ashtrays and stuff,' O'Toole explained, 'but actually chucking one set through another upset her. She couldn't know the deepseated satisfaction it gave me.'

Sian, who had adored him, found that, as his career declined and, ironically, hers moved from strength to strength, he was less happy about the arrangement. And, as intimate as she had always been with him, more privy to his innermost thoughts than anyone, the strain of a flagging career meant that she was finding out a less attractive side to his nature. On her return to Hampstead, after filming with him in *Murphy's War*, she said: 'There are things I still don't know about him. I know, we have been married thirteen years and it's a bit late in the day now, but so little of what goes on gets into this house. I don't know. I'm a very confused lady.' Still, for the time being, they behaved as if everything was all right.

Before the filming of *Foxtrot* began, O'Toole was going to need Sian Phillips more than ever before. At the end of February 1975, the abdominal irregularity which he had been carrying around for years, for which the doctors at Stratford had said he should have surgery, finally erupted. O'Toole was rushed to the Royal Free Hospital at Hampstead on a Sunday night and admitted to a National Health Service ward. He was put on a series of tests to find out what was causing the agonising pain which had encouraged him to drink so heavily for years.

The press drew their own conclusions and hinted that O'Toole was suffering from a liver complaint as a result of a persistent overdose of alcohol, but it was much more serious than they guessed. He was incapable of taking solid food and pure water was being fed down a pipe directly into his stomach. O'Toole was in a very low state and thought that he was dying. Sian remained loyal to him and, despite her decision to leave him, stayed at his beside for the duration.

O'Toole had a full beard, grown to play the part of Judas Iscariot in Lord Grade's *The Life of Jesus Christ*, a television epic starring Robert Powell. When nurses began to shave it off, O'Toole protested: 'Don't do that. I need it.' But he was being optimistic. O'Toole would not be well enough to meet the shooting schedule. O'Toole was obsessional about people knowing exactly what illness he was suffering from. He forbade everyone from mentioning what it was and made the doctor promise that his files would be kept under lock and key. O'Toole suspected he had cancer and he was desperately worried.

The tests were proving nothing and it was decided that there should be exploratory surgery. Something serious was going on inside his digestive system and a series of operations was carried out, first to determine exactly what was wrong, then to remove what they found. To this day, O'Toole is nervous of saying what the surgeons discovered, as if by mentioning his complaint, he might encourage it to return. And the secrecy about his illness is maintained by all his close friends. Each one pretends not to know exactly what was wrong.

American newspapers reported with certainty that O'Toole had had his pancreas removed, which O'Toole has always denied. He seldom talks about his ill-health at all. 'The worst periods of my illnesses were between thirty-nine and forty-two. At forty, I was so ill I had to stop working for a year. I used to get through the day with the help of a lot of aspirin to ease the pain. At night I didn't sleep much anyway; I stayed awake because I didn't know why I couldn't sleep. I put off surgery for as long as possible; I didn't relish the thought of anyone coming at me with a knife. Now, I have a scar on my stomach – it is about six inches or eight inches long – and I suggested they should put in a zip-fastener for the sake of easier entry. When I was finally in hospital in Hampstead, I was an awful patient – always making plans to detach the pumps and escape. No one actually told me I might die, but I couldn't help but notice some glum faces around me or others that were artificially smiling to try to be funny too fast.'

As if to taunt the frightening disease that was found within him, O'Toole now likes to parade the long scar across his stomach – evidence that he faced the ultimate danger and lived. But, for all the bravado, O'Toole was a changed man. There would be no more drink. There was now so little of his digestive system left that any amount of alcohol, however small, would prove fatal to him. And, having lived through such a close meeting with death, he was determined to live each day as the last. It was in the eight weeks which followed his sudden admission to hospital that O'Toole summoned Kenneth Griffith to him and gave his blessing to a biography, because he thought he was dying. (He has since claimed that he only granted Griffith his blessing to do a filmed biography.) He had frightened off every potential biographer until then and since that brush with death has been even more vehemently against anyone writing a full-length assessment of his life. The thought fills him with dread. He considers it a waste of precious time to dig through old memories, sift old thoughts, and he is not prepared to help anyone doing it for him.

Looking back on that time, O'Toole saw it as the most miserable period of his life: '*Heartbreak House* wasn't in it. The things that happened to me were almost Biblical. My wife, Sian Phillips, left me for a young kid. I was quite ill and they had to open me up like a tennis bag. I became uninsurable in pictures. My father went up in the air at eighty-six. And the dog died, too. Poor Scobie.' He had been close to death. 'It was a photo-finish, the surgeons said. I was down to nine stone. I'd been in pain since I was nineteen, you know. It was diagnosed as all sorts of things. Nobody really knew. So I drank to kill the pain. Madame Bottle, the great anaesthetic. Trouble was, when I stopped drinking the pain kept on. Eventually they opened me up and spotted something that shouldn't be there.'

What he was determined to do was to get back to work and work as hard and as often as he could. The chance to go to Mexico, which he adored, to make *Foxtrot* was exciting for him – the first film in a new life.

O'Toole explained what it felt like to arrive on the *Foxtrot* set: 'I became ill and was laid up for eight weeks before coming down to Cabo San Lucas. I had some abdominal surgery and the illness kept me from my normal schedule of preparing for the film. By the time I had recovered, I had to lock myself in a room to concentrate completely on the script. I was well prepared by the time shooting began, but I had to learn the script and my character much more quickly than usual.' And he told the cast and crew what his illness meant in practical terms for him: 'I'm on doctor's orders not to touch alcohol. I also can't even drink coffee or take aspirin or Alka-Seltzer. I've had to cut down on my smoking as well.'

The filming of *Foxtrot* proved undemanding. The part of Count Liviu Milescu, a Romanian aristocrat who leaves Europe at the beginning of World War II to live on a desert island, was not wordy and allowed O'Toole to put his frailty and emaciation to some use. Off the set, he searched for archaeological treasures on the site of a new road nearby. The director, Arturo Ripstein, allowed O'Toole to go his own way on the set at Cabo San Lucas and then in the Churubusco Studios in Mexico.

Although never released in Britain, *Foxtrot* had its adherents. Arthur Knight, of the *Hollywood Reporter*, wrote: 'As a visual and aural experience, *Foxtrot* is a masterwork. No picture could look better, or feel better.' And O'Toole acquitted himself, though his illness was clearly visible in his face. Knight continued: 'O'Toole is simply incredible as the jaded aristocrat . . . lacking, however, are the wellsprings of emotion that might make it all happen.'

Although O'Toole was not entirely happy with the project – 'It wasn't very good, was it? There's been an awful dearth of good material.' – he was grateful to be back to work and was planning a return to the theatre in Dublin, in Travers's *Plunder*. But the next thing of substance that he would film was *Rogue Male*, directed for BBC Television by Clive Donner.

On traditional form, this departure into television meant another step backwards. His career seemed to be on an unstoppable slide. But *Rogue Male* proved to be an extraordinarily important film for him, one of his most distinguished performances. He was in no position to pick and choose his parts any more and, as luck had it, he had nothing to do when one afternoon a taxi arrived at his door in Hampstead to deliver a script by Frederic Raphael from Geoffrey Household's 1939 novel and a proposition to play the hero, Sir Robert Hunter, an aristocratic Englishman who takes it into his own hands to shoot Hitler some months before the outbreak of World War II. It was a project which was close to him and he had been trying to interest people in it since 1956. By coincidence, Clive Donner, the director of *What's New Pussycat?*, had pressed ahead with the idea and remembered O'Toole for the part. It was a film with a noble antecedent, Fritz Lang's *Manhunt*, made from the same novel.

There was a gruelling six-week filming schedule in Wales, the Wye Valley and the Thames, with other locations in London, and O'Toole was delighted to find that he was fit enough to hold his own. 'Not only was it strenuous, but, being a show-off, I could not resist doing my own stunts. They've had me hanging by my eyelashes from a cliff. I have fallen off trees, driven cars and made amazing leaps over five-bar gates. At three am they had me rowing a boat without hands because the Nazis are supposed to have pulled out my fingernails. They were packing up to go home, leaving me being washed down the Thames with the rest of the detritus.'

O'Toole revelled in the part, which gave him the chance to work again with Alastair Sim, who took the best line: 'Shooting heads of state is never in season. They are protected. Like osprey.' Even the playwright Harold Pinter took a part. And his rival in the film, the Nazi-loving English gent, was played by John Standing. On a budget of a mere £147,000 and a shooting schedule of just twenty-five days, O'Toole made one of the best films of his career.

There was one minor domestic clash. *Rogue Male* was released in the same week as the BBC television version of Robert Graves's *I, Claudius*, which starred Sian Phillips. As the two biggest premières on British television that week, both vied for the front of the *Radio Times*, an honour as important in British terms as the cover of *Time* or *Newsweek* to American celebrities. O'Toole proved to be – still – more headlineworthy than his wife and it was his face that was chosen for the front. When O'Toole went to the set of *I, Claudius* to see Sian Phillips, he remembers: 'I was as popular as a pork sausage in a synagogue.'

In the summer of 1976, O'Toole was offered a part in Gore Vidal's *Caligula*, an epic on the debauched life of the Roman Emperor financed by Bob Guccione, the proprietor of the glossy soft-pornography magazine, *Penthouse*. But before O'Toole was allowed to sign the contract, he was obliged to subject himself to five days of hospital tests before an insurance company would cover him. He came out with a bill of health clean enough to guarantee that he would not drop dead during the month that he was needed in Rome for filming.

O'Toole was aware of the furore surrounding *Caligula*, but was eager to take part. Gore Vidal had ensured that his name was in the credits 'not so much in homage to myself as out of concern for the writer's status' and he imagined that this film would satisfy one ambition of his. 'I've always wanted to make one good movie, mine, reflective of me, with the director serving the text.' He was to be rudely disillusioned.

Before the filming, Vidal was touring Europe, unaware of the disaster about to overtake him. 'It's not going to be fancy,' he said. 'Italian movie makers have a Sistine Chapel complex: they fill everything in with pretty pictures. I want to show how it was when they all wore dirty togas and put chalk on to cover the marks, so that in a high wind the air in the Senate was filled with dust.' To that extent, Vidal was not disappointed. *Caligula* showed Rome in the most sordid context. And soon he was pleading with Guccione to take his name off the title and his script was ignored.

'Once upon a time it was a very good film script by Gore Vidal, but that was cast aside about two minutes before we started filming,' remembered O'Toole. 'I'm a professional. If I've got a job to do, I do it. John Gielgud and Helen Mirren were in it and it was supposed to be Gore Vidal's version of Caligula. Then the day before the off, Bob Guccione and his merry men did something to the script and left us in an amazing blue movie. I was there for six days and John for three and we both enjoyed ourselves enormously. We started off looking at all the naked bodies and then after a while compared our operation scars.'

O'Toole came to the conclusion that he was being asked to play Father Christmas. 'The first day on the set, the director, Tinto Brass – we called him Tinto Zinc – said: "What you want? How you liked to be paralysed in picture?" So I said: "Anything you like, smiler" and got myself a naked Sumerian girl to lean on from start to finish. She became known as Betty the Collapsible Crutch.'

O'Toole enjoys describing *Caligula*. Here, for once, was a bad film which had sucked him in. If he was caught in the same disaster as Sir John Gielgud and Malcolm McDowell, then he could not be to blame. 'Imagine me, O'Toole, playing the Emperor Tiberius, followed everywhere by thirteen naked men wearing silver Robin Hood hats – my bodyguard. Imagine a director who couldn't speak very good English and could only say: "Turn Over" and "Are you finished?" A bit bizarre, wouldn't you say? But I don't think it can hurt me, even if it has been turned into soft porn.' He and John Gielgud were the only ones who were not allowed to take off their togas. 'Half the cast went round wearing four-foot rubber phalluses strapped to them and Malcolm McDowell had a nice gold lamé number. I called him Tinkerbell.'

But, for all his relish in telling the disastrous events on the set, O'Toole was rather disappointed. He was, as an amateur historian and archaeologist, very keen to appear in a serious piece of history by a serious writer. He had spent weeks examining busts of Tiberius, and coins and medallions in the British Museum and in the library of Trinity College, Dublin, trying to track down any likeness for a hint of character. And the filming was arduous. Giuseppe Banchelli had had a life mask of O'Toole's face made and flown from London so that he could prepare for the three-hour make-up sessions which made OToole look cadaverous and syphilitic.

'The funny thing is, Gore Vidal is a serious historian and he wrote the script as a serious drama,' said O'Toole. 'But that's not the way it came out. Oh, dear, no. Not with all those naked people milling about, flaunting their pale bottoms and appendectome scars. As for being erotic . . . .' And, although mildly amused at finding himself in such rubbish, he defends his own performance. 'I'm not ashamed of my Tiberius. Not ashamed at all. He's all right. He's dead in the first reel, isn't he? What I did was immediately practise as much as I could on Tiberius. It's quixotic, I suppose, but I had a demand on me to be as professional as possible and protect Tiberius, who fascinated me. I'd love to play him from about my age now till his death. He ran the entire Roman Empire – and that spread every-where – from the Isle of Capri: he didn't move from there. I did it because Roman history fascinates me. Simply, because of all the countries in Europe, it never got to Ireland.'

Bob Guccione, *Caligula*'s producer, was also generous to O'Toole when the film was released in Britain in 1980, but in a roundabout way. He is reported in the *Daily Mirror* to have accused O'Toole of being high while on the set. Guccione is reported to have said: 'He was smashed from the first day I saw him in Italy, where the film was shot. Peter O'Toole was never sober enough to know what he was doing when I watched him – and I was there twenty-five per cent of the time. I couldn't fire him because you can't do much once you've started to film. Anyway, it didn't hurt his performance. He played a doddering seventy-six-year-old syphilitic emperor and he did it extremely well.' O'Toole dodged the charge and, for a British readership, interpreted 'smashed' as 'drunk', saying: 'Guccione's statements are completely untrue. All my colleagues will testify that I've been a teetotaller for five years.' His lawyers told him that

Guccione had grossly defamed him, but no court case ensued.

Now getting into his stride, O'Toole wanted to get back to the stage and had a plan in mind. He planned to open at the Gaiety Theatre, Dublin, in *Dead Eyed Dicks*, a new play by Peter King in which O'Toole had invested money. O'Toole was to play, in turn, Lord Peter Wimsey, Philip Marlowe and Sherlock Holmes. After its Dublin début, it was planned for a tour of northern England before arriving in London for Christmas 1976. 'It'll be good for the nerve, good for the trim,' he said. And he boasted that this would be his first venture into commercial theatre ever and that he was fed up with working in subsidised companies – conveniently forgetting his successful commercial run in David Mercer's *Ride a Cock Horse* in 1965. He was deliberately trying to turn the event into high drama, both for publicity, which was essential if he was to get his money back, and in order to heighten the sense of drama for himself to act up to. He was finding the drug of a live audience increasingly tame and needed to keep up the tension.

The result was disastrous and gave warning of the horrors that were to be so conspicuous in his Old Vic *Macbeth*. O'Toole was saved from utter humiliation by the failure of the play to reach London. Instead he took it outside the country, to Canada, to Washington DC and to Australia. O'Toole was still a big cinema name and curiosity at least would guarantee packed houses. The play did make money, but no one who saw the production doubted that O'Toole was finished as a stage actor. His rambling around the stage, hamming up the lines, implied that he was not sober.

By the middle of 1977, O'Toole was in a trough. He had just finished filming *Power Play*, also known as *Coup d'Etat*, a poorly written thriller, directed by Martyn Burke. The work had taken him to Canada and Yugoslavia, but it had been barely worth the effort. Although he took top billing, the only other name of any substance was David Hemmings and O'Toole's part was small, that of a tank commander who takes part in a military coup and snatches power from his fellow revolutionaries at the last minute. And when he arrived home to London, the news of his marriage break-up had slipped out.

O'Toole had become an interesting has-been, cheap fodder for the gossip columnists because he added a dimension of glamour to their pages.

'The glue has come unstuck,' he said. 'In fact, Sian left me two-and-a-half years ago. We agreed not to talk about it because it is private and most people thought it just happened this summer. She used to come and visit me in hospital in many countries during the past few years. And then she stopped coming. At least there was no subterfuge. It was all above board and she told me she was leaving because there was someone else. I am fond of her and I am glad professionally things are going well for her, but there can be no going back for me. I am only a man and I am starting over again on my own.' His two daughters, Pat, then aged fourteen and Kate, aged seventeen, were given the choice and decided to live with their father in Hampstead. And another, most unlikely member of the ménage decided to stay: Sian's mother.

The final reason for the end of the O'Toole marriage – and the name cited in the divorce proceedings – was a young actor, Robin Sachs, then aged twenty-six, seventeen years younger than Sian Phillips. They had met in *The Gay Lord Quex*, a farce in the West End of London in 1975 and their friendship soon became sexual. In 1977, when the news finally broke, she first went to live in Chelsea, then it was a great relief for them to live together without subterfuge in a house in Oakley Road, Islington. 'Of course I regret it being over,' said Sian Phillips, 'but these things happen and I'd already had one disastrous student marriage by the time we met. Peter and I were never a couple on stage or screen, though we did occasionally turn up on the same projects. He had to be away a lot in his work and somehow the marriage just drifted away from us. But I can't say I've minded having to set up home all over again in Islington.'

O'Toole was less philosophical: 'I'm forty-five, nearly forty-six and I know I've been lucky with my life. And in that luck I include Sian Phillips. When she went off with this young geezer, Robin Sachs, it was a shock. It hurt. Of course it hurt. I never thought anything like that would happen. When it did, I said to her: "When you're fifty-seven he'll be only forty. It's ridiculous." But later, I decided she's entitled. If that's what she wants, she's entitled.' He felt very sorry for himself, betrayed and humiliated by a younger man. 'From the day I was twenty, I knew there would come a time when I would be quite ill. But I never visualised that I would also be alone.'

O'Toole decided to cure his misery by working harder than ever. 'Dr Work is the best prescription for someone in my condition. Without theatre training, I'd be bitched.' And first stop in the early summer of 1978 was to South Africa for a preamble to the story dealt with in the epic *Zulu*, in which the Zulus were to be considered the heroes and the British imperialists the villains. Chief villain was Lord Chelmsford, the part played by O'Toole.

*Zulu Dawn* was shot in the actual locations and O'Toole flew to Cape Town, then on to Isandhlwana, the plain on which the battle was fought in 1879. The director, Douglas Hickox, had a budget of five million pounds and a celebrated cast, including O'Toole, Burt Lancaster, John Mills, Michael Jayston, Denholm Elliott, Nigel

Davenport and six thousand Zulu extras. It was the sort of location that O'Toole thrives in: tough, dry and sandy, although the South African winter had also been delivering cold winds and rain. Shooting went according to plan, except for an unfortunate incident where O'Toole was thrown by a horse and spent two days recovering. Otherwise, he was happy working hard and busy planning what to do next.

He was planning a theatre season in Canada, which would include Coward's *Present Laughter* and Chekhov's *Uncle Vanya*, which he hoped would travel first to the United States, then to London. And he had his eyes firmly on a proper return to the London stage, perhaps at the Old Vic. 'I'm going back to an old theatre in Toronto,' he said, 'because I love playhouses. I can't separate the act of performing from the conditions the performance is given in, and that means the theatre. I have no wish to mesmerise concrete in London. I've been to the National Theatre, but if we could get into the Old Vic and make that theatre come alive again, then I would be the happiest man on this earth. Perhaps it's time I threw my hat in the ring and became an actor-manager.' It was the first time that he had hinted at the notion which would lead to the most notable fiasco of his career: his punishing humiliation in the Old Vic *Macbeth*.

From *Zulu Dawn*, which, for all its ambition, failed to light when released, O'Toole took up a project which had been offered to him two years before at a party – the chance to work for the first time in Hollywood.

He had met Richard Rush at a party. Rush had considered O'Toole 'one of the greatest actors in the world' and could not understand why the film industry was using him so badly. He was in particular fond of O'Toole's performance in *Becket*, which he described as 'the best single performance I'd ever seen on the screen'. Rush gave O'Toole the script of *The Stunt Man* to read and O'Toole quickly gave a positive reply, saying: 'Richard, I'm a literate and articulate person and if you don't let me play this part, I'll kill you.'

It was a plum part, as far as Rush was concerned. The film had been nursed by him for years, based upon a novel by Paul Brodeur published in 1970. Among others who had hoped to film it were François Truffaut and Arthur Penn. Truffaut had been so disappointed at missing the rights that he had made *Day for Night*, a similarly complicated film about illusion and reality on a film set. Rush had met a barrage of indifference from American film companies and at one point even had to fight to keep the title. Burt Reynolds was making an adventure comedy about stunt men and Rush stood firm saying that he would, eventually, make his film, so Reynolds' film was called *Hooper* instead.

Finally, against the odds, Rush found the money from Mel Simon Productions, the cinema off-shoot of a company founded by an Indianapolis supermarket tycoon who wanted to be a film mogul. And Rush found O'Toole, a casting decision which also went in the face of conventional Hollywood wisdom. 'Studio people have told me, "Don't mention Peter O'Toole, he's death at the box office. His last two pictures didn't make a dime and he can't bring in a dollar at the box office," ' said Rush. And O'Toole had a reputation for being difficult on the set.

In the event, Rush and O'Toole worked well together. 'He was the best and easiest actor I've ever worked with in my life, a dream – like being handed a Stradivarius.' And the flattery went the other way. O'Toole explained that he took the part because of the script, which intrigued him, and because of Rush. 'The attraction was Richard Rush,' he said. 'I find him to be clearly streets ahead of anybody I know in this country in terms of film making, except for just a few, and also the script was the most intelligent and exciting I'd read for many years. Richard has put a lot into this film, anywhere between four and seven years, but I find that's normal with movie makers of this substance.' And he went on: 'So many people have written on their passport the word "director" that it's become a meaningless word. I've only known about a handful of movie directors in my life – people who are film *directors*, whose life is making a film. Richard Rush is one. David Lean's another. William Wyler, John Huston and Clive Donner, too. And that's about it.'

Filming began in the summer of 1978 with a budget of six million dollars. O'Toole was, for the first time, working on United States soil, at San Diego, Southern California, at the wooden castellated Hotel del Coronado, an American national monument which had been made famous to filmgoers when Billy Wilder had used it in *Some Like It Hot*. O'Toole's part was of a megalomaniac film director, who subjects his cast and crew to insufferable misery in the name of movies. The obvious thing would be to base the character upon Rush himself – the character was called Eli Cross, a pseudonym that Rush had used when making pulp exploitation films that he was not proud of. Other suggestions were made.

'I've heard John Huston. I've heard Orson Welles. I've heard Peckinpah. I've heard the Devil. I've heard God,' said O'Toole. 'I've heard all sorts of things. I hope he's a complete original. If there is any influence, it's through the pores, and it would be David Lean. I was two years and three months with David, and it was as though he'd given me a course in how to be a director. At every shot I looked through the viewfinder. I was with him viewing takes of other performers, watching his complete involvement and this great capacity for film being a mother tongue, which Richard Rush has. I think I even look like David occasionally, particularly the young David.' There were other likenesses. 'He says: "Cut" in the same way. He uses a cigarette holder as David does and he wears a sort of David outfit for shooting, hand-picked, no doubt, by the continuity girl.'

And, while waiting for *The Stunt Man* to find a distributor – a task which was to prove most difficult – O'Toole embarked on two gruelling television epics: monster projects which would envelope him in warmth and friendship like that found in a theatre company. *Strumpet City*, directed by Tony Barry, was an ambitious serial produced by Radio Telefis Eireann, the Irish public service television network, who had high hopes for it. Filmed entirely in Ireland, it was a story about Dublin from 1907-14, dramatised by Hugh Leonard from a novel by James Plunkett. O'Toole played an historical figure, James Larkin, a legendary Irish Labour character: It was only the second time – the first was *Murphy's War* – that O'Toole had played an Irishman on film, and he was understandably a little embarrassed.

'I don't have an Irish accent and I don't want to acquire one,' he said. 'If you go around playing Irish parts called Peter O'Toole you would have to have red hair and carry a shillelagh.' *Strumpet City* was filmed in seven parts and RTE hoped to sell it to the BBC – their first serious adventure into the costume serial market boasting international stars like O'Toole and Peter Ustinov, as Edward VII. In the event, it was sold to the commercial network in the UK and was given a crippling schedule slot, in afternoons or late nights in different regions, ensuring that no overall ratings were available.

Then, back to hard labour. O'Toole set out for twenty-one weeks in the desert to make an eight-hour serial epic about the besieged fortress of *Masada* – a pivotal event in Jewish history, for final release on the American ABC network. It boasted a budget of twenty-one million dollars, the most expensive American television part-work ever. George Eckstein, the producer, and Boris Sagal, the director, had a neat way of ensuring that the audience was not confused between the Jewish Zealots in their togas and the Roman Army in theirs. All the Jews would be American actors; all the Romans would be British. Among those who benefited from this field day for British actors were O'Toole, Nigel Davenport, Anthony Quayle, Denis Quilley, Anthony Valentine and, working with O'Toole for the first time, Timothy West, one of Britain's most successful actor-managers.

West remembers that he and O'Toole got on particularly well and that O'Toole proved to be a great morale booster amid some very uncomfortable filming. O'Toole was not only cast as the dastardly Roman general of the 10th Legion, Cornelius Flavius Silva, because he was British. Joel Oliansky, the writer who had adapted Ernest K. Gann's novel into a screenplay, was a fan: 'I always dreamed of O'Toole playing the part. I always had him in mind, and I wrote for his speech rhythms. Peter loved every syllable of his role. Occasionally someone would suggest lightening his load a bit and cutting, but Peter would say: "Don't touch it. I want to do it." I find it really spooky that I can now take a video cassette, shove it in a machine and actually see Peter O'Toole in full armour, with five thousand extras, playing my dialogue. It's a great feeling.'

The producer, Eckstein, was also impressed by O'Toole and his professionalism: 'O'Toole was a great choice – a popular choice. He had a meaty, magnificent role that gave him plenty of screen time – and paid quite well, too. Peter's approach to the part was interesting. He received the first draft script six months before filming and memorised every word. When we got to the rewritten scenes, he ignored them. We had "discussions" about the changes, which he simply didn't want to adopt. Otherwise, he was always word-perfect on the first take.'

O'Toole was back in the desert with a shooting schedule in Israel, near the genuine fortress of Masada and its remains, for three-and-a-half months, followed by six weeks in the United States. It was gruelling progress. 'Filming at Masada was like undergoing army basic training – I can't describe how bad it was,' explained Eckstein. 'The temperature went to a hundred and thirty-five degrees with no shade, and we had extras in Roman leather armour dropping everywhere. The actors – their enthusiasm – were just wonderful; we had physical personnel problems instead of equipment breakdowns. Peter O'Toole had a painful infection below his eye; Peter Strauss flew to London with intestinal problems and about fifteen other medical disasters occurred.'

O'Toole was proud of his performance. He had very much enjoyed researching his part and was confident he had delivered a watchable performance. 'I have a feeling,' he said, 'and it is only a feeling, that in *Masada*, General Silva will wipe T. E. Lawrence away, because that will come into everybody's home and there's eight hours of it and it's a character everybody will want to identify with.'

When *Masada* arrived on the ABC network, screened in two-hour segments over four consecutive nights, *Variety* declared that 'O'Toole's performance was more compelling than Strauss's' and that 'O'Toole's dynamic performance will emerge as the most memorable element of the project'. When the series was slashed to a mere 121-minute cinema version for world release, reverting to Gann's original title, *The Antagonists*, the critics were less kind.

And by the time that it reached Britain, O'Toole's reputation was in tatters. He had become front page news for several days because of the production of *Macbeth* at the Old Vic in London which was deemed such a disaster by the critics that the scale of the event had pushed it off the arts pages to lead the papers. The *Sun* dubbed it 'Macbomb'. The *Daily Mail* headlined their story: 'Downfall of a star who insisted on his own way' and crossheaded their text with a logo of crossed daggers, dripping in blood. Headline writers used what one paper called 'the biggest *débâcle* of the theatrical season, or possibly the decade' as an excuse for O'Toole-baiting, tagging one interview with him; 'Glamis wasn't built in a day'. Even the usually staid *The Times* headed their review, drily: 'Putting the clock back too far'. And few reviewing *The Antagonists* could resist echoing the *Macbeth* farce.

Arthur Thirkell, of the *Daily Mirror*, wrote of O'Toole: 'When he passes the time of day with anybody, it's as if he is addressing a multitude of the hard of hearing. That wouldn't be so bad if what he says is worth anything. But the script is stiff with comic strip clichés, a collection of the banal and the ridiculous. I haven't laughed so much for ages.' Ian Christie, of the *Daily Express*, also used *The Antagonists* as an excuse to repeat the abuse poured upon O'Toole during *Macbeth*. 'I didn't like Peter O'Toole shouting at me from the stage in his *Macbeth*,' he wrote, 'and the experience of watching and listening to him bellowing in *The Antagonists* is no more pleasurable.' And more than one critic pointed out the irony in one of O'Toole's lines in the film: 'Nobody is listening any more.'

# 10   Harry Lauder

O'TOOLE NEEDED something to yank himself out of an unprecedented trough of failure. For years, everything he touched seemed to be cursed with mediocrity, nothing would spark into success. His reputation was fast sinking. Although he had attracted a loyal following – as loyal as the close band of personal friends who would hear nothing against him – his general public image was one of a ludicrous poseur. His grand-gestured acting style was totally out of fashion. With the rise during the 1970s of the new wave of Hollywood directors – Martin Scorsese, Francis Ford Coppola, Steven Spielberg, George Lucas – had come a new generation of actors like Robert de Niro, Harvey Keitel, Richard Dreyfuss and Jack Nicholson. O'Toole's stagey style seemed increasingly absurd, uncool and irrelevant. He found himself eclipsed by young actors just as he, in his time, had eclipsed a generation of actors before him.

And the parts that he was being offered were getting worse and more stereotyped. Despite all his determination to follow David Lean's advice to come out of a different hole each time, he was increasingly being given a slight variation on the same character – an aristocratic, British, aloof, half mad, bossy, idiosyncratic petty tyrant and eccentric. And as much as O'Toole tried to vary his performance, he found that he held his roles in such little regard that his contempt for the film industry made him walk through, unmoved. His two television epics had at least proved a change, but television was little more than the film industry with less talented people, less professional sense and less money.

Two more personal factors also demanded that he make a break from his most recent work. His recovery from near death had had a profound effect on the way he viewed his life. The sensation of growing old that he felt when the young actors turned to him for advice during the filming of *The Lion in Winter* was quadrupled after the drastic surgery upon his digestive system. Life would not go on forever. He could not expect to maintain his health as easily again and he had been told that the extent of the surgery would certainly shorten his life. Drifting from one uninspiring film project to the next, he determined that something must be done to stop the slide. And he knew from the sudden death of his close friend James

Kennaway that there may be no room for regret at a later date. O'Toole became consumed with a vivid consciousness of his own mortality – a feeling that still drives him today. And, an energetic worker at all times, he pushed himself harder than ever to reinforce his thrill of being alive.

He had decided after his illness to live each day as if it were the last, yet chance had not thrown up the scripts which matched his new urgency of purpose. This, too, made him think carefully about how he would break back into worthwhile projects. His chance came in 1980, two years after he had first made exploratory enquiries with Toby Robertson, the director of the Prospect Theatre Company, considered to be the third most established theatre company in Britain after the National Theatre Company and the Royal Shakespeare Company.

Robertson was in the process of transforming Prospect from an ambitious, well-respected but essentially minor company into a company which would hold its place as an equal with the other two principal companies in Britain. The main instrument of this elevation came, strangely, from the expansion of the National Theatre, which left the cramped conditions of the Old Vic Theatre in Waterloo Road, London, for a modern three-halled concrete palace on the South Bank of the Thames. Under the careful direction of Sir Peter Hall, the National was strengthening its reputation with apparent ease. But the National's move left the Old Vic, where the company had been founded by Laurence Olivier with O'Toole as Hamlet, without occupants. Robertson took his chance and smartly moved the Prospect players in.

The history and tradition of the Old Vic and the fond place it held in the hearts of everyone who loved the British theatre would, he hoped, give Prospect a boost and a permanent London home for his ambitions to rival the National and the Royal Shakespeare companies. But there was a catch – and a catch which meant that Robertson would come to lean upon the unique talents of O'Toole. The central body for state funding of the arts in Britain is the Arts Council, an appointed body who apply, independently of the government, a policy which reflects what they, in their wisdom, consider the best way of encouraging artistic endeavour. More often than not, this encouragement boils down to one thing: the allocation of an Arts Council grant.

As the principal touring company, Robertson's Prospect was given a substantial grant for delivering good theatre to provincial audiences in their local theatres. Robertson's move to the Old Vic, however, was not matched by an extra grant. The Arts Council decided that the state subsidies granted to the National Theatre and to the Royal Shakespeare Company, half of which operated in London from the Aldwych Theatre until its permanent home in the Barbican was ready, were sufficient to maintain top quality classical theatre in London. It would continue paying towards the touring work which the Prospect did, but it would not pay a grant for the company to perform to London audiences.

Having fought and lost this Arts Council decision, Toby Robertson was forced to make a choice between leaving the Old Vic or staying but finding another source of revenue – and that could only be through the box office. He decided that the best way of ensuring that the Old Vic venture made a profit from the very beginning – for there was no room for mistakes – was for it to boast a star guaranteed to draw the public in large numbers, what he called 'a marriage of convenience'. He made an approach to O'Toole in 1978 and was given an immediate, warm reply. The plan was for O'Toole to join the company as associate director when Prospect first performed in the Old Vic, under the name of the Old Vic Company, in the autumn of 1980.

This arrangement suited O'Toole for many reasons. The first was that he was anxious to return to the London stage which he had not worked on for fifteen years, since *Ride a Cock Horse* at the Piccadilly Theatre. He had always preferred the stage to film work and had dipped in and out throughout his career. A live audience provided a buzz which was not available from the blank gaze of a camera. But, more than that, O'Toole needed to be told that he was still a great stage actor. His recent stage work – in Toronto, in Washington, in a disastrous tour of Australia, at the Bristol Old Vic – had proved less than satisfactory to him. And Robertson was offering him not only the chance to return to London – for such a chance could be arranged with relative ease through a commercial impresario who would want to exploit O'Toole in much the same way as O'Toole felt he was exploited by film producers for their own ends. Robertson was also offering a return to the Old Vic in the relaunch of a new company.

The Old Vic was a very special theatre to O'Toole. He had auditioned there in 1954 before great names of the British Theatre: Tyrone Guthrie, Nat Brenner, his mentor at the Bristol Old Vic, John Moody and Michael Benthall. 'I don't feel as though I ever left the Old Vic,' he said. 'I've been giving to it since 1954.' It was there that Olivier had given him the gruelling privilege of performing the full-length *Hamlet*, thus inaugurating the National Theatre company. But the memory of *Hamlet*, although historic, had left O'Toole with a nasty aftertaste. He was not happy with his performance and thought that Olivier, through guile and charm, had taken advantage of him and, to an extent, humiliated him by the marathon nature of the production. O'Toole did not want to be remembered for that performance at the Old Vic and was determined to return in triumph.

And O'Toole, who is even more romantic about the theatre than most other actors – which is to say a great deal – wanted to see every British actor's favourite theatre working properly, with large audiences, with an inventive, inspirational company, and in profit again. His commitment to the Old Vic was absolute. 'It's still London's theatre, despite all that amazing pile of cement on the South Bank,' he said, dismissing the efforts of the National Theatre a half a mile to the west. 'What might Christopher Wren have done with all that cement.'

As for the Vic: 'It's not a narrow thing like a national theatre, it's an international theatre and it holds Europe's heritage, it really does. I just love it.' And his plans for the Old Vic were clear. 'My idea is simple, to return to the Old Vic and what the Old Vic means and stands for, which is a conservatoire for actors and acting, doing the best of the playwrights, primarily Shakespeare. We get a grant from the Arts Council, but I would prefer to lose it and live or die by the box office. If we can't live, then we shouldn't be there. Nothing can disguise mediocrity.'

And O'Toole had further stern things to say about the debilitating effect of subsidised theatre. 'I've been a professional in the theatre for twenty-seven years and a spectator before that,' he told Jack Crossley, one of his old colleagues during his early incarnation as a journalist on the *Yorkshire Evening News*, 'and I've attended so many wakes. People keep writing that the theatre is dead. It keeps rising from the dead. But you can't run a classical company without a small body of patrons to pay the costs of putting the productions on. Economics dictates that. After that, you live or die by the box office. This is my law. I'm not interested in any government subsidies. Can't abide them. Don't wany any. We will stand or fall eventually by what we take at the box office, and that means becoming an attraction. It means finding the right people who want to do this as much as I do. We want to use the Old Vic as a place where we can practise our art, rather than it just being a way of earning a living.'

He backed his sentiments wholeheartedly. He took a modest two hundred pounds a week salary for the duration. 'The idea is that actors do it because they want to,' he explained. 'The money that I'm not going to earn is metaphysics. It doesn't really matter. It doesn't bolster the bank balance, but that's not important. If earning money in the cinema and television subsidises me and the Old Vic, then smashing. Remember, I wouldn't have done *Lawrence of Arabia* if it hadn't been for the Vic. I wouldn't have had the equipment or anything. The Vic is and should be a conservatoire for actors to act in. When I first came here I saw on the stage people like Alec Guinness and Larry Olivier all working for buttons. But the pay-off is that it's the best shop window in the world. Commercial work flows from it, and its people come back and fill the place and do what they want to do.'

O'Toole and Robertson had not finally defined what position O'Toole would hold, but O'Toole had clear ideas of his own. It would be a final realisation of his early dream of an O'Toole repertory company run by actors for actors, an idea he had floated many times on both sides of the Atlantic. Suddenly everything seemed to have fallen into place. He had been invited to sit atop a company with a good, competent tradition to revive the fortunes of a theatre which meant so much to him. He had no doubts about the scale of the task or the amount of responsibility he should take. Robertson might have had a more modest role for O'Toole in mind, but that soon became academic. While Robertson was touring China, there was a palace revolution within the Prospect board, he was displaced and a successor appointed – the actor, director and former Prospect Company member, Timothy West.

West was not clear about Robertson's intentions for O'Toole and was understandably hesitant about working so closely with an actor with such a reputation for wildness, particularly as the deal meant that O'Toole would have an almost free hand with one of the company's principal productions: *Macbeth*. His immediate inquiry upon joining Prospect was to see how far the O'Toole deal had gone. He was too late. The Prospect lawyers confirmed that O'Toole had signed a binding contract with the company and there was no obvious escape clause. 'I took advice from the lawyers,' remembered West, 'about what would happen if we withdrew from our side of the contract and they told me that O'Toole could and probably would sue and that we would be liable to a considerable sum in damages. I therefore reluctantly agreed to O'Toole joining the company.'

O'Toole was delighted and promptly started making plans. And, as a conspicuous gesture towards defining the role he would play in the company, he ignored the offer of a well-appointed large office in the prefabricated block away from the Old Vic, which the National Theatre had left behind, in favour of a small garret of an office and boasted that it was used once to be the powerhouse of the theatre when it was occupied by the Vic's most celebrated manager, Lilian Baylis. In her long reign from 1914, she had established the Old Vic as the home of classical theatre in Britain. It was a poky room, nick-named The Rectangular Banana, with a single small slit window which looked over a London Transport bus garage. Barely fifteen feet by ten, it was to be O'Toole's eyrie and, sitting on a broken-down black plastic armchair, he would hold court.

This, to him, was what the Old Vic was about; the discomfort and archaic conditions were part of its charm and character. As for the new building: 'It's a concrete matchbox, a Lego nightmare. I call it the Electric, Gas Light and Coal Company and I won't go in it. I'm going to be happy in here. It drips with the spirit of the Vic. Baylis worked in this banana. So did Guthrie. I couldn't do the job from a square cell across the road.'

The truth was slightly different and a lot less glamorous. O'Toole had refused an office in the modern building in favour of camping on any space which he could find in the theatre. At first, Timothy West thought that this was laudable, an attempt to break down the inevitable division between administrators and players. But the Baylis room was not available for O'Toole's use. The boardroom, which Lilian Baylis used, was strictly out of bounds and, when O'Toole entertained visitors and the press, he would borrow the theatre manager's office and call it his own. And it was not long before West began to hear gossip from the theatre building that O'Toole was running down his administration, referring to those in the modern block as 'those wankers from across the road'. O'Toole seemed to be engaged in some sort of elaborate power game.

As soon as O'Toole and West were installed, it became clear that there was a confusion about who exactly was giving the orders. West was the ultimate boss, but O'Toole seemed to have a free hand. West was, publicly, quite satisfied. In private he held doubts. 'We are two very different sorts of people,' he explained, 'and, I hope, complementary. I work well within this organisation and Peter works without it, and that enlarges the horizons. We approach productions differently. I am interested in intellectual grasp and psychological truth and Peter in visual excitement. I think it is a very good arrangement.'

O'Toole knew what he had to do. 'My job has been to find the right director, to bring in the right people, to find the young 'uns. I've got to try to influence quality, financial philosophy and help return the Old Vic to what it was, what it can be and should be – a London theatre playing in London for a London season. You begin in September, stick in a panto at Christmas and, if what you produced in the autumn was rubbish, you lose it. If it was good, keep it, add to it, carry on until late spring, early summer – and stop.'

Although it looked as if O'Toole's self-written job description overlapped entirely with West's principal function, there should have been little chance for head banging. There was more than enough work for both of them. West was working around the clock, to the great cost to his family life, and was capable of managing a commercial enterprise, whereas O'Toole could merely describe the artistic philosophy necessary to make the Old Vic a success once more.

O'Toole's assessment of the company as he started out was this: 'We're a pretty disparate bunch at the moment, with some new boys and some left over from the National Theatre days. It hasn't sorted itself out yet, but you can see it lurching to its feet again now. We had to persuade the governors – and various colleagues – that we should go back to repertoire and that's as far as I can see it at the moment, as far as I want to see it.' And, of his personal position in the company: 'I want to continue as associate director of The Old Vic Theatre for five years, help to revitalise the place and form a permanent company.'

More important than the grand pronouncements about policy was the choice of plays. West was clear. Working as an actor-manager, he would act in *Lancelot and Guinevere* about the legend of King Arthur's court, before taking the part of Shylock in *The Merchant of Venice* a month after the relaunch. O'Toole had set his heart on acting *Macbeth*, the achievement of a lifelong ambition. As with all ambitious classical actors, he had always hoped to master the three principal Shakespearean roles of Hamlet, King Lear and Macbeth. When at Stratford, he had told an interviewer that he would most of all like to play Macbeth, he had promptly touched the wooden bar of the Dirty Duck to ward off the curse which is meant to linger over the play. When Toby Robertson had first asked him in 1978 whether he would like to join the Old Vic company, O'Toole had toyed with the idea of Macbeth and he stuck to his original plan. Very early on, however, O'Toole, a chronically superstitious person, had smelt the whiff of disaster about the production. He decided not even to mention Macbeth's name, calling the play *Harry Lauder* instead.

From the beginning of the arrangements for *Macbeth*, it became clear to West and the rest of the company that O'Toole had, first, a very old-fashioned notion of how Shakespeare was performed on the modern stage and, second and far worse, O'Toole's decision-making ability was confused, erratic and, the worst sin of all, unprofessional. The first evidence of this amateur approach to management was shown in the casting of Lady Macbeth.

An original pecking order had been drawn up for the part and various actresses approached – the traditional way of discovering suitability and availability. The actress Jane Lapotaire was chosen. But when O'Toole arrived, he said that he did not want her. West was embarrassed. To back out of an agreement was unprofessional, unfair on the actress and a bad precedent, one which would soon spread around the small circuit of actors and stage people. West did not want his company to be branded as unprofessional and resisted O'Toole as far as was possible, but he was adamant. The actress was somehow unsuitable. With deep regret and enormous misgivings, West agreed to O'Toole's request and a new Lady Macbeth was found in Frances Tomelty, an Irish actress whom O'Toole knew as she and her husband, the rock singer Sting, had a house near O'Toole's in Clifden.

There was a similar confusion about finding a director. Jack Gold had agreed to take the project, then backed out at the last minute. A film project had come up offering a substantial amount of money and as Gold's film career was more important to him than a career in stage direction, when he asked to be relieved of his commitment, Timothy West reluctantly agreed. O'Toole then found a substitute.

Bryan Forbes was an unusual choice as director, because his work had almost entirely been in the cinema. He had begun as an actor in such supremely British films as *The Wooden Horse*, about the escape from a German prisoner-of-war camp, had then begun writing screenplays for such films as *Cockleshell Heroes*, then had made the move to film director, with films like *The Madwoman of Chaillot*, *International Velvet* and *The Stepford Wives*. O'Toole chose him because he was a close personal friend and known to be an actors' director, who put the art of acting above the art of film direction. O'Toole had come to despise film directors who had, during his career, eclipsed actors in the critical mind as the crucial stars of cinema. Forbes had also, like O'Toole, always worked in Britain in a British tradition whenever possible. And Forbes was a fan of O'Toole.

Writing in his selective history of stage actors, *That Despicable Race*, Forbes gave this verdict of O'Toole: 'At his best, which is very good indeed, he is an actor of great presence and power, constantly swimming against the tide. A romantic by nature, he finds much to criticise in the contemporary theatrical scene and can unleash laser beams of invective against the citadels of mediocrity. In recent years he has been tested in other ways, fighting ill-health with all the panache and tenacity that characterises his best performances. Happily he is now braced to return to his first love and by the end of 1980 he will be back at the Old Vic and in command of his own destiny. As well as the classical roles he is so finely equipped to play, he needs a contemporary dramatist who can write specifically for him, somebody who has the courage to pick up the glove that O'Toole has flung in the face of convention. There is passion and violence beneath the handsome mask, for the face as well as the man has matured. His destiny lies not in the mundane but the heroic – and heroism is thought reactionary these days, more's the pity.' This eulogy came hard on another line of assessment and piece of advice by Forbes which he might have done well to follow: 'He is an actor who needs firm handling, and there are not too many David Leans around in the film industry.'

O'Toole and Forbes also shared a vision of how *Macbeth* should turn out. 'Even in films,' said Forbes, 'I've never pretended to be anything other than an actors' director and I think that's what Peter wanted. In the last analysis, everything has to be subservient to the actor.' And they shared the same instinctive approach to Shakespeare. 'Too much scholarship has been applied to Shakespeare,' said Forbes. 'He's been analysed out of existence. Shakespeare was a working playwright, dear. Take the porter's scene in Macbeth. Why is it there? It's there because Burbage said, "Listen Will, I'm covered in tomato ketchup, I've got to get round the back of The Globe, I've got to have a couple of jars of mead and change my knickers – give me eight or nine minutes to get my breath back".'

Forbes and O'Toole between them worked out a means of bending *Macbeth* to their own theories, combining the cinematic method of visual sensation to an old-fashioned, almost hammy, literal interpretation of the play, as if performed by the old Baylis company. O'Toole gave this advice: 'I urge you to watch Bryan Forbes's innovative treatment of Banquo's ghost and the sleep-walking sequences of Lady Macbeth. We're also staging a terrifying swordfight.'

How did O'Toole view the character of Macbeth? 'Macbeth is a precursor of practically all literature we now term Gothic,' he explained. 'A precursor of Beckett. It is one of Shakespeare's more mature works; ironic, explicit and implicit. He is not a flawed hero, but a flawed villain. I believe it is Shakespeare's greatest play, yet I find Lear to be the greatest artefact on earth. Approaching the role of Macbeth, one feeling I got was that intellectualism is the main spoilator of the arts.'

He was conscious of the presence of evil in the play. 'Whoever wrote this play had looked upon such unimaginable horrors with an unflinching steady gaze and had such powers of observation and expression that this work registers an unqualified knowledge of evil and transforms it into another strange world. The evil smokes off the printed page. It is all right there in the text.' Forbes agreed entirely. 'This is the first supernatural play in the English language,' he said. 'It was written by Shakespeare to suck up to James I who fancied himself as an expert on demonology. I would never have gone along with a production where everyone is dressed as a Nazi.'

West's fear that the O'Toole/Forbes production was going to be immensely archaic did not mean that it could not work. It might be dreadfully old-fashioned, but that did not make it impractical. What made it impractical was the desire to apply film techniques to the theatre. First, there seemed to be little attempt to stay within a small budget. The wastrel attitudes of the film industry were brought to bear on the costumes, on the set, on everything where a degree of economy could be maintained. Late decisions and arbitrary changes meant that costly work was rejected at the last moment. There was a ludicrous attempt to effect massive scene changes which proved to be impossible to mount, but O'Toole and Forbes did manage to achieve a castellated set, like an old Hollywood castle.

O'Toole was getting it all his own way and neither West nor any other member of the Prospect company could intervene. This is how O'Toole described the casting of Lady Macbeth. 'The role of Lady Lauder is the most difficult part to cast in all Shakespeare,' explained O'Toole. 'I had had a number of ideas for the role but none of the actresses, bright talents that they were, quite fitted my dream. I could see her as though she were real. And then one day I was lucky enough to see my dream personified. This was Frances Tomelty from the Belfast Theatre. When I laid my eyes on her for the first time I was knocked out by her manner and the fierceness of her eyes. She fitted exactly what I had been carrying around in my head for ten months – a bloody eagle, tall and dark. Then I told her what I had in mind, and we had a top to bottom bash at the text. I had to say "The part is yours".'

He found the casting of Banquo similarly magical. 'Brian Blessed is marvellous as Banquo,' he said. 'He's a massive man with a massive humour. A skilled fighter, amazing, exciting and hugely intelligent. He's so sexy. His great, beautiful, deep voice keeps rolling out at you and the whole house shakes. He's my height and he's built like a barn. Not only is Banquo terribly important in the first two acts, but after that his apparition comes on three times. He terrifies Lauder and I assure you that, off or on, Brian Blessed terrifies me.'

O'Toole wanted to apply the same rehearsal method that he used in films. Before the cast went anywhere near the theatre, he wanted to have become intimate with them and the text. He was nervous about his return to the stage and wanted everything to be just right. 'What's left of my insides,' he said, 'are churning over at taking on *Harry Lauder*. We're doing *Lauder* straight down the middle, which is the hardest way – but the most rewarding. Of course, as so many of us have film backgrounds, we've chucked in some cinematics skills.'

His plan to calm his nerves and take whatever precautions were necessary to alleviate the dangers of a flop was to take the cast to his house in Connemara, there to have persistent read-throughs and even do some rudimentary blocking. 'It is the only way to approach acting unobserved, uninitiated, protracted private study of the role and the play,' he explained. He went off to Galway on his own at first, then sent for three key members of the cast: Frances Tomelty, Brian Blessed and Donald Sutton, who was cast as Macduff. And it was while in Ireland with the small group of cast that O'Toole first realised that the bad spell which hangs over *Macbeth* was beginning to affect his production.

While working on the play in Connemara, he was driving along the cliff road when he went out of control and the car veered towards the edge. 'The car was a total write-off, just pieces,' he said, 'and I was inches from a huge tumble.' He had thought of other things which might be simply coincidence, but certainly looked suspicious in the light of the Macbeth curse. Just after he had first talked to Toby Robertson about playing Macbeth, his marriage with Sian Phillips had broken up. That might have been coincidence, but what O'Toole was not to know was that a fringe theatre production of the musical *Pal Joey* with Sian Phillips would transfer to the West End shortly after *Macbeth* opened at the Old Vic. His wife playing in public the part of a woman whose sexual appetite favoured younger men was the sort of coincidence which O'Toole could do without.

Then, a month before *Macbeth* opened, David Mercer died. He had written *Ride a Cock Horse*, the last play in which O'Toole, with Sian, had appeared on the London stage. Other members of the cast were also suffering from the Macbeth coincidence. Frances Tomelty, playing Lady Macbeth, was very nearly killed when she fell off her motorbike at eighty miles an hour. And Trudie Tyler, the actress playing the first witch, was rushed to hospital with a burst appendix – 'that was life or death,' said O'Toole. O'Toole was not reassured when Bryan Forbes remembered that it was on the first night of *Macbeth* at the Old Vic in 1937, at the opening of the new season, that Lilian Baylis had a heart attack and died.

And when rehearsals began at the theatre, it was clear that everything was not well. The first day was, as expected, pretty awful and Forbes started as he meant to go on by tearing everyone off a strip. But as the days went by, the improvement which usually accompanies the hard work which was undoubtedly going into the production was not showing. Rumours started coming out of those rehearsals that, unless something major was done, the company was heading for a disaster.

Timothy West was torn between intervening, as he had every right to do, or leaving O'Toole to make his own mistakes. Princess Margaret made an unexpected appearance at the rehearsals and tried, jokingly, to lift the curse which was all too evidently at work.

'Suddenly I heard this voice,' O'Toole remembers, '"I was born in Glamis and I've come to take the curse off it." I thought it was very decent of her.' But all that the Princess did of lasting effect was to recommend that the company use Kensington Gore, the name of the stage blood which the St John's Ambulance Brigade, the voluntary first aid body, use for their demonstrations. That, too, was to rebound.

The Sunday before opening night, West was in despair. He was confident of disaster and angry about O'Toole's squandering of scarce company resources. An example of this was O'Toole's initial choice of lighting director. 'He is good,' said O'Toole. 'He works with lights and lasers so the dagger seems to hang in the air.' O'Toole's lighting wizard, however, did little for weeks, shutting himself in a rehearsal room asking only for conventional lighting equipment, empty tin cans and a number of black plastic dustbin liners. His fee was well outside the normal sum budgeted for lighting technicians, and empty Scotch bottles were taken from outside his room daily.

At last the company was gathered to see the result of this genius recommended by O'Toole. There was an elaborate sense of drama, as the house lights were dimmed and the curtain slowly rose. There on the stage were the dustbin bags, blown up with air, lit by bulbs in old tin cans. The wizard boasted that they would seem like Glamis, hills, ramparts or anything else the director wished. West covered his face in a mixture of embarrassment, for having been duped so easily, and simmering, resigned anger.

By the morning of 3 September 1980, the opening night, the scale of the looming disaster was clear. Advance bookings excelled any figure for any play at the Old Vic in recent times. While having his photograph taken by press photographers outside the theatre, O'Toole was already murmuring about crucial errors in his life. 'Every day of my life I've made mistakes,' he said. 'I like to have time to myself to think over my past life and my past mistakes – which are many.' He was not going to have a quiet life for the next four months.

By the last half hour before curtain up, everyone backstage knew that the storm was about to break. Having O'Toole in the company had its advantages. This *Macbeth* had attracted acres of free publicity. Journalists had queued up to interview O'Toole, back on the London stage after a fifteen-year break. But that same publicity machine was also going to prove a tragic disadvantage. This *Macbeth* was now horribly conspicuous. The critics were seated on the far side of the curtain with sharpened pencils. Any play with such a build-up of publicity was likely to attract harsher critical judgments than usual, but there was also, in this case, a forewarning from the buzz which came through the network of actors.

The production was flawed, unmanageable, outrageously undisciplined and the critics were looking forward to carving up the pretensions of O'Toole and Forbes. Timothy West had made an appeal to them during rehearsals to amend their conception and do their own reputations a favour. He was ignored. O'Toole had an interference-free contract and he could not see the scale of the disaster facing him. Still, he put the word about among the cast before curtain-up to be prepared for a rough ride.

Timothy West was loyal to O'Toole until the scale of the disaster had been proved to him. On the evening of the first night, West appeared on the main national evening news programme, 'Nationwide', and bolstered the production, insisting that all the rumours about it opening too soon, before all the difficulties had been ironed out, were false. Until the production was proved to be a disaster, West was determined to remain impeccably loyal in public to O'Toole and Forbes. At the same time, as the administrator of the company ultimately responsible for the welfare of the company, he wanted to make it clear that O'Toole had overruled him and his better judgment and gone on regardless. He did not want to be accused of having disassociated himself from the production after the press notices were published and so he sent a letter, making clear that it was his view that the production of *Macbeth* about to be staged was unworthy of the company, to O'Toole, Forbes, their respective lawyers and the members of the Old Vic Board.

One of the most humiliating moments of West's life was standing in the foyer of the Old Vic on the opening night, knowing the scale of the disaster about to break upon his company. He had issued a public statement, a less direct version of the letter he had sent to those immediately concerned with *Macbeth*, which, for those astute enough to read between the lines, meant that he wanted to stand clear of the imminent avalanche of abuse. A reporter from the *Daily Mail* spotted that something was up and asked West: 'What does this mean?' West replied: 'What it says.' The reporter: 'Do you disassociate yourself from it, then?' West dodged the question, but the meaning of his anxious face was clear.

From the first scene, of three witches stirring their venomous pot, the audience was giggling and tittering. Before long this broke into open laughter. There had not been a full-frontal flop as huge as this for years. Young critics looked forward to using a battery of vitriolic words which had lain unneeded and unused in the vocabulary for as long as they had been working. The reviews the next day spelled out the mighty mess that was served up that first night.

The assault was led by Jack Tinker of the *Daily Mail*, who wrote: 'It would be uncharitable to describe Peter O'Toole's long heralded return to the Old Vic as an unmitigated disaster. There is at least one thing to be said in mitigation: he is the first actor ever to set me off in fits of involuntary giggles throughout *Macbeth*. Now that in itself is a sort of achievement. The performance is not so much downright bad as heroically ludicrous. What O'Toole conjures up may not be the tragedy of a brave man wrecked by a single flaw in his nature (the classic definition of tragedy, Mr O'Toole) but it is Hollywood at its most hilarious self-parody. The voice is pure Bette Davis in her Baby Jane mood; the manner is Vincent Price hamming up a Hammer Horror.'

He went on: 'It was, of course, the rottenest luck for him to run smack into a wall on his third bravura exit (so much of this play takes place in the dark). But it is surely the most hilarious miscalculation to totter out of Duncan's death chamber covered from head to toe in bright red gore, clutching two dripping swords and eventually gasp out the purely superfluous information: "I have done the deed." '

Even Irving Wardle of *The Times*, who is usually well-mannered enough to prefer not to write a scathing notice, better ignore the show altogether, could not avoid meeting the expectations of the overblown publicity head-on. 'Mr O'Toole,' he wrote, 'strides on in what one first takes to be the last stages of battle fatigue. His walk is an exhausted lunge, his voice thick, hoarse and full of abrupt sledgehammer emphases. But as he begins, so he continues. His manner on the stage is not that of a man in an intricate, danger-fraught situation, but that of someone who owns the place. He walks around the stage as if inspecting a property he has just acquired; pinching a cheek here and there, tossing commands over his shoulder, but not paying too much attention to the small fry.'

He continues: 'His verse speaking consists of a heavy lurch from beat to beat, delivered in measured, sustained tone, and depending on prolonged phrasing within a single breath. Arresting to begin with, if only as total departure from modern verse convention, it grows extremely monotonous and blots out the sense.' The critics were unanimous: the production stank from top to toe. No one, not even the set designers, were free from scathing criticism. The gallons of Kensington Gore on stage was matched gallon for gallon by the blood over the newspapers the next morning.

With the benefit of a few days thought, the *Sunday Times* critic, James Fenton, having thrown his tomatoes at O'Toole in the stocks, tried for an explanation. 'Don't trust those reviews,' he wrote. 'The spectacle is far worse than has hitherto been made out, a milestone in the history of coarse acting. It moved the *Daily Mail* to giggles and

I was in such difficulties that I often wondered whether it would be better to leave the theatre and explode outside. But something froze the laughter on the lips. It was the premeditated awfulness of O'Toole's performance. There was no question of risks taken, or brave attempts which had simply failed. This was the kind of awfulness which could have been seen a mile off.' Which, indeed, it had been.

Fenton then went on to name the mistakes, then lay the blame. 'My colleagues have commented on the Knightsbridge witches, the sword that bent in the duel, the classic gaffe when Macduff announced that "Macbeth was from his mother's womb untimely ripped", the laughter of the audience when Mr O'Toole arrived drenched in gore and announced after age-long pause that he had done the deed (had he not told us, we might have supposed that some discontented members of the cast had placed a bucket of blood over his dressing room door), the moment when the Macbeths walked straight into the scenery, and a hundred or so other minor points which a little time (a century, for instance) might straighten out.'

And, in his final diagnosis, Fenton gets closer than anyone to the true reason for O'Toole's shambling appearance. 'As to Mr O'Toole's performance, it was deranged. "I have," says Macbeth, "a strange infirmity which is nothing/To those that know me." At first, I thought that this must be a portrayal of drunkenness. It had a slurred slowness, like that of the drunken driver who imagines he will go undetected if he sticks to the kerb and never exceeds ten miles an hour. Later, I began to wonder whether the boorishness and imperception of the delivery might not be better explained if one thought of a Macbeth who was in the habit of getting stoned out of his mind, so that his brain over the years had turned to Gruyère cheese. Finally, I was forced to reject both theories in favour of a worse explanation, that this Macbeth stemmed from an utterly private conception of personal glory, a conception so private and so intense that it rejected any offer of help or advice in its realisation, a conception that spurned the company and spurned the audience.'

The morning after, O'Toole, Forbes, the rest of the cast and West were all stunned by the harshness of the reception. This was not a single bad notice that could be put down to a little indigestion in the reviewer. This was a shower of bile unanimously sprayed and no one was in any doubt that it was O'Toole who was to blame. O'Toole's Hampstead home was besieged by reporters. At two in the afternoon, O'Toole finally agreed to see them and invited them in. He was still in his green dressing room. He delivered an expletive-ridden defence of his performance. 'It was competent. It was fit for public consumption. It will improve,' he said.

Meanwhile, Timothy West was disowning the production. Skating around the delicate ice of professional protocol, he could not defend his colleague's behaviour. 'I am afraid I have to disown it. Peter contractually has total artistic control, and though I tried to talk to him about how he was playing it, he would not listen. I had enormous reservations, but by the time I was able to see it in rehearsal it was too late to try to get him to see reason.'

He went on: 'Peter doesn't seem to realise that we do Shakespeare far more quickly now, without laboriously explaining the setting of each scene. It's something Peter, no doubt for good reasons of his own, ignores – the result is very slow. He has a concept, which to be honest I'm unable to define, and has been preparing it for a long time. Perfectly laudable, he wanted no interference. The problem is that when it became evident this would lead to the present outcome he was totally unwilling to jettison or even adapt his approach. I admire Peter as an actor. Doing the play this way, he's not being fair to himself. He's got a wonderful Macbeth in him. We all know that. It's sad that he rejects any direction advice. I'm hoping to meet Peter and persuade him.'

O'Toole smartly slapped back. Laughing, he said of West's advice: 'If he disowns this production he will be skint.' His words became tougher. '*Macbeth* is none of West's business. I would never contemplate restaging it. I shall continue to have full artistic control. I am not going to make any changes . . . but it will be better. It will be just as I want it, in time. All the ingredients are there, but it hasn't come together yet.'

Bryan Forbes was even more vitriolic about West's disloyalty. He stood up on the stage at the curtain call on the second night and made a statement. 'Ladies and Gentlemen,' he said before a bewildered audience who were, by and large, thrilled to be witnessing news being made – a real, live row in front of their eyes, 'as you probably know, World War III was announced today. We are bloodied but not yet bowed. I have always thought that Judas was one of the least attractive characters in the whole of human history, and would therefore like to say that I don't disown my company or my stage crew, my lighting crew or my sound crew. On the contrary, I stand with them and I applaud them.' The curse of Macbeth had split the Old Vic company in two. The only consolation was that the queues were longer than ever at the box office. The play had transcended the description bad and had become essential viewing, at the very least to determine a low mark of stage competence.

The row was too much for Toby Robertson, the sacked director of the Old Vic company. He sent an angry telegram to David Russell, the Old Vic board's chairman, criticising West for daring to criticise O'Toole. Still bitter about the method of his ousting, he thought West's intervention was 'more damaging to the Vic's interest than bad notices'. It was not only damaging to this production, but also to those who might be persuaded, as O'Toole was, to join the company and therefore draw in large audiences. 'Who can go to the Vic now,' asked Roberston, 'without wondering whether Tim will turn round and disown this one as well?'

The curse of Macbeth followed the play into its third night. A quarter of an hour before curtain-up, a soft-spoken Irish woman's voice told the stage doorkeeper on the telephone that there was a bomb in the theatre. Frances Tomelty took to the stage and asked the audience to leave. Being Irish, she was able to tell them, with feeling: 'I know what it's like to be in a bomb scare.' After a police search for twenty-five minutes, the audience was allowed back into the theatre.

Just before the delayed curtain-up, a second bomb scare was received on the telephone. The same voice said: 'You didn't take it seriously, did you? It'll go off in the interval.' O'Toole and Brian Blessed took to the stage, O'Toole half dressed as Macbeth. 'The police are at the stage door,' he said. 'It is with the utmost reluctance that I beg everybody in this house to take it seriously.' There was an awkward silence among the audience, until Blessed stepped forward and said: 'Ladies and Gentlemen, do come and see the show because he is absolutely smashing.'

O'Toole was pressed into a further gloom. Not only was the third night cancelled, but during the time he was out of the theatre, his grandfather's gold watch, bought by his grandmother after 'she made some fortunate wagers on some horses', and given to O'Toole by his mother, had been stolen. Macbeth's curse had struck again. The nineteenth century solid gold pendant watch, with a Chinese design on the back, was the only sentimental thing that O'Toole wore and he kept it with him for good luck. He offered a reward in vain.

By the end of the week, O'Toole was ready to take stock. His anger with Timothy West, who he delighted in nicknaming Miss Piggy, had died down and he had replaced that with a determination to save the production and his reputation. He had certainly been shaken by the harshness of the reviews. 'There has been a lot of abuse poured on me,' he told James Green. 'When I read it, of course it hurts me. I'm only a human being. I'm affected by reasonable opinion. But when that opinion is done, the performance remains and the public are my peers and will judge. Getting slated in the reviews had a reverse effect. It brought the entire cast closer together and fighting back and it brought people flocking into the theatre putting bums on seats.'

He described his feelings of the first night and what it was like on stage: 'I felt cold and tense on stage; it was a curious mixture of mania and fears and zaniness. It is like a bell ringing for the start of a prize fight. Once you begin you forget your own feelings.' Of West's criticism of taking the part too slowly: 'I was probably a little too pedantic. But I would rather settle for pedantic accuracy than the kind of sloppy rubbish I hear elsewhere and will not support. There are lots of people keen to make the poetic prosaic. It is a crime. Trying to speak blank verse correctly is a deliberate attempt on my part. I didn't want an intellectual Macbeth, slanted in some trendy way or set in some unlikely milieu. Our version goes straight down the middle, which is the hardest way – but also the most rewarding.' And of the reviews: 'First nights are a modern form of bear-baiting. A sophisticated form. Sometimes I was pleased the way it was going, other times I wasn't. I knew the reviews would be bad, as you only have to look at the record of the play and O'Toole. I didn't think they would be that savage.'

He took some solace in the fact that the play had had a history of spectacular failures. 'All the previous Old Vic *Macbeths* have been calamitous, so we're merely following in tradition. Charles Laughton, who had this very dressing room, came unstuck here when he was the biggest cinema star. His Macbeth was a disaster. He got raspberries from the gallery for the only time in his career, and the thought of that night made him weep. Laurence Olivier also came unstuck here. Among other things he lost his voice on opening night and couldn't be heard beyond the second row. In actors' parlance he "died a death". Wasn't it Henry Irving, who failed himself as Macbeth but kept it on with enormous courage, who said: "No audience, no art?" '

A correspondence started in the columns of *The Times* backing his brave efforts, condemning West and pointing out other disastrous attempts at the play. But O'Toole was determined that the play would not beat him. Armed with a Victoria Cross medal, with its inscription 'For Valour', which Tommy Steele had sent him after the first night reviews, he vowed that he would keep working at his part and the production until it was right. 'You could rehearse for years and still not get it right. It needs a marriage between actor and audience. Every performance at the Vic I am being instructed and filtered. It is mutating. So there are now some minor differences from the first night and we'll be meeting to discuss more.'

O'Toole was grateful for small mercies. His biggest achievement, he thought, was that the production was at least not mediocre. He hated mediocrity. Better try and fail disastrously than scrape by. He would plod away until it was right and if it didn't come right, mind. 'Glamis wasn't built in a day,' he said.

O'Toole was being ludicrously optimistic about his ability to tu. the production round, imagining that it was merely a matter of rehearsal, of rapport, and ignoring the fatally flawed conception of the production. Before the aborted third night, he made this idiotic assessment of where the trouble lay and offered an absurd offering to fortune. Few actors without the arrogance of O'Toole could declare, after two disastrous, laughter-ridden, chaotic nights of a doomed production: 'The play is so complex and yet so simple, it befuddles any second-rate theatrical mind. Such people attempt to find some oblique way of doing it and the result is chaos.' Standing in the ruins of his own chaotic production, he had lost any ability to recognise reality.

For their part, the Old Vic Theatre Company board, embarrassed by such a public division in their senior personnel and not wanting to sink either a terrible production which they still hoped would make them some money, backed both horses. The chairman, David Russell, said that he backed O'Toole. The board knew from the beginning that he would provide 'an individual and possibly controversial interpretation.' And 'the board now hope that nothing further will interrupt future performances by O'Toole and the *Macbeth* company at the Old Vic and the forthcoming Arts Council tour. Equally they would like to express their total confidence in Timothy West as artistic director of the Old Vic.'

The production had become a *succès de scandale* and the bookings for the tour of Britain beginning the next month, October, were record breaking. In Liverpool, where *Macbeth* opened on 13 October, the bookings had, by the previous night, reached ninety per cent of capacity, bringing in £30,000 in cash to the box-office; at Bristol, which the company was to reach on 20 October, all previous theatre booking records had been broken; for Leeds, which would host O'Toole on 27 October, the previous record for advance bookings had been doubled and only single seats remained for sale. This success sharpened the accusations from within the company that the critics' reception on the opening night at the Old Vic had caused the cancellation of a nine-week *Macbeth* tour of Europe arranged by the Dutch impresario, Jan de Blieck. 'I have a reputation to consider,' he said, explaining why he was pulling out.

The company's British tour began on 13 October at Liverpool, due back at the Old Vic at the end of November for seventeen final performances and a last night on 10 December. At the Bristol Hippodrome, all tickets were sold before the opening night and the same happened at the Liverpool Empire where the company played

.o a capacity audience of 2,312 each night. By the beginning of November, O'Toole was still fiddling with the production, hoping for a triumphant re-entry.

At Coventry, he put up a notice backstage, appealing for the cast to suggest changes before the final assault. 'As you may have noticed,' it read, 'since the last weeks in London and throughout the tour our production has been subjected to mutations of text, scenery, costume and lighting.' He asked for any suggestions 'be it a sound effect, a light, an inflection or a cut.' O'Toole went on to thank the cast for being 'so loyal, brave, helpful and professional throughout our run.' He concluded, quoting from *Hamlet*: 'We return home to the Old Vic on Monday and, as the man said, "The readiness is all".'

But the production was still substantially the same as the one which left London in disgrace. The provincial critics had, as always, been kinder than their London colleagues, but few in the company could tell whether this meant that the production was improving. D. J. Hart of the *Birmingham Post* found the production 'static and ordinary', although O'Toole's performance he described as 'magnificent'. Peter McGarry of the *Coventry Evening Telegraph* found O'Toole 'a figure of emotional substance' and 'ever formidable'.

The tour had been riven with embarrassment because Timothy West's production of *The Merchant of Venice*, with himself as Shylock, had been running in tandem. O'Toole and West were still barely on speaking terms and it was not long in London before matters came to a head again. On 21 December, four days after the last night of *Macbeth*, O'Toole told Philip Oakes: 'I persuaded Tim West not to allow the Old Vic to become a third-rate touring company drudging round the provinces to earn an Arts Council handout. I said we should put two Shakespearean plays in repertoire, then go out and storm a few barns from our base in Waterloo Road. And the policy worked. It was a hundred per cent, bottled in bond, copperbottomed, oceangoing success, in every sense; both critically and financially. We opened to bad notices, but by the time we'd finished our tour we were playing like a Stradivarius. Even the press had come round to our side. They were practically writing poems.'

He went on: 'In sixty-odd performances of *Macbeth* we've put over £200,000 into the Old Vic's kitty. That's not a bad buttress against cuts in public spending. There is no doubt that we have been theatrically successful and we have a smashing company. But whether it will be kept together I have no idea, because I am being excluded from a certain amount of policy making in 1981. My heart always was – and is – at the Old Vic. It is the last proper playhouse in London. But it is getting overwhelmed with bureaucracy, alas. There's nothing I can say about the way our production was disowned. It is beyond any comment I could muster. If any wants to pick a fight with me, let them pick it. But no one has actually come forward. Lots of people have said things to newspapers, but never to my face. Let them say it to my face first. That's all I ask. We can go on from there.' Two days later, on the day before Christmas Eve, he resigned from the Old Vic.

The resignation was sensational but not surprising. O'Toole and West had met during December to discuss plans for the company in the new year and O'Toole had floated the idea of doing *King Lear*, but there was an assumption underlying the discussions that this was no more than a proposal for form's sake; once more O'Toole's *Lear* would remain a pipe-dream. West had told O'Toole that he did not see any future for him in the company and that there was no question of him having total artistic control in future productions.

O'Toole took that as an invitation to stand down. He issued a press statement which arrived in print before he had written a letter informing the Old Vic company. It read:

'The Old Vic, as it existed between 1930 and 1960, was my nursery and my inspiration. I was privileged to serve my apprenticeship by the light of the Old Vic tradition and ethic. When Mr Toby Robertson asked me to help him reestablish the Old Vic company, I readily agreed to do so. After the adverse critical notices for *Macbeth*, I and my fellow actors worked very hard. The public responded with full houses and £200,000 at the box office in seventy-two performances, but for the people who currently run the Old Vic Theatre, namely Prospect Productions Ltd, that is not enough and therefore I have today resigned my position as associate director. The public will be the final arbiters on what is Old Vic tradition and I hope that in future I will be able to serve it again.'

Right until the end, O'Toole was confident that the venture had been a success and had no regrets about the follies of *Macbeth*. 'I chose to do *Macbeth*, he explained, 'because it's the most difficult play in the canon. You're chicken if you don't try. And I just wanted a crack at it on the principle of getting the worst over first. In the history of the British theatre there have been only three actors who have pulled it off: Macready, Garrick and Wolfit. And now me. It took time, but eventually it came together.'

For him, despite the critics' judgment which he admitted had 'deeply hurt' him, he still regarded it as 'the most important thing I've done in my life'. He even enjoyed the ludicrous sections of the *Macbeth* saga. He told Philip Oakes: 'I enjoyed every second of it. My favourite moment on the first night was when I'd killed Duncan. As I came down the stairs, dripping with blood, an ambulance howled all the way up Waterloo Road. I got the giggles. The audience got the giggles. It was bloody marvellous.'

The most sensational theatrical production for decades took its toll on the British acting fraternity and split them down the middle. Both O'Toole and West encouraged deep loyalty in their friends and lobbying and argument went on between the two factions. More than a mere squabble, it became a first-class political conflict about the artistic independence of actors and directors, the correct use of subsidised theatre money, the future or lack of future of the Old Vic as London's most historic playhouse and much more besides. Dinner parties and auditions dissolved when the matter was discussed. Everyone held an opinion about what went wrong and the relative merit of the two main protagonists. Often the subject was declared taboo by any hostess who wanted to keep a gathering of actors from destroying the furniture.

Those who backed West trouped to see O'Toole in *Macbeth* simply to gain further ammunition for their argument. Close friends of O'Toole wouldn't go anywhere near it, preferring the safety of ignorance and avoiding the anguish of seeing O'Toole make himself look ridiculous. Kenneth Griffith was out of the country, working on a film script in Valbruno in the Italian Alps. Although he passed through London, he was unable to see the production and the play closed on the weekend he returned. O'Toole accused him of cowardice, of wanting to avoid seeing him as Macbeth, but Griffith denied it. 'I wasn't looking forward to it, O'Toole, but I would have gone. I intended to go,' he told him. And he had sent a letter of support to O'Toole which was published in the *Guardian*. Sadly for O'Toole, the two high points of his career in the public mind have been his extraordinary, brilliant, precocious performance as Lawrence and the crazy, rambling, distracted portrayal of Macbeth.

There is one miserable postscript to the story of O'Toole and the Old Vic. A week before he resigned as associate director, the Arts Council discontinued their grant to the Old Vic Company. The Director-General, Sir Roy Shaw, quoted the controversy surrounding the production of *Macbeth* as one of the reasons for cutting the £300,000 per annum subsidy. After anguished attempts to save their continuance at the Old Vic, the Prospect Theatre Company resigned itself to liquidation. Among their assets were the costumes used in O'Toole's *Macbeth* and the leather and cloth tunics, bloodstained in Kensington Gore stage blood, were put up for auction in November of the following year.

The most opulent costume used by O'Toole was the star attraction and a great deal of speculation went on as to who would buy it.

O'Toole himself was thought to be bidding through an anonymous source and the star-speckled audience in the Old Vic stalls for the auction included many actor friends of O'Toole, including Dorothy Tutin. The O'Toole costumes provided the highest bids of the day, but there was no glamour attached to their final purchasers. Through an agent, the principal costume was sold to a theatrical costumiers in the United States; another to a costumier in Leeds, O'Toole's home city, as a publicity curio for his shop window.

# 11   Starting Again

MACBETH HAD been a great deal of fun for the audiences, who had rushed to register a new low in theatrical offerings. It had been good for the critics, who had delighted in reducing O'Toole to size. But for the cast and crew – and particularly for O'Toole – the whole episode was a disaster, a painful mess. At the farewell party, thrown mostly at O'Toole's expense, many of the actors either did not turn up at all or sloped off early. The celebrations of striking the set had a depressing quality about them. It was a wake. Everyone backstage had called O'Toole, 'Spud', for the run, but there was little affection when it was used as the scale of the disaster became clear. Everyone except O'Toole's most loyal allies within the cast was disillusioned with this fallible actor, once a great film star and a hero, who had turned their working lives to misery.

But if the experience of *Macbeth* was bad for the cast, it was terrible for O'Toole. He was humiliated and reviled. His reputation was dragged through the mud and, try as he and his friends might, the direction if not the weight of criticism was justified. O'Toole was distraught but, typically, defiant. He had convinced himself that, by the end of the run, he had got it right. Worse for him was that because everyone else perceived the play to have been a great disaster, he was to be forbidden to continue working for the Vic. His plans for *Lear* were laughed out of court. He was banished – O'Toole saved his face by imposing self-exile – from the Old Vic at Waterloo Road and the Old Vic Company was disbanded. O'Toole was blamed for that, too.

There was another important disappointment for O'Toole which he had rarely articulated except to himself. His failure in *Macbeth* had put a stop to an ambition which he had been moving towards and seemed at one time to be within an arm's length of achieving: to instal himself at the head of a great actors' company with himself as an actor-manager in the tradition of Henry Irving and all the heroic actor figures he worshipped.

This dimension of the *Macbeth* drama had only been hinted at once during the run of the play and then by Kenneth Griffith, who was staying in a small Italian Alpine village. Griffith wrote a letter to the *Guardian*: 'It strikes me about O'Toole, surrounded as I am by other physical peaks, that in this scandal he has brought to the British theatre the first bit of honest excitement in at least twenty years. Edmund Kean did it regularly.' O'Toole and Griffith shared the same perspective about the expensive excellence of the British subsidised theatre and the need to re-establish the actor as the prime interpreter of the dramatist's work in place of what O'Toole and Griffith described disparagingly as 'the puppet masters', the undergraduate actors turned stage directors which had come to dominate the British theatre. The rise of the puppet masters had reduced the stage to an unexciting, lavish yet unglamorous demonstration of a text, rather than a fullblooded, riproaring, gritty, powerful celebration of plays which only actors of the calibre and adventure of O'Toole could achieve.

Griffith explained it more fully well after the débâcle of *Macbeth*. To him, his friend O'Toole was a true hero of the British theatre, a crusader who had sacrificed nearly everything in trying at the Vic to wrest the attention of the public away from the anodyne happenings in the concrete palace of the National Theatre in favour of the true meat of thrilling acting in the old mould. Griffith explained: 'Quite a while before it opened, I was with him and he caught hold of me physically and said: "I promise you one thing, Griffith, about *Macbeth* – or, as he called it, *Harry Lauder* – it will not be good. It will be either a major triumph or a disaster." And I thanked him for that, because what I do resent about the contemporary British theatre is that it is very expensively "good". O'Toole is perhaps the last personification that we have of the potential of the actor. I think that what has happened with the advent of the failed actors from the Oxford University Dramatic Society and the Footlights in Cambridge, that these people, the Peter Halls, the Peter Brooks and whoever is running the Royal Shakespeare today, have taken away the potential of the actor and I think that the theare is between the actor and the writer primarily.'

When O'Toole was challenging Timothy West for control of the Old Vic Company, he made a symbolic decision to fight from within the theatre, leaving West in makeshift offices. There was no doubt in O'Toole's mind that the Old Vic Company could be wrested away from the accountants and given back to the actors and that formed the basis of his quarrel with West, although it was never described as such by either side.

As he walked away from the real-life tragedy of *Macbeth*, all the issues which it represented to O'Toole were mixed in his mind. He maintained that the play was good, that he was fine, that the audience loved it, the critics were unfair and that West had proved dishonourably disloyal. But as time went on, he admitted that, perhaps, things were not as they should have been. Some months after the event, he said: 'The opening night was a fiasco. When I think of it, my nose bleeds. I was very bad and there was only one thing to do and that was get it right, for that was just the first night that gave everyone a lovely time. They wrote in blood. It was a wonderful, concerted bay of abuse. Thoroughly deserved, I'm sure.'

It took a long time, but eventually he did admit that crashing into scenery, forgetting his lines and wearing running shoes was, perhaps, not the best way to play Macbeth. He had been shielded from the full effect of much of the abuse by being numb. 'Of course, I was pretty devastated,' he admitted to John Morgan in a radio interview. 'Not at the time. I mean, disbelief is a great cushion and then, I think simply out of "I am going to get the damned thing right", it began to get better and better and better at the Vic and then we began to tour. We went to my home town – I call it my home town, Bristol, where I served my apprenticeship – and blew it on the first night. I knew I'd blown it. And that was the only night of absolute desolation I'd had. I sat at the bottom of the suspension bridge in the pissing rain, thinking: "What on earth is going on?" But somehow or other, that was the absolute nadir of it all and from then on it went up, up, up, up, up.'

An element of self-deception remains. Only O'Toole thought and still persists in saying that, by the end of the run, he had mastered the part. The provincial press was less cruel than the London press, but the feeling from within the cast contradicted O'Toole's belief that he had eventually got it right. However, he explained it shortly afterwards thus: "We began disastrously, but we didn't end disastrously. It was reported as a one-night event. It wasn't, it was a fifteen-week event. But gradually, gradually, it began to turn. Without any question it was the most difficult thing I've ever done. I knew when it was right. I knew when it began to come right. The other rewarding thing was we began it in early September and the best performance was 22 November. I know that, so that's a build. Oh, the liberation. The sense of liberation, the sense of overcoming.'

Strangely, the horrors of *Macbeth* proved to be a good thing for O'Toole's state of mind. For many years he had been drifting through a series of films and had made little impression – with the exception of *Rogue Male* and *The Stunt Man*, which had acquired a cult following. *Macbeth* proved to him that he was still a big star, because the critics would merely have ignored a poor performance by a moderate star. The fact that they roasted him alive was evidence to O'Toole that he was still up there among the greats. More than that, for O'Toole, who lived with an ever-present death sentence since his serious illness, it proved that he was alive. He might not think much of the critics and would try to put them down, but he was grateful for their response.

As he explained: 'If I was criticised by Hazlitt or by Ken Tynan or by Hobson or someone I truly respected, it would affect me a great deal. But that was unbelievable. Poland didn't exist. Vietnam didn't exist. We were suddenly world news. It was probably the most savage compliment that I have ever been paid, to be world news because I was *bad*. It was wonderful. Now . . . not then.'

And he had proved something about his determination to carry on, despite his physical difficulties. The nightly humiliation of *Macbeth*, going on in front of an audience who were there prepared to laugh their way through the play, among a cast of actors and actresses with far less experience than he, who had once considered him a formidable actor: that nightly performance was an act of not only great physical stamina, but immense courage and each night he built up his confidence a little more. From total defeat, he discovered in himself the strength to ride the most horrifying reverse of his career. No wonder he imagined that the play was getting better; it was his ability to cope with the anguish of humiliation which led him, rightly, to consider that he was beating the pain of shaming himself in public.

As usual, when in trouble, O'Toole immediately set about two things: a visit to Clifden, his home in Ireland, and more work. His attitude was summed up by his remark: 'There isn't a day of my life, not one day, not one, that I don't wake up in the morning with such a sense of futility. Every single day. It lasts for about ten minutes, that's all. I think it's a little bit like immunisation. It's built-in. I'm immune to the great failures and defeats. I think one should keep one's expectations low.'

He found work in America. He had rarely worked in the United States, although nearly all of his films were intended principally for the American market. *The Stunt Man* was one of the rare exceptions and he had liked it. Having resisted Hollywood for years, he woke up to its charms very late. After the misery of *Macbeth*, he headed for Los Angeles and the same house with a pool. 'I have sat by a pool only two or three times in my entire life, and each time it's been this very same pool,' he explained. 'Sitting poolside in the California sunshine like a fucking movie star. People bring me coffee and juice if I ask for it. I tell them I've a movie star. They don't give a fuck, but somehow I amuse them.'

O'Toole is a commodity in the United States in a way that he is not in Britain. There he is a famous face, one of the aristocracy of successful people who have inscribed their faces and personalities on the minds of the American public. In the United States, they love a faded movie star almost more than they love stars in their prime. O'Toole is a commodity, a marketable, going concern, simply because he *is* O'Toole. In Britain success counts for little and achievement is measured in other ways than mere fame. The British don't like celebrities to get above themselves and positively relish a spectacular downfall. That is why *Macbeth* was a sell out and why, immediately afterwards, O'Toole thought his best bet was to make for California.

He was right. It was not long before a proposal was made to him to take part in a television safari to Botswana, to ride in a dugout canoe down the Okavango River for a series called *The American Sportsman*. This project suited O'Toole, whose love of travel and primitive communities gave him essential qualifications for the job. And such a trip would be therapeutic, a wonderful relief to put *Macbeth* and the wretched memories of the Old Vic in perspective. As usual, he started serious research immediately, surrounding his poolside with books on Africa, finding out everything he could about the people he would meet in Botswana. O'Toole described his safari as 'Good fun. Something unknown, a bit of true adventure. The Great White Actor on safari.'

He remembers the trip with great enthusiasm. 'Every fucking thing we did. It was an extraordinary, *extraordinary* adventure. We had only two bad moments. Once, we came across a pack of wild dogs and for a moment it looked like goodbye. But somehow we managed to get out with our skins intact. The other happened when we were stalking – of all things – bull elephants. Amazingly, they are the stealthiest of all the animals of the bush. They appear absolutely without warning. He had that ancient, old look. And one eye spotted us – and he gave us the ear treatment. *Va-voom*. And he showed us those great tusks and those great trotters and I thought, Dear God Almighty, this is my farewell performance. But once again, Providence intervened and we escaped.

'We saw hawks, shrikes, eagles; we were floating down river in a soap dish, with the camera crew in another soap dish behind us. And there in a tree on the other side of the river was an eagle, a fishing eagle, with its wings spread, drying its feathers. A *mighty* creature, with very carefully defined features outlined in black and white. We wondered whether it would be interested in a lump of fish. So I took a lump of tiger fish and heaved it into the air. Down it came, and with one talon he hooked onto it and off he went. It was an astounding sight.'

O'Toole had always been fascinated by wild animals, ever since a peculiar event in his childhood, in Leeds, during a German air raid. It is a classic O'Toole story: 'I remember this almighty night. I remember my mother's face, lying over my sister in the cellar and my father, Daddy, was sticking his head out of the door to see what was going on and there was a huge explosion and he came back with an unlit cigar and a bottle of Scotch. And that following morning, I went down into the main centre of the city and the first thing that I saw was a huge giraffe lying on its side. I thought, where on earth has this come from? And what had happened was that the bomb had hit the Science Museum and it was a stuffed giraffe. There were stuffed buffaloes, mastodons and all sorts. And not only that, hundreds and hundreds, I'll never forget this, of salt cellars and pepper pots because, right at the front of the museum was an exhibit of condiments through the ages and they had copped it. So the place was full of vinegar bottles and pepper and salt and stuffed animals.'

And he had done his homework on the Africans who live in Botswana. 'Jesus, these fellows go back more than a fortnight,' he said. 'When our hairy ancestors descended from the tress and went out onto the grassy plains and so on, these fuckers stayed right there – there at the base of the fucking trees. And there they stayed. They're completely primitive. They're not of this century at all. They're timeless, in fact. Looking at these bastards is like looking at the beginning of man. Very interesting coloration. Not at all negroid. Different characteristics entirely.'

For O'Toole, who fancies himself as a self-educated archaeologist and anthropologist, this was hardly work. By the time he returned to the USA, a more demanding job was ready for him – and one which would also act as a purgative to the bad memories of the London stage. *My Favourite Year* was an extraordinary project and one which suited O'Toole very well. It was based upon the experiences of young writers like Mel Brooks, Neil Simon and Woody Allen, who used to be down-table gag men for Saturday night spectacular television shows on the American networks in New York in the early 1950s. Mel Brooks's film company co-produced the film, engaging the actor Richard Benjamin, himself once a page for the NBC television network in New York, to direct. The plot concerns a young writer, whose unenviable task it is to look after the star of the live television show in the day preceding the broadcast. But the actor is a wildly irresponsible drunk, by the name of Alan Swann. O'Toole was cast as Swann.

Although the producer, Michael Gruskoff, described Swann as 'a cross between John Barrymore, John Gilbert and Errol Flynn' there was enough O'Toole in the role to make him a natural in the part. Not only was he encouraged by Benjamin to indulge himself in the sort of acting he preferred, but the retrospective nature of the television show within the film demanded O'Toole to be seen in clips from two of his previous films, *Lord Jim* and *Great Catherine*.

Although O'Toole had first read the script at the time *The Stunt Man* was released, there could not have been a better time for him to start on such a self-parodying role as when, in the aftermath of *Macbeth*, his whole career should seem to be in such sharp perspective before him. When first told of the project, O'Toole didn't think much of it, but when Richard Benjamin said he would like to see him about it, O'Toole speed-read the script and was charmed by it, as it seemed to contain many of the things that had made his best comedies so successful.

By chance, he had worked with Benjamin's wife in *What's New Pussycat?* Among the many lines he delighted in saying was one which he might have written himself. 'There's a line in it,' explained O'Toole, 'where Swann tells the young man who is looking after him: "Comedy is such a mystery to me. I feel much the way that Edmund Kean did." "You mean the great English actor?" the young man asks. "Yes," says Swann. "On his death bed, when he was asked how he felt, he replied: Dying is easy. Comedy is hard." '

Richard Benjamin explained that there was a very short list of actors whom they thought suitable for the part: 'Just about all English. We couldn't think of an American who would look believable with a sword. Not today, anyway. We knew O'Toole lived in Ireland. We called his agent in England, then called someone in Ireland who wasn't sure where he was. I get a phone call: he's at the Beverly Wilshire Hotel.' The day O'Toole was made a formal offer for the part, he was nominated for an Oscar for *The Stunt Man*. Mel Brooks called Benjamin and said to him: 'Well, that was brilliant. You know what that's going to cost us? Couldn't you have offered him the part yesterday?'

Benjamin was impressed by O'Toole's screen presence – 'He's a star in a room and he's a star on the screen' – and his professionalism: 'O'Toole is not just comedic or dramatic, he's human. I've worked with really good actors, but watching O'Toole is like seeing a thoroughbred run. It's really something. In the beginning, I would print three or four takes of something that Peter was doing and when I saw the dailies I would see it was there on the first take. It was all there because he reaches way down inside and pulls it all up. And it's a beautiful thing to see.' Benjamin had also underestimated O'Toole's range. 'I wasn't quite prepared for his comic sense, which is so astute. He would want to take a laugh line out of the script and instead do something that was deeply funny. He never went for an easy laugh. He's like a great comedian in this.'

Filming took place on location in New York City and drew large crowds. Although since O'Toole's illness, when doctors found what

O'Toole cagily calls 'a sort of form of malignancy', he has been expensive to insure, yet he insisted upon doing his own stunts. 'You can't fake these things,' he explained, 'especially in wide screen close-ups. The audience expects to see you there.' With his usual thoroughness, he sent for a swordfighting expert from California to demonstrate how he should wield a broadsword, even though the scene – a snatch from a phoney Swann film, *Defender of the Crown* – lasts only a few minutes.

But one thing that O'Toole did not count upon was a strange assault upon him and Mark Linn-Baker, playing his young escort, by a crowd of extras. 'Very Hollywood Gothic,' said O'Toole. 'Mark and I were attacked during the shooting of a scene by a mob of extras. Can you believe that? Actually attacked. It was positively like *The Day of the Locust*. I don't think I've witnessed anything quite so bizarre in my long and eclectic career. God only knows what was on their minds. We were shooting a scene in an apartment-house corridor and these extras – these animals, as it turned out – were supposed to simply mill around us, very passively, I might emphasise. Instead of that, they jumped all over us like rabid dogs. One cheeky prick took hold of me by the ear and wouldn't let go. I mean, he would *not* let go. I finally had to bash him in order to get free. I think they'd been in Hollywood so long, they'd lost their grip on reality.'

But if O'Toole had not expected the level of violence on the set, even less could he have guessed how well *My Favourite Year* would be received. It was quite against the trend: old-fashioned, a laboriously constructed comedy script, a cast of modest, middling actors and the first time Richard Benjamin had directed. Perhaps it was just because it was so off-beam from the high-technology films which were dominating the market that the film looked so fresh.

Leading the praise was Pauline Kael, whose reputation, although tainted by recent assaults by the next generation of film writers below her, still was an important boost to the film's opening. Although, she wrote in the *New Yorker*, 'the lighting is gummy, the views of Broadway are a blur, and the staging sometimes creaks – it even klonks,' she praised the film for its 'bubbling spirit' and particularly the work of O'Toole. It was a useful, intelligent and extraordinarily flattering notice.

'O'Toole is simply astounding,' she wrote. 'In recent years he hasn't had the press he deserves, particularly in England. Maybe, having had the nobility of a certain kind of stardom conferred upon him, he is thought not to have kept his side up. His recent performances seem to be an answer to that; he's saying, "See, I'm not gone – you're just looking in the wrong place." And he has been getting better as an actor. When you watch him work in *The Stunt Man* or on

TV in *Masada* or here, it's clear that he doesn't impress himself with what he is doing. And he doesn't hold back a thing – not even what stars usually hold back to make you know they're stars. While others turn into immobile figureheads, he has become a master of physical comedy – a whirlwind of the order of Barrymore in *Twentieth Century*.' She goes on: 'The jokes are good, but it's Peter O'Toole's Swann who makes it memorable. I can't think of another major star, with the possible exception of Ralph Richardson, who would have the effrontery (about what great actors should allow themselves to do) to bring this sly performance off.'

O'Toole stayed in New York for his next film, made for CBS Television, *Svengali*, an update of George Du Maurier's novel, *Trilby*, which had been made into a film several times before, including a 1955 British version, starring Donald Wolfit and Hildegarde Neff. The director was Anthony Harvey, who had directed O'Toole when making his first film, *The Lion in Winter*. At the end of that film, O'Toole had been enraged by Harvey's final cut of the film and had driven across London to hammer at the door of Harvey's Chelsea home, demanding that the cuts be restored. The reunion, however, was happier than might have been expected.

'Peter's much more mellow,' Harvey explained. 'The anger is still there, of course, but there's a gentleness, an inner strength. You can sit and have long talks with him. You couldn't do that before.' He continued: 'He takes great chances, but he's saved by his own sense of the ridiculous. He's not afraid to make an ass of himself.' Harvey, too, had found that O'Toole's illness had significantly changed his outlook. The wild boy was gone.

O'Toole smokes a great deal, always French cigarettes in a black holder, which minimally filters the nicotine, and, a habit he picked up in the States, he chews gum – 'It helped me get off the booze. And now, at least, they make it sugarless, so your fucking teeth don't rot out' – but hell-raising is behind him. Or, at least, the old, drunken style has gone. 'Only ninnies make booze the excuse for their wild escapades,' he said. 'I can still make whoopee, sweetheart, but now I do it sober. I no longer anaesthetise myself into unconsciousness. That makes the escapade pointless.'

The making of *Svengali* was sobering for other reasons. His co-star was Jodie Foster, making her first film since, eleven months before, a lunatic, John Hinckley, had tried to shoot dead President Ronald Reagan. When he was arrested, he claimed that he had done the deed in order to impress Jodie Foster, an actress whom he had never met but with whom he had become obsessed since seeing her in Martin Scorsese's film, *Taxi Driver*, in which she played a twelve-year-old prostitute.

In the year preceding the filming of *Svengali*, the Hinckley trial had seriously upset Jodie Foster, a student at Yale University. To return to film making was a delicate business and O'Toole was to become an avuncular figure on the set. In the plot of the film, things were different. O'Toole was to play the part of Anton Bosnyak, a voice teacher who spots an exceptional talent in a singer in a band called the Skunkadelics, played by Jodie Foster. They work with each other and fall in love, becoming so dependent upon each other that the young woman can only sing properly when he is around.

The filming was kept very low-key and there was a great deal of extra security on the set. As O'Toole explained: 'The place is covered in fuzz as there are always dodgy people after her. But she rises above the whole damn thing. Right now her bodyguards are me and half of the Teamsters Union, who are the crew of this picture. She can't step out an inch without one of us keeping a friendly eye on her.'

The two of them developed a warm working relationship and, because of their differing heights – he is 6 foot 3 inches, she is 5 foot 1 inch – he called her, affectionately, 'Midget'. She is a gutsy little bird,' he said, 'a gorgeous snot-nose. I adore her.' When Katharine Hepburn saw the completed film, she wrote to O'Toole saying that it was the best film he had ever made. And her lasting judgment on him was: 'He can do anything. A bit cuckoo, but sweet and terribly funny.'

As filming down by the Hudson River in New York came to an end, O'Toole made his way slowly back to Ireland. There were hints that he would be returning to the London stage. There was a rumour that he would star in a remake by Nagisa Oshima of *The Bridge Over the River Kwai*, David Lean's masterpiece about an English officer, played by Sir Alec Guinness, in a Japanese prisoner-of-war camp. But what concerned O'Toole more than anything was an important date due in August: his fiftieth birthday. 'Half a century. It is the only birthday that has ever meant anything to me at all. But Midsummer, in Ireland, up it popped. I suddenly thought, I'm half a century and what haven't I done? What is there to do? I'd done an awful lot. Maybe not the right things. For the first time I became contemplative. It was quite astounding.'

The one part which he had never played and which he had often suggested out loud that he would like to play – to Timothy West after the *Macbeth* rumpus, then again to an interviewer in New York, shortly after – was that of King Lear. But that was not to be, at least for the time being. It became clear that O'Toole would return to the West End stage in London as Jack Tanner, George Bernard Shaw's progressive, affluent revolutionary in *Man and Superman*. This time, there would be more care to prevent a recurrence of the *Macbeth* débâcle. O'Toole's old friend from Bristol days, Patrick Dromgoole, of Harlech Television, would direct O'Toole, thereby avoiding the dangers of a conventional stage director. The play would open quietly at the end of September in Birmingham at the Repertory Theatre, then slowly travel around the provinces until it opened at the Haymarket Theatre at the beginning of November.

It would be possible, therefore, to abort the London opening if disaster overtook the production. As an extra precaution, well down the cast, opening as a housemaid in her British début, would be Pat O'Toole, O'Toole's younger daughter, although, by the time the production reached London she would be a humble assistant stage manager. But still there was O'Toole bravado. Jack Tanner is the longest part in the British theatre repertoire, even without the 'Don Juan in Hell' act which was to be omitted, and O'Toole would be on stage for most of the time.

When previews began in Birmingham, O'Toole was word-perfect, if a little wobbly on his feet. He was so confident of his lines, having played the part last at the Gaiety Theatre, Dublin, that when Joyce Carey, playing Mrs Whitefield, faltered in her words, he was able to help her out and ad lib. Still, O'Toole looked doddery. He tended to lisp and appeared regularly to lose his balance. On his first entrance on the first Saturday of the provincial run, he tripped over the carpet and almost went head first up stage.

There was a general air of expectation when the first night arrived at the Haymarket Theatre on Thursday 18 November. A great number of his friends were there to support him. Kenneth Griffith was sat in the stalls, rooting for the champion of actors without puppet strings. There were Alan Bates, Derek Nimmo, Bill Wyman of the Rolling Stones. And there were the press. There was great tension in the foyers of the Haymarket that night as supporters brushed shoulders with bloodthirsty critics. When the time for curtain-up came, there was even more tension. Prince Andrew was switching on the Christmas lights in Regent Street, a stone's throw away, which had held up a great part of the audience. By the time the curtain was raised, twelve minutes late, there was as much relief from within the audience that the performance had started as there was from the actors.

The opening scene, Roebuck Ramsden's study, and James Grout, as Ramsden, set a fair pace, talking of Mr Whitefield's death and the guardianship of his daughter Ann to Octavius Robinson. It seemed a long time before John Tanner's entrance was due. The programme note for O'Toole blandly recorded: 'He played Macbeth at the Old Vic in 1980.' That anodyne sentence did not do justice to the memory of the event which every member of the audience, cast, stage crew and each one of the drama critics knew was the reason they were so ardently waiting for their man to appear. O'Toole, backstage, was wracked with nerves. Then on he burst.

The audience clapped with relief as much as support, contrary to the good manners of London theatregoers who deem such greetings as provincial and uncool. The fact that he had got this far was worth celebrating. Then all eyes were on him. At each line, each floppy gesture, the audience followed O'Toole. Actors who would have had a hard enough job to wrest the audience's attention away from a professional upstager like O'Toole had the further disadvantage that the reason that most of the seats were filled that night was because so many wanted to mark, judge, applaud O'Toole on his return.

Whether they wished him harm or good luck, they knew that they would not be disappointed. As O'Toole had assured Griffith about *Macbeth*, there would be no half measures: his return would either be a triumph or a disaster. After the first twenty minutes, it became clear which it was to be. O'Toole was cantering with ease through the part. The nervous giggles turned to genuine laughs as O'Toole's supporters relaxed. He had done it. They would not uncross their fingers until the final word was spoken, but they knew he was well on the way to vindicating himself.

By the interval, there were nods of understanding and broad beams from those who knew they would have their faith rewarded. Kenneth Griffith called across: 'I've got the title for your last chapter, Wapshott: "Triumph".' The press confirmed as much the following morning. Ned Chaillet of *The Times* came clean. 'After a *Macbeth* that stretched the vocabulary of denigration to new lengths and restored each reviewer's pride in derision, this *Man and Superman* should be ripe for *coup de grâce*. There is just one problem and that is that, er, Peter O'Toole – I should not be telling you this – is, well, rather good. It is the kind of goodness that an actor can suggest only if he has greatness in him and it is a kind of goodness that defeats niggling criticism completely . . . But against all those complaints, and many others, there is O'Toole the star, as a man larger than lifesize with a clear understanding of every joke and a presence that cannot be ignored. He displays his intelligence and forces his fellow performers to rise to the same outsize dimensions, or risk getting blown away.'

The general consensus was that, first, O'Toole was recovered from whatever ailment of body or mind that had led to the horrors of *Macbeth*. Second, it was commonly accepted that O'Toole dominated proceedings. As Milton Shulman of the *Standard* remarked: 'This production is not only dominated by the performance of Peter O'Toole as Tanner, but swamped by it. Following his Macbeth, Mr

O'Toole has cultivated an acting style that is so forceful and idiosyncratic that it has become a phenomenon to be savoured for itself alone.' Third, what seemed, in the circumstances, a technical point of acting, O'Toole was thought to be straining his voice a little: the words were being shouted. 'Mr O'Toole's way with them is to treat them not as dialogue but as oratory,' wrote Anthony Curtis in the *Financial Times*, 'and to shout them, nay belt them, in precisely the manner of the old actor-managers whom Shaw castigated in his critical days. His model could hardly have been Irving, but you feel it might have been Wolfit in *Lear*. If the part is not well acted, it is well ranted.'

There were various attempts to describe O'Toole, who had noticeably aged since *Macbeth*. 'His blue eyes glint like stilettos. His head moves with the jerky reflexes of a ventriloquist's doll. He moves across the stage with the assurance of a male model about to be knighted,' wrote Milton Shulman in the *Standard*. 'In a role for which he is twenty years too old,' commented Mark Amory, in the *Spectator*, 'he is slender, haggard and forever dashing about, which gives the impression of a seriously ill young man.' Robert Cushman of the *Observer* drew attention to 'Peter O'Toole's prima donna performance, yellow-haired, pale-faced and strep-throated.' Then continued, 'still, Tanner is a prima donna character, and Mr O'Toole's timing is at least intact.' Curtis of the *Financial Times*, again: 'With his great mop of flaxen hair, his lantern-jaw, his Dracula eyes, his matinée idol presence, his Balmoral tweeds and plus fours, Mr O'Toole is an arresting sight.'

And there was O'Toole's diction. It was evident that O'Toole was unable to speak clearly. From the opening previews to the opening night at the Haymarket, O'Toole had slurred his words and spoken with a lateral lisp. O'Toole's tongue, once cut in two, seemed incapable of crisp enunciation and he tried to make up for that by raising his voice.

Shulman remarked: 'The lines tumble out of him in arbitrary disarray. Sometimes sentences gushed out as if the words had all been stapled together in one gurgling sound. Sometimes his voice rises to a declamatory crescendo as if he were a desperate barrister trying to convince a deaf jury. As the evening proceeds, the sheer energy need for such an operatic display eventually takes its toll. Either I got used to this odd clamour or O'Toole's larynx was wearing out, but by the final act the performance was beginning to sound normal and almost enjoyable.'

Of all the critics, the most astute over O'Toole's reasons for failing so miserably in *Macbeth* had been James Fenton of the *Sunday Times*. This time he came in for the kill. He led with O'Toole, even though it soon became clear that such prominence was given only to wound the more effectively. Fenton was out to humiliate and, by a cruel device, rubbed in O'Toole's imprecise diction by writing every word that contained an *s* with *sh* instead. As with *Macbeth*, he attacked O'Toole by pretending to describe the character of Tanner. 'Peter O'Toolesh performansh in *Man and Schluperman* ish bashed on one profound inshight into the character of John Tanner; John Tanner is a shexually vain, intellectually shelf-obsheshed, biologically opinionated bore.' Then, writing of Shaw, he continued: 'Hish linesh should be delivered in a high-pitched croak: he should, preferably, shtamp hish feet in order to give emphashish. He should rush on to shtage and, again preferably, he should come to a halt before he fallsh into the auditorium. This Mr O'Toole pulled off shplendidly. After that, it ish shout, shout, shout, all the way.'

O'Toole's euphoria was not spoilt. The *Sunday Times* review was three days after the first night and directly after the performance he enjoyed the praise of fellow actors and friends who visited him in his dressing room. Toasting himself in soft drinks, he felt that he had returned in a dignified way. And the following morning's reviews were not painful. Never mind the small criticisms: he had been exciting without making himself look an idiot. The ghost of Macbeth was finally beginning to lift. Perhaps King Lear was not such a pipe-dream after all.

Looking back on his career, it is impossible not to come to the sorry judgment that a lack of self-discipline has led him to squander his early promise. The young actor whose Hamlet caused him to be greeted by critics, audiences and fellow actors as a new Olivier now attracts audiences of either blindly loyal devotees or cruel voyeurs, hoping to witness a disaster. His acting is certainly sensational but no one could pretend that it was great acting. O'Toole's persistent love-affair with the stage has come to very little. His determination to continue acting in front of live audiences only serves to highlight his increasing deficiencies as an actor. For all his early determination to keep in touch with the stage, to use it as a lifeline to his public, he has become increasingly out of touch with the way the theatre operates. Even his most devoted friends on *Macbeth* were appalled at his ignorance of modern stagecraft and his insistence that everything be conducted in the extravagant ways of the cinema and in the grand-iloquent ways of the old-fashioned theatre.

His film career can be judged as more successful. His early, brilliant performances are fixed and nothing can detract from them. Above all, his appearance in *Lawrence of Arabia* still remains a most dazzling screen performance. O'Toole has become the definitive

Lawrence in the public mind and only followers of the cult of T.E. Lawrence can see through and beyond the tall, lanky O'Toole figure to the short man on whom the legend was built. Many of O'Toole's early comic performances also stand the test of time, as do his roly-poly historic characters, particularly that of Henry II in *Becket* and *The Lion in Winter*. O'Toole's reputation stands firmly on those films and rarely has he regained the combination of innocent devotion, patience and confidence that would allow him to rekindle the magic of those performances. Still, even in lesser films, O'Toole's highly individual style and extraordinary physiognomy have ensured that, even when totally out of fashion, he has maintained a loyal band of supporters, later joined by a new generation of younger audiences who recognise in the nonsense of films like *The Ruling Class* a sense of radical, irreverent, almost adolescent rebelliousness. These two groups of O'Toole-watchers have ensured that whatever project O'Toole is involved in, he cannot be ignored. It was their devotion that propelled the disaster of *Macbeth* onto the front pages – a lesser star would have survived a failure ignored, unnoticed.

But for all the valid reservation about O'Toole's career when judged as a conventional acting life, what cannot be denied is that O'Toole has that elusive quality which means he cannot be considered, cannot even be watched as a mere film actor or a mere stage actor. It is O'Toole's real personality which is on show in all his projects. It is that unruly spirit, an inspired personality which drives a body which should have given up the ghost years ago, that triumphs whatever the scale of the success or disaster. It is that independent soul that is so inspirational when, rarely, as in *Rogue Male* or *The Stunt Man*, he regains his past brilliance. And it is the same sympathetic soul that transforms a conventional failure into an interesting attempt or an enjoyable flop. As long as O'Toole's obsessive mind drives him to perform, he will have a following who feel so close to the man behind the part that whether he really succeeds or not becomes irrelevant.

As for his future, he is determined to keep working, full pelt and continue to live each day as the last. As for marriage, he said: 'I love company. I'm very gregarious. But I love to be alone. Always have. It's very difficult. It would take an exceptional woman. I have an open pair of arms and an open mind – and low expectations.' But he was not to be alone for long. In 1982 he met and fell in love with Karen Somerville Leftwhich in Los Angeles, whom he described as 'from a very old Yankee family in New Jersey'. And, on St Patrick's Day, 1983, he became the father of a son for the first time. Lorcan Patrick, named after the Irish for Lawrence and his father, was born in Dublin. Only one ambition remained to him: to play King Lear.

# Peter O'Toole Filmography

TITLE followed by year (director) other main actors.

KIDNAPPED 1959 (Robert Stevenson) Peter Finch

THE SAVAGE INNOCENTS 1959 (Nicholas Ray) Anthony
Quinn, Yoko Tani, Marie Yang, Anna May Wong (O'Toole
uncredited)

THE DAY THEY ROBBED THE BANK OF ENGLAND 1960
(John Guillermin) Aldo Ray, Elizabeth Sellars, Kieron Moore

LAWRENCE OF ARABIA 1962 (David Lean) Omar Sharif,
Arthur Kennedy, Jack Hawkins, Donald Wolfit, Claude Rains,
Anthony Quayle, Alec Guinness, Anthony Quinn, Jose Ferrer

BECKET 1964 (Peter Glenville) Richard Burton, Donald Wolfit,
John Gielgud, Martita Hunt, Pamela Brown, Sian Phillips

LORD JIM 1965 (Richard Brooks) James Mason, Eli Wallach, Paul
Lukas, Jack Hawkins, Daliah Lavi, Curt Jurgens, Akim Tamiroff

WHAT'S NEW PUSSYCAT? 1965 (Clive Donner) Peter Sellers,
Woody Allen, Ursula Andress, Romy Schneider, Capucine, Paula
Prentiss

HOW TO STEAL A MILLION 1966 (William Wyler) Audrey
Hepburn, Charles Boyer, Hugh Griffith, Eli Wallach

THE BIBLE 1966 (John Huston) Michael Parks, Ulla Bergryd,
Richard Harris, John Huston, Stephen Boyd, George C. Scott,
Ava Gardner

NIGHT OF THE GENERALS 1967 (Anatole Litvak) Omar Sharif,
Tom Courtenay, Donald Pleasance, Joanna Pettet, Philippe
Noiret

CASINO ROYALE 1967 (John Huston and others) David Niven,
Deborah Kerr, Orson Welles, Peter Sellers (O'Toole uncredited)

GREAT CATHERINE 1967 (Gordon Flemyng) Jeanne Moreau,
Zero Mostel, Jack Hawkins, Marie Lohr, Akim Tamiroff, Marie
Kean, Kenneth Griffith (O'Toole also co-produced)

THE LION IN WINTER 1968 (Anthony Harvey) Katharine
Hepburn, Jane Merrow, John Castle, Anthony Hopkins

GOODBYE MR CHIPS 1969 (Herbert Ross) Petula Clark,
Michael Bryant, Michael Redgrave, George Baker, Sian Phillips

COUNTRY DANCE (US: BROTHERLY LOVE) 1969 (J. Lee-

Thompson) Susannah York, Michael Craig, Harry Andrews, Cyril Cusack

MURPHY'S WAR 1970 (Peter Yates) Sian Phillips, Philippe Noiret, Horst Janson

UNDER MILK WOOD 1971 (Andrew Sinclair) Richard Burton, Elizabeth Taylor, Glynis Johns, Vivien Merchant, Sian Phillips, Victor Spinetti

THE RULING CLASS 1971 (Peter Medak) Harry Andrews, Arthur Lowe, Alastair Sim, Coral Browne, Michael Bryant

MAN OF LA MANCHA 1972 (Arthur Hiller) Sophia Loren, James Coco, Harry Andrews, John Castle, Brian Blessed

ROSEBUD 1975 (Otto Preminger) Richard Attenborough, Cliff Gorman, Claude Dauphin, Peter Lawford, Raf Vallone

MAN FRIDAY 1975 (Jack Gold) Richard Roundtree

FOXTROT 1976 (Arturo Ripstein) Charlotte Rampling, Max von Sydow (not released in UK)

ROGUE MALE 1976 (TV) (Clive Donner) Alastair Sim, John Standing, Harold Pinter

CALIGULA 1977 (Tinto Brass) Malcolm McDowell, John Gielgud, Helen Mirren

POWER PLAY 1978 (Martyn Burke) David Hemmings, Donald Pleasance, Barry Morse

ZULU DAWN 1979 (Douglas Hickox) Burt Lancaster, Denholm Elliott, John Mills, Simon Ward

STRUMPET CITY 1979 (Tony Barry) (RTE TV series) Peter Ustinov, Cyril Cusack

THE STUNT MAN 1980 (Richard Rush) Barbara Hersey, Steve Railsback, Sharon Farrell

MASADA 1980 (TV Series) Timothy West

SVENGALI/TRILBY 1982 (CBS TV film) Jodie Foster

MY FAVOURITE YEAR 1982 (Richard Benjamin) Mark Linn-Baker, Jessica Harper, Joseph Bologna


THE SANDPIPER 1965 (Vincente Minnelli) Elizabeth Taylor, Richard Burton ( O'Toole as voice only)

# INDEX